Storytelling

❧ An Encyclopedia of Mythology and Folklore ❧

Volume Three

Edited by Josepha Sherman

SHARPE REFERENCE

an imprint of M.E. Sharpe, Inc.

SHARPE REFERENCE

Sharpe Reference is an imprint of M.E. Sharpe, Inc.

M.E. Sharpe, Inc.
80 Business Park Drive
Armonk, NY 10504

Library of Congress Cataloging-in-Publication Data

Storytelling: an encyclopedia of mythology and folklore/Josepha Sherman, editor.
    p. cm.
Includes bibliographical references and index.
ISBN 978-0-7656-8047-1 (hardcover: alk. paper)
1. Folklore—Encyclopedias. 2. Mythology—Encyclopedias. 3. Storytelling—Encyclopedias.
I. Sherman, Josepha.

GR35.S76 2008
398.203—dc22   2008007915

Cover image: Werner Forman/Art Resource, New York.

Publisher: Myron E. Sharpe
Vice President and Editorial Director: Patricia Kolb
Vice President and Production Director: Carmen Chetti
Executive Editor and Manager of Reference: Todd Hallman
Project Manager: Laura Brengelman
Program Coordinator: Cathleen Prisco
Text Design: Carmen Chetti and Jesse Sanchez
Cover Design: Jesse Sanchez

Contents

Retellings

Contents

Storytelling

Volume Three

Tail Tales

In the tail tale, a world folktale type, a foolish animal is tricked by a clever one into losing its tail.

The most familiar version, which is common to the folklore of Norway and England, features a fox and a bear. At the start of the story, the bear has a long, flowing tail. The fox tells the bear that the best way to catch fish in the winter is to cut a hole in the ice, using its tail as fishing line. The bear believes this and is soon frozen fast to the ice. The only way for it to get free is to tear loose, leaving its tail behind. This is why bears have stubby tails today.

Variations on this basic story are found from Finland to India. The trickster's motivation in these tales ranges from an act of pure spite to a need either to teach a bully a lesson or to escape a predator.

In a related story, the gullible character buries its tail, only to be attacked by the trickster when it is unable to flee. It has to tear free, and winds up with a stubby tail. This version is found in India, Indonesia, and Spain, as well as in the West Indies.

In another variant, a bear or wolf is tricked into thinking that a basket tied to its tail is full of fish, when it is actually filled with stones. The weight of the basket slows the animal down so that the trickster can escape. In a German version, the bear, again dragging a stone-filled basket, jumps over a fire and loses his tail.

See also: Tale Types.

Sources

Afanas'ev, Aleksandr. *Russian Fairy Tales*. Trans. Norbert Guterman. New York: Pantheon, 1976.

Asbjornsen, Peter Christen, and Jorgen Moe. *Norwegian Folk Tales*. Trans. Pat Shaw and Carl Norman. New York: Pantheon, 1982.

Dasent, George Webbe. *Popular Tales from the Norse*. 2nd ed. Edinburgh, UK: Edmonston and Douglas, 1859.

Tale Types

The term *tale type* has multiple meanings. Literary scholars, storytellers, psychologists, and folklorists each apply this term differently.

In English and world literature studies, the term *tale type* generally refers to a genre, such as horror, fiction, or theater. Storytellers may use the term similarly, referring to tale types such as tall tales, ghost stories, urban legends, or Celtic mythology. In psychology, a tale type generally refers to stories categorized by similar functions, such as women's stories, stories dealing with abuse, or magical tales. Folklorists also use tale types as a method of categorization.

Folklore tale types are part of a numbering system formulated by nineteenth-century Finnish folklorists Kaarle Krohn and Julius

Krohn. This system of categorization was further developed by Antti Aarne in his work *The Types of the Folktale* (FFC 3; 1910), which was translated and expanded by Stith Thompson in 1928, and again in 1961, in *The Types of the Folktale: A Classification and Bibliography*. This work is referred to as the Aarne-Thompson tale type index or, more simply, as the tale type index.

In the tale type index, traditional folk narrative plots are grouped together, based on their similar motifs, and numbered. Each of these groups is a tale type. The index lists 2,499 tale types. Cinderella, for example, is tale type 510, the persecuted heroine. Each tale type is identified by a specific combination of motifs. The Aarne-Thompson tale type numbers are noted as AT or AaTH, followed by the number assigned to that particular tale, as in the following excerpt from the index:

AT 360: "The Shoes That Were Danced to Pieces." Plot summary: Twelve princesses wear out their shoes every night. A soldier, with the aid of an invisible cloak, solves the mystery, discovering that they are dancing. His reward is the hand of one of the princesses. Motifs that combine to structure AT 360: T68 Princess offered as a prize. F1015.1.1 Danced-out shoes. D1364.7 Sleeping potion. D1980 Magic invisibility. D2131 Magic underground journey. H80 Identification by tokens. Variants of AT 360 include:

"The Danced-Out Shoes" (Russian), in Stith Thompson's 100 Folktales, no. 6.

"Elena the Wise," Afanaysev, Russian Fairy Tales, p. 545.

"Hild, Queen of the Elves," Simpson, Icelandic Folktales and Legends, p. 43.

"The Shoes That Were Danced to Pieces" (German), Grimm, No. 133.

"Twelve Dancing Princesses," Lang, Red Fairy Book.

Tale types can be a very useful source of inspiration for storytellers. If a storyteller is hunting for a fresh version of a familiar tale, a look at any collection of tale types can help. Such collections also can help a storyteller who wants to combine tale elements into a fresh story.

Ruth Stotter

See also: Motifs.

Sources

Aarne, Antti. *Verzeichnis der Märchentypen (The Types of the Folktale)*. FFC 3. Helsinki, Finland: Folklore Fellows Communications, 1910.

Aarne, Antti, and Stith Thompson. *The Types of the Folktale: A Classification and Bibliography*. FFC 74. Helsinki, Finland: Folklore Fellows Communications, 1961.

Ashliman, D.L. *A Guide to Folktales in the English Language: Based on the Aarne-Thompson Classification System*. New York: Greenwood, 1987.

Shannon, George, comp. *A Knock at the Door*. Phoenix, AZ: Oryx, 1992.

Sierra, Judy, comp. *Cinderella*. Phoenix, AZ: Oryx, 1992.

Stotter, Ruth. *The Golden Axe*. Stimson Beach, CA: Stotter, 1998.

Talismans

Talismans are objects that act as charms. Generally, they are specially prepared objects made of a specific material—stone, metal, wood, or parchment—that has been inscribed with magical signs, characters, or drawings that endow them with magical properties. These objects are believed to bring the owner good luck, success, health, and virility.

A talisman is not meant to be worn. Instead, it is carried or placed near the person or object that must be protected.

See also: Amulets.

Sources

Budge, E.A. Wallis. *Amulets and Talismans*. New York: Collier, 1970.

Pavitt, William Thomas, and Kate Pavitt. *Book of Talismans, Amulets, and Zodiacal Gems*. 3rd ed. New York: S. Weiser, 1970.

Thompson, C.J.S. *Amulets, Talismans and Charms*. Edmonds, WA: Holmes, 1994.

Tall Tales

Tall tales are stories that feature a larger-than-life or superhuman main character that has a specific task. The task takes the form of an outlandish problem that is solved in a humorous or outrageous way. The main elements in a tall tale are the story's exaggerated and improbable details.

The word *tall* acquired a meaning of "grandiose" or "high-flown" in the seventeenth century. The term *tall tale* probably dates to the mid-nineteenth century, although there is no proof of its first use. In modern usage, a tall tale is simply a lie or an outlandish excuse.

Tall tales have a long tradition that may date to the ancient Greeks. The Romans were also familiar with this type of story, as were the Celts.

In Europe, tall tales are sometimes called Münchhausen tales, after the eighteenth-century German storyteller Karl Friedrich Hieronymus Baron von Münchhausen, who was nicknamed the Baron of Lies.

In the United States and Canada, tall tales are called yarns, windies, whoppers, stretchers, and gallyfloppers. Many tall tales from the New World originated with immigrant groups. Something about the vastness of the new land seemed to inspire these humorous, larger-than-life stories. Over time, groups of American workers, from cowboys to steelworkers, each created their own tall-tale champions—superhuman heroes who shared their work experience and triumphed over all obstacles.

Tall tales are linked closely with oral tradition, but many of them are created tales with known authors. The character Pecos Bill, for example, made his first appearance in the "Saga of Pecos Bill," which was written by Edward O'Reilly in the early 1920s. There is also some evidence that Paul Bunyan, the giant logger, and his great blue ox, Babe, might have been a newspaperman's creation. Today, Paul Bunyan, like Pecos Bill, has entered the folk tradition.

Not every tall-tale hero was imaginary. Davy Crockett, the famous frontiersman and politician, had a cycle of tall tales told about him—many of them created by Crockett himself.

Other tall tales are told about regions or local claims to fame. These include tales of the gigantic size of Texas, where everything is larger than life, or Idaho's potatoes, which grow larger than any others—or so the stories claim.

In telling a tall tale, the storyteller should make the audience aware that the story is fiction, not fact. This can be done by using a specific opening, such as overdoing the idea that yes, this is the truth—really it is—or by using a sly tone or delivery. Once the audience realizes that what they are hearing is a tall tale, it is up to the teller to embellish the story with the creativity and cleverness necessary to hold the audience's attention.

Gregory Hansen

See also: Urban Legends.

Sources

Bauman, Richard. *Story, Performance, and Event: Contextual Studies of Oral Narrative.* New York: Cambridge University Press, 1986.

Brown, Carolyn S. *The Tall Tale in American Folklore and Literature.* Knoxville: University of Tennessee Press, 1989.

Randolph, Vance. *We Always Lie to Strangers: Tall Tales from the Ozarks.* Westport, CT: Greenwood, 1974.

Talmudic Storytelling

(Jewish)

Although the Talmud is usually thought of simply as a repository for Jewish legal decisions, it also contains a wealth of folktales and stories. Many of the stories tell of the lives and deeds of major biblical figures and of biblical events, such as the Genesis story of creation. The stories also use biblical themes to teach important lessons.

The Oral Law

The Torah is the first five books of the Bible, or the five books of Moses. These are the stories that Moses received directly from God.

The first part of the Talmud is called the Mishnah and is referred to as half of the "whole Torah of Moses at Sinai." The religious and civil laws contained in the Mishnah were handed down orally from generation to generation and were finally written down around 200 C.E.

Rabbi Judah the Prince took it upon himself to oversee the Mishnah's transition from an oral work to the written format that is studied to this day. By the time the Mishnah was codified, other traditions had risen up around the laws. Stories and folklore were seen as important enough to include in the work, especially those that shed light on some of the more obscure laws.

The Mishnah together with these later stories and lessons became the Talmud. This blending has provided the basis for still more commentary, and, in this way, the Talmud continues to expand today.

Types and Purpose of Talmudic Stories

Many stories in the Talmud detail the lives of the rabbis, while others speak of the rabbis' interactions with one another and with laymen. The stories that serve to explain or expand upon biblical events and personalities are among the most intriguing in this work.

Explaining Contradictions

Several contradictions arise in the Torah text, and Talmudic rabbis attempt to reconcile these inconsistencies in inventive ways.

In one example, the rabbis noticed that God created light before he created the Sun and the Moon. To explain this, they suggested that the light mentioned prior to the creation of the Sun must be a different kind of light. This light enabled Adam to see from one end of the universe to the other. When he and Eve ate the forbidden fruit, the light was extinguished for them. A small part of that light was hidden by God inside a glowing stone known as the *tzohar*. The tzohar was given to Adam as a reminder of all that had been lost.

This story goes on to explain that Adam passed the glowing stone to his son Seth, who gave it to his son, and so on down to Noah, who used the tzohar to illuminate the ark. The Talmud records Abraham wearing a glowing stone around his neck that had healing powers.

In the end of days, when the Messiah arrives, the light from the stone will be released and restored to the original light of creation. Thus, a contradiction is paved over and a hope for the future is introduced.

Emulating God's Attributes

Certain stories in the Talmud relate directly to God's deeds. Others point out divine characteristics to show how these attributes should be mastered by mortals on Earth.

This example of the former is found in God's reaction to the death of his own creatures; it is meant to teach us not to be overjoyed by the fall of anyone, even our enemies:

When the Egyptian armies were drowning in the sea, the Heavenly Hosts broke out in songs of jubilation. God silenced them and said, "My creatures are perishing, and you sing praises?"

Another passage illustrates God's modesty:

Modesty is a quality of God. When He appeared to Moses the first time He did not appear in the form of a proud cedar tree, but in the form of a lowly bush. When He gave the Torah to the Jews He did so from Sinai, which is small compared to the great mountains.

Stories of the Patriarchs

A fascinating element in the Torah is that many of the most prominent figures are shown "warts and all." They doubt. They are indecisive. They get angry.

The rabbis of the Talmud are not afraid to speak out against the mistakes made by even the most important personages, including the patriarchs Abraham, Isaac, and Jacob. The rabbis dissect the biblical stories to show where the great men of the past could have done better.

Remembering to Rely on God

Jewish tradition holds that everything is just the way that God intended. This is referred to as divine order. Humans should not attempt to understand God's will or to alter his plan.

A story is told of King Solomon, who overheard two birds talking about the impending death of two of the king's closest advisers. Solomon knew that the Angel of Death was not allowed into the city of Luz and instructed his advisers to go there.

Solomon continues, "But when they arrived they saw, to their horror, the Angel of Death waiting for them. 'How did you know to look for us here?' they asked. The angel replied: 'This is where I was told to meet you.'"

This story exemplifies the futility of trying to escape the inevitable, stressing that we should be dependent on God and trust that even if we cannot understand his ways, that he knows what is best for his creation.

The Prophet Elijah

The prophet Elijah teaches several important lessons in the Talmudic stories. In an oft-repeated story, Elijah teaches a rabbi that there is a great value in making people feel better about themselves:

Rabbi Beroka Hazzah used to frequent the market of Be Lapat, where Elijah often appeared to him. Once he asked Elijah, "Is there anyone in this market who is worthy of a share in the world to come?" He [Elijah] replied, "No." While they were walking, two men passed by and he said, "These two are due for a share in the world to come." He [Rabbi Beroka] approached them and asked: "What is your occupation?" They replied: "We are merrymakers. When people are sad we cheer them up, and when we see two people who have quarreled we try to make peace between them."

Learning from the Adversary

In Jewish thought, Satan is simply "the adversary," one of many divine beings who present themselves before God from time to time. One story in the Talmud shows the best way to avoid being ensnared by Satan:

Plemo used to say every day: "I defy Satan." One day before the Day of Atonement Satan appeared to him in the guise of a poor man. Plemo brought him out a piece of bread. The poor man said to him, "On a day like this everyone is inside but I am outside!" He took him inside and gave him the bread. The poor man now said, "At a time like this everyone eats at the table, but I am alone!" He seated him at the table. He feigned that his skin was full of scabs, and he acted repulsively. Plemo said to him, "Sit properly." He then said, "Give me a cup of wine to drink." He gave it to him. He coughed and threw his phlegm into the cup. Plemo rebuked him, and [the disguised Satan] pretended he was dead. The rumor began to circulate: Plemo killed a man. Plemo ran away and hid himself in a toilet outside the city. When Satan saw how distressed he was, he revealed himself to him and said, "Why did you speak so defiantly of Satan?" "But how else should I have spoken?" he asked. Satan answered, "You should say, 'May the Merciful One rebuke Satan.'"

This lengthy passage is meant to show that nothing can be accomplished unless God is involved. Plemo cannot defy Satan himself; he can only ask that God do so on Plemo's behalf.

Judaism is a covenantal religion, and so both parties—Israel and God—have their parts to play in the continuing existence of the people.

From the very first verses of the Torah, when the world is brought into being, to the last, when Moses is praised for a final time, it can be demonstrated that Judaism has a very strong storytelling tradition. The stories of the Torah are meant to educate students on the proper way to live, the proper way to worship, and the proper way to treat others.

David M. Honigsberg

See also: *Retelling: King Solomon and the Demon.*

Sources

Bader, Gershom. *The Encyclopedia of Talmudic Sages.* Lanham, MD: Jason Aronson, 1993.

Bosker, Ben Zion. *The Talmud: Selected Writings.* New York: Paulist Press, 1989.

Hebrew-English Tanakh. Philadelphia: Jewish Publication Society, 1999.

Neusner, Jacob. *The Mishnah: A New Translation.* New Haven, CT: Yale University Press, 1988.

Schwartz, Howard. *Reimagining the Bible: The Storytelling of the Rabbis.* New York: Oxford University Press, 1998.

Tasmisus

(Hittite)

Tasmisus is a Hittite deity. His parents were Anu and Kumarbi, who conceived Tasmisus along with Aranzahus and the storm god, Teshub.

Tasmisus was spat out by Kumarbi onto Mount Kanzuras. After this rough and unnatural birth, Tasmisus joined up with Anu and the storm god to destroy Kumarbi.

He served as the storm god's messenger and attendant and had the power to control the storm winds, rain, and lightning in the storm god's name. Tasmisus took part in the storm god's final, successful battle against Ullikummi.

Ira Spar

See also: Hermes.

Sources

Gurney, O.R. *The Hittites.* Rev. ed. New York: Penguin, 1990.

Hoffner, Harry A. *Hittite Myths.* 2nd ed. Atlanta: Scholars, 1991.

Hooke, S.H. *Middle Eastern Mythology.* Mineola, NY: Dover Publications, 2004.

Tefnut

(Egyptian)

The Egyptian goddess Tefnut was the counterpart and consort of her brother Shu, the air god. The meaning of her name is not known, but, like her husband, she had an atmospheric association, perhaps as moist air.

Both Tefnut and Shu came forth from the nose or mouth of the primordial god, Atum. Together, they produced the earth god, Geb, and his sister, the sky goddess, Nut. Artists depicted Tefnut as a lioness or as a woman with the head of a lion.

The Egyptians loved animal fables. Here, Tefnut, daughter of the sun god Re, is portrayed as a lioness and Thoth, god of wisdom, is a baboon. This artist's sketch was found in western Thebes and dates to about 1250–1100 B.C.E. *(Bildarchiv Preussischer Kulturbesitz/ Art Resource, NY)*

Tefnut was identified with the governing principal of *maat,* or order, as Shu was with forces of change. She also was identified with the eye of the sun god, Re, which brought her into close association with other goddesses, such as Hathor and Sekhmet.

Certain texts tell of a quarrel between Tefnut and Re. The goddess ran away to sulk in Nubia. Re sent Thoth, god of wisdom, to convince her to return. Ultimately successful, Thoth returned with the pacified Tefnut, who was sometimes considered to be Thoth's wife.

Noreen Doyle

See also: Maat.

Sources

Allen, James P. *Genesis in Egypt: The Philosophy of Ancient Egyptian Creation Accounts.* New Haven, CT: Yale Egyptological Seminar, 1988.

Málek, Jaromír. *The Cat in Ancient Egypt.* Philadelphia: University of Pennsylvania Press, 1997.

Shirun-Grumach, I. "Remarks on the Goddess Maat." In *Pharaonic Egypt: The Bible and Christianity.* Ed. Sarah Israelit-Groll. Jerusalem, Israel: Magnes, 1985.

Telegonia

(Greek)

The lost Greek epic that is known as the *Telegonia* is named for its hero, Telegonus, the son of Odysseus and Circe.

The written form of this epic is believed to date to the fifth century B.C.E. and has been attributed to a poet named Eugamonn. An earlier oral version may have existed, since some of the *Telegonia*'s elements are found in Homer's *Odyssey,* which was written in the eighth or ninth century B.C.E. Although the original of the *Telegonia* is lost, there is a complete summary contained in the *Chrestomatheia,* a later work attributed to the philosopher Proclus Diadochus.

The story begins after Homer's *Odyssey* ends. Odysseus has returned home to Ithaca and has done away with his wife's suitors. The *Telegonia* states that after the burial of the suitors Odysseus made sacrifices to the nymphs.

He then left his home and wife and traveled to Elis and then on to Thesprotia. There, Odysseus was involved in an affair with Queen Callidice, who bore him a son, Polypoites. Odysseus fought for the Thesprotians in a war against their neighbors, but when Callidice died in the battle, Odysseus returned to Ithaca.

Meanwhile, Circe gave birth to another of Odysseus's sons, Telegonus, who lived with Circe on her island called Aeaea. When Telegonus had grown to manhood, Circe revealed the name of his father and gave him a spear made by the smith god Hephaestus. The spear was tipped with the sting of a poisonous stingray. Telegonus went in search of Odysseus.

A storm forced Telegonus onto Ithaca, although at the time he did not know where he had landed. Desperate for food, he stole some cattle, unaware that they were the property of his father. Odysseus defended his property and fought Telegonus, neither one knowing the other's identity. Telegonus killed Odysseus with his spear. As Odysseus lay dying, he and Telegonus discovered their relationship. Telegonus lamented his mistake.

Telegonus, Odysseus's widow, Penelope, and her son, Telemachus, traveled with Odysseus's body to Aeaea. There, Odysseus was buried, and Circe made the others immortal. Telegonus and Penelope were wed, as were Telemachus and Circe.

See also: Epics; *Odyssey.*

Sources

Davies, Malcolm. *The Greek Epic Cycle.* Bristol, UK: Bristol Classical Press, 1989.

West, M.L., ed. and trans. *Greek Epic Fragments from the Seventh to the Fifth Centuries B.C.* Cambridge, MA: Harvard University Press, 2003.

Telepinu/Telepinus

(Hittite)

Called the noble god, Telepinu was an agricultural deity of the Hittite pantheon and the firstborn and favorite son of the storm god. It was Telepinu who introduced plows, harrowing, and irrigation.

In one myth, Telepinu was angered and stormed off onto the vast steppes. There, he was overcome by weariness and fell into a deep sleep. Without the god of agriculture, the lands, crops, and herds lost their fertility. Both gods and humans were faced with the peril of famine.

The goddess Hannahanna was asked for help. She sent one of her bees after Telepinu, which found him and stung his hands and feet to awaken him. This made Telepinu even angrier, and he sent floods that destroyed houses.

At last, the gods found a way to remove Telepinu's anger through magic. Telepinu went home, and fertility was restored to the land.

In another myth, Telepinu's father asked him to bring back the sun god from the sea god. Telepinu so frightened the sea god that he not only won the day but was given the hand of the sea god's daughter as well.

Ira Spar

See also: Culture Heroes.

Sources

Gurney, O.R. *The Hittites.* Rev. ed. New York: Penguin, 1990.

Hoffner, Harry A. *Hittite Myths.* 2nd ed. Atlanta: Scholars, 1991.

Hooke, S.H. *Middle Eastern Mythology.* Mineola, NY: Dover, 2004.

Teshub

(Hittite)

Teshub was the Hittite storm god, also known as Taru, Tarhun (the conqueror), and the king of Kummiya (king of heaven). Chief among the gods, with a bull as his symbol, Teshub was a god of battle and of victory and the consort of Wurusemu.

Teshub was a child of Anu and Kumarbi, conceived along with Tasmisus and Aranzahus when Kumarbi bit off and swallowed Anu's phallus. Teshub plotted with Anu, Tasmisus, and Aranzhus to destroy Kumarbi, and seized the kingship in heaven.

Among his battles, Teshub fought the monstrous diorite giant, Ullikummi, and, with the help of the other gods, defeated him. He also battled and defeated the dragon called Illuyankas.

In one myth, Teshub's son, Telepinu, flew into a wild rage and went into hiding. But in another, very similar myth, it was Teshub who ran off and journeyed to the so-called Dark Earth in a rage. He returned with the help of his mother, Wuruntemu (or Ereshkigal), the sun goddess.

Ira Spar

See also: Upelluri/Ubelluris; Wurusemu.

Sources

Gurney, O.R. *The Hittites.* Rev. ed. New York: Penguin, 1990.

Hoffner, Harry A. *Hittite Myths.* 2nd ed. Atlanta: Scholars, 1991.

Hooke, S.H. *Middle Eastern Mythology.* Mineola, NY: Dover, 2004.

Theseus

(Greek)

Theseus is one of the most famous heroes in Greek mythology. He was the son of Aegeus, king of Athens, and Aethra of Troezen. Some versions say that Theseus's father was Poseidon, god of the oceans.

When Aethra was pregnant, Aegeus left Troezen to return to Athens. Before leaving, he placed a sword and sandals under a rock. If Aethra bore a boy, he was to go to Athens to claim his birthright as soon as he was strong enough to lift the rock.

The young Theseus came of age and lifted the rock. Retrieving the sandals and sword, he set out for Athens.

On his way to Athens, Theseus had several adventures with wild beasts and brigands. One of the latter, Procrustes, was particularly notorious. He would invite guests to sleep on his bed, and if the unfortunate guest was too short for the bed, Procrustes would stretch him to fit it. If the guest was too tall, Procrustes would make him fit by cutting off his feet.

Medea

When Theseus reached Athens, he faced a new problem—Medea, the wife of Aegeus. Medea was the sorceress who had helped her husband, Jason, to win the Golden Fleece, only to be betrayed by him. She had slain their children and fled to Athens.

When Theseus arrived in Athens, Aegeus did not know that the young man was his son. Medea saw Theseus as a possible rival and persuaded Aegeus to kill him by sending Theseus to capture the savage Marathonian Bull. To Medea's disappointment, Theseus was victorious, so she told Aegeus to give Theseus poisoned wine. But just as Theseus was about to drink, Aegeus recognized Theseus's sword and knocked the goblet away. Medea fled.

After Medea's departure, there was bloodshed between the houses of Aegeus and Minos, his brother, in Crete. A drought struck Athens, and an oracle warned that Minos must be offered compensation. Minos demanded seven maidens and seven youths to be sacrificed to the Minotaur, the monstrous creature that was half man and half bull, once every nine years.

Theseus was among the chosen victims. He promised Aegeus that his ship's black flag would be replaced with a white flag if he was victorious, and sailed off to Crete to vanquish the Minotaur. Ariadne, a young Cretan woman already betrothed to Dionysus, fell in love with Theseus and helped him defeat the Minotaur. Ariadne left Crete with Theseus, but he abandoned her on the island of Dia. Theseus later married Ariadne's sister, Phaedra.

Returning to Athens, Theseus forgot to switch the black sail to the white one. Aegeus, sure that his son was dead, hurled himself into the sea. The sea was named the Aegean Sea in his honor.

After Aegeus's death, Theseus's brother, Pallas, conspired to assassinate him. So Theseus killed Pallas and took the throne.

Further Adventures

Theseus and his good friend Peirithous both wanted to marry daughters of Zeus. They began by kidnapping the young Helen, who would later play a major role in the Trojan War. Theseus won Helen in a bet with Peirithous, and then had to accompany his friend to Hades to steal away Persephone. Peirithous did not survive this adventure.

Theseus also fought against the Amazons, the mythical female warriors. Some accounts say that he alone fought them; others say he fought at the side of Hercules. But all the stories agree that Theseus returned with a captured Amazon wife, either Antiope, the queen's sister, or Hippolyte, the Amazon queen. A battle followed, as the Amazons fought to free their comrade. Depending on the version of the story, she was either slain or freed, but she left a son with Theseus, called Hippolytus.

Theseus then married Ariadne's sister, Phaedra. But that marriage was to end in tragedy. Phaedra was much younger than Theseus and tried to seduce his son, Hippolytus. When the young man refused her, she accused him of rape. Hippolytus, escaping his father's anger, rode too close to the cliffs and was killed by a wave sent by Poseidon. Phaedra, overcome by guilt, killed herself.

Late in his life, Theseus was exiled from Athens. He died in a fall from a cliff.

See also: Culture Heroes; Minotaur.

Sources

Apollodorus. *Library of Greek Mythology*. Trans. Robin Hard. New York: Oxford University Press, 1998.

Grant, Michael. *Myths of the Greeks and Romans*. Cleveland, OH: World, 1962.

Tyrrell, William B., and Frieda S. Brown. *Athenian Myths and Institutions: Words in Action*. New York: Oxford University Press, 1991.

Thompson, Stith

(1885–1976)

The twentieth-century American folklorist Stith Thompson is known for his work with folklore, mythology, and folktale types. Thompson created a center for folklore studies and established folklore as an academic discipline. Among his numerous publications, perhaps his most important contribution was the *Motif-Index of Folk Literature*. This reference work in six volumes, first published between 1932 and 1936, catalogs recurrent subjects, characters, themes, motifs, and other elements found in world folklore.

Thompson was born in Bloomfield, Kentucky, on March 7, 1885. As a young man, he studied English literature at the University of Wisconsin, where he earned his bachelor's degree in 1909. He went on to complete his master's degree in English literature at the University of California. Thompson's dissertation, "European Tales Among the North American Indians," earned him a Ph.D. in English from the same university. In 1921, Thompson was appointed associate professor of English and director of composition at Indiana University, where he was promoted to professor of English and folklore in 1939. He remained at Indiana University until his retirement in 1955.

While teaching folklore courses, Thompson continued to work on codifying folk narratives. His first major contribution was the translation and enlargement of Finnish folklorist Antti Aarne's tale type index, *Verzeichnis der Märchentypen* (*The Types of the Folktale*) in 1928, which he revised again in 1961. The index is now commonly referred to as the Aarne-Thompson tale type index or as just the tale type index. Tales are classified by Aarne-Thompson numbers (noted as AT or AaTH).

Thompson also compiled the *Motif-Index of Folk Literature* between 1932 and 1936. Both the tale type and motif indexes are essential reference works for folklorists and storytellers.

In 1946, Thompson published *The Folktale*, which contained a selection of folktales from various geographical regions, as well as explanations of forms, classification, collections, and a summary of scholarship and theories.

Thompson served as president of the American Folklore Society from 1937 to 1939. He was the U.S. delegate to the 1937 International Folklore Congress in Paris.

An excellent administrator, Thompson established the first U.S. doctoral program in folklore at Indiana University in 1949. During his tenure as dean of Indiana University, Thompson founded a summer institute for scholars and students for the study of folklore and established a folklore collection in the library. In recognition and appreciation of his tireless industry, Thompson was named a distinguished service professor in 1953.

Thompson died in Columbus, Indiana, on January 13, 1976.

Maria Teresa Agozzino

See also: Aarne, Antti; Motif Index.

Sources

Aarne, Antti. *Verzeichnis der Märchentypen (The Types of the Folktale)*. FFC 3. Helsinki, Finland: Folklore Fellows Communications, 1910.

Aarne, Antti, and Stith Thompson. *The Types of the Folktale: A Classification and Bibliography*. FFC 74. Helsinki, Finland: Folklore Fellows Communications, 1961.

Dorson, Richard M. "Stith Thompson." *Journal of American Folklore* 90 (1977): 3–7.

Thompson, Stith. *A Folklorist's Progress: Reflections of a Scholar's Life*. Bloomington: Indiana University Press, 1996.

———. *The Folktale*. 1946. Berkeley: University of California Press, 1977.

———. *Motif-Index of Folk Literature*. Bloomington: Indiana University Press, 1932–1936.

Thor

(Norse)

Thor, the Norse god of thunder, generally was portrayed as a powerfully built man with flaming red or red-gold hair and beard.

This mighty warrior had gloves of iron and a magic belt called Megingjard that doubled his strength. His favorite weapon was his hammer, Mjollnir. Thor threw Mjollnir to make the lightning flash, and it always returned to his hand.

During thunderstorms, Thor was believed to be riding across the heavens in his chariot pulled by two goats, Tanngrisni (gap-tooth) and Tanngnost (tooth-grinder). Whenever Thor grew hungry, he would slay and eat the goats, who would then magically return to life.

Thor's home was his hall, Bilskirnir, which he shared with his wife, Sif. He also had a long-lasting affair with a woman of the giants, Jarnsaxa, by whom he had three children: two sons, Magni and Modi, and a daughter, Thrud.

Thor and Thrym

A giant called Thrym stole Thor's hammer and demanded the hand of Freya, the goddess of love and beauty, in exchange. This was out of the question, so Thor and the mischievous Loki devised a plot to get the hammer back.

Thor disguised himself as Freya and set off for Thrym's hall. There, the giants were amazed at how much the "bride" ate and drank, but Loki explained that this was because she had not eaten or drunk for nine days in anticipation of this day. Thrym wanted to kiss his bride, but he was put off by her fiery eyes and ruddy complexion. Loki explained that she was feverish from lack of sleep.

Eager to get the marriage over and done, Thrym had the magic hammer placed on the bride's knees, as was the custom. This was a fatal error. Thor, shedding his disguise, took up the hammer. Soon, all the giants in the hall lay dead.

The Midgard Serpent

Thor was a great fisherman and decided to catch the ultimate prize: the Midgard serpent. This incredibly large snake encircled the world, holding its tail in its mouth.

Thor was the Norse god of thunder and lightning. In this first-century C.E. bronze, Thor is holding his hammer, called Mjollnir. The figurine, which dates to about 1000 C.E., was found in Iceland. *(Werner Forman/Art Resource, NY)*

Thor sailed out with the giant Hymir as guide and took the boat farther out to sea than Hymir would normally have ventured. Thor baited his hook and cast his line, hooking the Midgard serpent.

A tremendous battle ensued between god and beast. Thor began to win the savage battle, and might have killed the serpent, but the terrified Hymir, sure he would be drowned, cut the line. The force of the release sent Thor crashing back into Hymir, and the giant was drowned.

In another version of this tale, after Hymir cut the line, Thor struck him an angry blow that hurled the giant overboard. Hymir managed to climb back aboard the boat, while Thor waded ashore.

The Common Man's God

Odin, the supreme god and creator, was the preferred god of the Norse noblemen. But his son Thor was a deity of the common man. This was perhaps because Odin was a fairly ambiguous figure and worship of him included human sacrifice. Thor was benevolent toward mankind and did not demand sacrifice.

See also: Norse Mythology; *Retelling: Thor Catches the Midgard Serpent.*

Sources

Crossley-Howard, Kevin. *The Norse Myths.* New York: Pantheon, 1980.

Hollander, Lee M., trans. *The Poetic Edda.* Austin: University of Texas Press, 1928.

Lindow, John. *Norse Mythology: A Guide to the Gods, Heroes, Rituals, and Beliefs.* New York: Oxford University Press, 2002.

Sturluson, Snorri. *The Prose Edda: Tales from Norse Mythology.* Trans. Jean I. Young. Berkeley: University of California Press, 2001.

Thoth/Djehuty

(Egyptian)

Thoth is the Egyptian god most closely associated with intellectual pursuits, including writing and magic. Divine scribe and so-called lord of the sacred words, he often was shown making calculations, recording events, or announcing judgments.

Thoth appeared as a yellow baboon, a sacred ibis, or a man with the head of an ibis. As a moon god, he often wore a crown of a lunar disc cradled in a lunar crescent.

Thoth was cast as an impartial judge in the contest between the gods Horus and Seth for the crown. Thoth eventually became an advocate for the young Horus. He took on a similar role for the mortal dead, recording the outcome of the weighing of their hearts against *maat* (truth) and proclaiming the results before Osiris, god of the dead. As such a participant in the divine judicial system, Thoth had weights and measures under his jurisdiction.

Thoth's knowledge extended to all branches of learning. He taught Isis the magic necessary to revive the dead and was capable of restoring the lost eye of Horus. By the Middle and New Kingdoms (c. 2106–1786 B.C.E. and c. 1550–1069 B.C.E., respectively), he was viewed as the establisher of laws and the principles of sacred architecture, decoration, texts, and rites.

At Hermopolis, which was Thoth's principle cult center, he created the Ogdoad, a set of eight divinities that included Nun and Amun. He also was regarded as the eldest son of Re, whom he often accompanied in the solar barque (the ship that represents the rising and setting Sun) as either the scribe of the divine book at the right of Re or the scribe of Maat.

The Book of Thoth was purported to contain all knowledge, cultural and natural. While Thoth could see into anyone else's heart, he himself was mysterious and unknown.

Seshat, goddess of writing, is variously credited as Thoth's wife or daughter. In Greek mythology, he is Hermes.

Noreen Doyle

See also: Wise Man or Woman.

Sources

Boylan, Patrick. *Thoth, the Hermes of Egypt: A Study of Some Aspects of Theological Thought in Ancient Egypt.* New York: Oxford University Press, 1922.

Doxey, Denise M. "Thoth." In *The Oxford Encyclopedia of Ancient Egypt.* Vol. 3. Ed. D.B. Redford. New York: Oxford University Press, 2001.

Griffiths, J. Gwyn. *The Conflict of Horus and Seth from Egyptian and Classical Sources.* Liverpool, UK: Liverpool University Press, 1960.

Tiamat

(Sumerian and Babylonian)

Tiamat, a goddess of the ocean, is described as the primordial mother of the gods in the Babylonian creation myth, *Enuma Elish.* Her consort in this myth is Apsu, the god of the subterranean waters.

The myth begins before the existence of the heavens and Earth, as the mother, Tiamat, and her husband, Apsu, mingled their waters together, creating their progeny. Their first two children were Lahmu and Lahamu. Later, the pair Anshar and Kishar were born, who then gave birth to Anu, the supreme god of heaven. Anu fathered Nudimmud, also known as Ea, the god of wisdom.

The noise created by the divine offspring greatly disturbed the goddess Tiamat, but she indulged her young. Apsu complained about loss of sleep at night and lack of rest during the day. Frustrated, angry, and pushed to his limit, Apsu decided to kill the deities.

When she heard of Apsu's decision, Tiamat urged tolerance, but to no avail. When the gods learned of Apsu's decision, they were stunned. The wise Ea decided that they must act. He fashioned a magic spell and placed it on Apsu, putting him into a deep slumber. Ea then bound both Apsu and Mummu, Apsu's vizier (or chief adviser). He killed Apsu and made Mummu a prisoner.

Tiamat and Marduk

Soon afterward, Marduk, the hero, was born to Ea and his wife, Damkina. Anu formed and produced four terrifying winds that he gave to Marduk. Marduk toyed with the winds, creating a storm that agitated Tiamat and kept her and her offspring awake. Tiamat's offspring complained bitterly to their mother to do something. They urged Tiamat to respond to Marduk's aggressive, provoking behavior.

Tiamat agreed and prepared for war. She gave birth to twelve monster serpents: three types of horned snakes, a snake-dragon, a hairy hero-man, a storm-beast, a lion-demon, a lion-man, a scorpion-man, the essence of fierce storms, a fish-man, and a bull-man. Tiamat appointed her lover, Qingu, as chief of these forces. She also gave him control over the tablet of destinies, which held the power to control divine authority as well as human life.

Tiamat assembled her creatures to prepare for battle. Her array of powers was so great that Ea was forced to go to Anshar, king of the gods, for advice. Anshar ordered Ea to subdue Tiamat, but Ea's powers were not strong enough to counter her spells. Finally, Ea summoned Marduk, who offered to champion the gods and fight against Tiamat.

The Battle with Marduk

Marduk challenged Tiamat to one-on-one combat. The two gods were soon locked in battle. Marduk spread out his net, encircled Tiamat in a trap, and released an ill wind toward her face. The wind entered Tiamat's mouth and bloated her belly. Marduk then shot an arrow into her belly. It cut her innards and pieced her heart. Marduk killed Tiamat, flung down her carcass, and stood on it. He smashed her remaining forces, captured Qingu, and took away the tablet of destinies.

Next, Marduk turned his attention to the body of Tiamat. He crushed her skull with his mace and cut open her arteries. He then split her body in two. He set up half of her body as a roof for the heavens and the other half as the surface of the earth. The Tigris and Euphrates rivers flowed from her eyes, and mountains were formed from her breasts.

As for Tiamat's twelve creatures, Marduk smashed their weapons and made statues of them to be set up before the gate of Apsu. Qingu was sentenced to death, and mankind was formed from his blood.

Storytellers may view this myth in several ways. Depending on the age and knowledge level of the audience, this story may be told as a psychological tale, a dragon-slaying tale, a creation tale, or a hero tale.

Ira Spar

See also: Mother Goddess/Earth Mother.

Sources

Foster, Benjamin R. *Before the Muses: An Anthology of Akkadian Literature.* Potomac, MD: CDL, 1996.

Jacobsen, Thorkild. *The Treasures of Darkness: A History of Mesopotamian Religion.* New Haven, CT: Yale University Press, 1976.

Reiner, Erica. *Your Thwarts in Pieces, Your Mooring Rope Cut: Poetry from Babylon and Assyria.* Ann Arbor: University of Michigan Press, 1985.

Tibetan Storytelling

The Chinese occupation of Tibet, which began in 1951, led to a loss of many traditional practices, including storytelling. The wandering storytellers known as *lami manipas* or *lama manis* are no longer sanctioned by the current regime. Although they are not officially banned, their tradition, which dates back to perhaps the twelfth century C.E., is slowly dying out.

The lami manipas were traditionally of common birth and served a religious function. They traveled around Tibet carrying small shrines and sets of *thangkas,* which are traditional scrolls painted with religious themes.

The stories the lami manipas told were based on the paintings and served a dual purpose. They provided entertainment and educated the audience about the symbolism and meanings of the paintings and, through them, the traditional Tibetan Buddhist principles and legends. Whole villages would gather to hear these stories, especially during the holy month of the Buddha's birth, often chanting religious mantras together.

Another form of storytelling that has been exiled for its religious nature is a type of dance. There are two major types, *cham,* which is sacred monastic dancing meant to banish evil and bring blessings, and *achi lhamo,* the folk dances and operas that portray moral stories of good versus evil.

Despite the Chinese occupation, one traditional form of storytelling is very much alive in Tibet: the recitation of the Tibetan national epic, *Gesar of Ling.* This story of the hero-magician-king is known in all the Himalayan nations. In neighboring Ladakh it is known as *Kesar's Saga.*

One of the longest epics still in active recitation, the nearly 200 episodes may take a total of three months to recite. The episodes are recited only at night and in the winter, and several nights are required to complete each one. The recitation is performed by the visionary bards known as *drungpas* (male) and *drungmas* (female). It is said that in the past, the hoofprints of Gesar's horse might magically appear in a cleared circle around which the audience sat.

See also: Yeti; *Retelling: Geser.*

Sources

Coleman, Graham. *A Handbook of Tibetan Culture: A Guide to Tibetan Centres and Resources.* Boston: Shambhala, 1994.

Hyde-Chambers, Frederick, and Audrey Hyde-Chambers. *Tibetan Folk Tales.* Boston: Shambhala, 1981.

Tolkien, J.R.R.

(1892–1973)

The English author John Ronald Reuel Tolkien is perhaps best known for his epic fantasy novel *The Lord of the Rings.*

Childhood

Tolkien was born on January 3, 1892, in Bloemfontein, South Africa, to Arthur Reuel Tolkien and Mabel Suffield Tolkien. His father died when the boy was four, and young John, his brother, Hilary, and their mother settled near Birmingham, England. Their mother joined the Roman Catholic Church soon after their return to England. She raised the boys in the new faith and cut them off from both sides of their Anglican family.

Tolkien's mother died in 1904, and Father Francis X. Morgan, of the Birmingham Oratory Church, made sure the boys were protected. They lived with an aunt for a time and then in a rooming house for orphans.

John had proven himself adept at language, mastering Latin and Greek at an early age. He later added Finnish to his repertoire.

Love and War

Tolkien's life was changed when, at sixteen, he met a fellow lodger at school named Edith Bratt. She was nineteen, and their friendship soon deepened. Tolkien, distracted by his new relationship, failed to gain admission to Oxford on his first attempt. This caused Father Francis to forbid Tolkien from having any contact with Miss Bratt until he was twenty-one.

Tolkien dutifully followed Father Francis's order and entered Oxford's Exeter College. As soon as he reached the proper age, Tolkien once again took up his relationship with Edith. She ended a previous engagement and converted to Catholicism.

The young couple's plans were interrupted by the outbreak of World War I. Tolkien did not immediately enlist. Instead, he finished his degree in June 1915. By then, he had completed his first invented language, Qenya, and was enthralled with lyric poetry.

Tolkien entered the army and was made second lieutenant. He and Edith married at last on March 22, 1916, before he shipped out to France. While at the front near the Somme River, Tolkien began to work on his epic mythology and contracted trench fever. He was discharged and returned home in November 1916.

Early Works and Career

Tolkien completed his first work of fantasy, *Book of Lost Tales,* during his recovery. He continued to refine his imaginary beings, their world, and their languages for the rest of his life. During Tolkien's extended recuperation, Edith gave birth to their first son, John Francis Reuel, in 1917.

Shortly after the end of the war, Tolkien left the service and took his first job, as assistant lexicographer for *The New English Dictionary* (later known as *The Oxford English Dictionary*). He then worked at the University of Leeds, where he taught English language and literature until 1925.

It was at Leeds that Tolkien collaborated with Eric Valentine Gordon on a highly regarded translation of the fourteenth-century poem *Sir Gawain and the Green Knight.* Tolkien was also a founding member of the Viking Club, where students and teachers gathered to read Norse mythology and drink beer. During this period, Tolkien and his wife had two more sons, Michael Hilary Reuel and Christopher Reuel.

In 1925, Tolkien took a position at Oxford University, where he stayed until 1959. He enjoyed the academic life. During his time at Oxford, he helped found a group called the Inklings, which included the author C.S. Lewis. When he was not working, he continued to define his imaginary world and successfully raise a family. His only daughter, Priscilla, was born in 1929.

The Hobbit

As Tolkien told it, one day he was marking papers and found that a student had left an exam page blank. Professor Tolkien wrote on the page, "In a hole in the ground there lived a hobbit." Inspired, he went on to start a tale of adventure featuring the hobbit and his world.

Editor Susan Dagnall of the George Allen and Unwin publishing company saw an incomplete version of the book and asked the professor to finish it. After the publisher's ten-year-old son approved of the story—and earned a shilling for the effort—it was purchased. *The Hobbit* was published in 1937.

The Hobbit sold so well that the Unwin asked Tolkien if he had a sequel in mind. It took Tolkien sixteen years to complete his epic masterpiece, *The Lord of the Rings.* The novel, written in three parts—*The Fellowship of the Ring, The Two Towers,* and *The Return of the King*—was published in 1954 and 1955. Despite mixed reviews, it found an eager audience, which quickly grew after the production of a radio adaptation in 1956.

Widespread Success

The Lord of the Rings was more than a tale of men, wizards, trolls, dwarves, hobbits, and elves. Tolkien had been heavily influenced by his war experiences and what he saw as man's careless disregard for Earth's natural resources.

Despite its epic scope and fantastic imagery, people identified with the work's tales of love, courage, and friendship. The latter theme was presented in myriad combinations, but most notably between the two hobbits, Frodo Baggins and Samwise Gamgee. Tolkien's deep knowledge of the English language led him to name characters and settings using ancient tongues, in addition to his own inventions.

A paperback edition of the work was published in 1965. An American publisher released the three parts as separate books and fell into a highly publicized copyright dispute with Tolkien's British publisher. The media attention caught the imagination of the American youth and propelled the book to cult status as sales skyrocketed.

Tolkien appreciated the notoriety and revenue, but he disliked being the object of attention. He and Edith relocated to Bournemouth on England's south coast in 1969, where they lived quietly until Edith died in 1971.

After Edith's death, Tolkien moved into rooms provided by Merton College. He died on September 2, 1973.

The Silmarillion

Tolkien spent his final years revising his mythology and trying to complete a more heavily mythic work, *The Silmarillion,* to his satisfaction. Working alongside him was his son Christopher, who spent twenty-five years editing and polishing this complete history of Middle Earth after his father's death. The work was never finished.

Tolkien's works gained an even wider audience with the worldwide success of director Peter Jackson's faithful three-film adaptation of the novel. The final film of the trilogy, *The Return of the King* (2003), was awarded eleven Academy Awards.

Bob Greenberger

See also: Fantasy.

Sources

Carpenter, Humphrey. *Tolkien: A Biography.* Boston: Houghton Mifflin, 1977.

Curry, Patrick. *Defending Middle-Earth: Tolkien, Myth and Modernity.* New York: St. Martin's, 1997.

Grotta, Daniel. *The Biography of J.R.R. Tolkien: Architect of Middle Earth.* 2nd ed. Philadelphia: Running Press, 1978.

Pearce, Joseph. *Tolkien: Man and Myth.* San Francisco: Ignatius, 1998.

Tolkien, J.R.R. *Letters of J.R.R. Tolkien.* Ed. Humphrey Carpenter and Christopher Tolkien. Boston: Houghton Mifflin, 1981.

———. *The Lord of the Rings.* 1954–1955. Boston: Houghton Mifflin, 2003.

———. *The Monsters and the Critics, and Other Essays.* Boston: Allen and Unwin, 1983.

———. *The Silmarillion.* Ed. Christopher Tolkien. Boston: Houghton Mifflin, 1977.

———. *Sir Gawain and the Green Knight, Pearl, Sir Orfeo.* New York: Del Rey, 1977.

Tom Thumb

(English)

Tom Thumb is perhaps the earliest miniature human hero. One of the first stories written about the diminutive character dates from 1621, but he may well have existed in folklore long before that writing.

The most familiar version of Tom Thumb's story takes place in an Arthurian setting. The wizard Merlin is present at the birth of the thumb-sized boy. But the rest, the tongue-in-cheek exploits and too-cute clothing—a doublet made of thistledown and an oak-leaf hat—reflect the tone of the early seventeenth century. Tom Thumb is, in fact, reminiscent of the fairy folk of Shakespeare's *A Midsummer Night's Dream* (c. 1595–1596).

One of the earliest written versions of Tom Thumb's tale was *The History of Tom Thumbe the Little, for his small stature surnamed, King Arthvrs Dwarfe: Whose Life and aduentures containe many strange and wonderfull accidents, published for the delight of merry Time-spenders* (1621) by Richard Johnson. An anonymous verse version appeared in 1630 as *Tom Thumbe, His Life and Death: Wherein is declared many Marvailous Acts of Manhood, full of wonder, and strange merriments: Which the little Knight lived in King Arthurs time, and famous in the Court of Great-Brittaine.*

In 1730 and 1731, the English author Henry Fielding wrote a play based on the story of Tom Thumb. He used it to satirize both heroic drama and government politics.

For 300 years, the tale has turned up in various forms, from plays to children's books. Bawdy elements relating to Tom's stature and fame with the ladies often were included, as was the mention of Merlin and King Arthur. The story has been given both tragic and happy endings. The former include Tom being swallowed by a cow or bitten by a venomous spider. The children's versions, however, usually omit both King Arthur and the tragic ending.

In the United States in the nineteenth century, there were two unique uses of the story.

The story of Tom Thumb originated in England during the Middle Ages. In the nineteenth century, showman P.T. Barnum gave this performer the stage name of General Tom Thumb. His real name was Charles Sherwood Stratton (1838–1883). *(London Stereoscopic Company/Stringer/Getty Images)*

The famous showman P.T. Barnum featured in his show Charles Sherwood Stratton, who was just 25 inches (64 centimeters) tall, under the name General Tom Thumb. And in 1829, the Baltimore and Ohio Railroad experimented with its first steam engine, which was called the Tom Thumb.

There seems to be something innately fascinating about the idea of miniature human life. The topic was explored in the movies *The Incredible Shrinking Man* (1957; 2008), *The Incredible Shrinking Woman* (1981; 1994), and *Honey, I Shrunk the Kids* (1989).

Audiences' fascination with small beings, combined with the symbolism of the common man getting the better of the big men, make Tom Thumb an enduring character.

See also: No-Bigger-than-a-Finger; *Retelling: Tom Thumb's Adventures.*

Sources

Bauer, Susan. "Tom Thumb in the Arthurian Tradition." University of Rochester Libraries. http://www.lib.rochester.edu/camelot/TTMenu.htm.

Desmond, Alice Curtis. *Barnum Presents General Tom Thumb.* New York: Macmillan, 1954.

Hirsch, Richard S.M., ed. *The Most Pleasant History of Tom a Lincolne.* Columbia: University of South Carolina Press, 1978.

Tomte/Tomten/Tomtar

(Swedish)

Every farm in Sweden was said to have a *tomte* (the plural is *tomten* or *tomtar*), a helpful little being.

The tomte was about the size of a four-year-old child but had an old man's face and a long white or gray beard. He generally wore a knitted hat that resembled those found on garden gnomes, a jacket, knickers, red stockings, and sturdy shoes. In Finland, the tomte is called a *tontu.*

The folklore does not mention female tomten. There generally was only one tomte per household. A shy being, unwilling to be seen by humans, the tomte could make himself invisible. In some stories, this ability came from his hat, which he would twist around. This may be derived from the *tarnkap* or *tarnhelm* of invisibility, out of Norse and Germanic lore.

When he was treated nicely and when the farm animals were treated well, the tomte was happy and willingly took care of the home and farm, including the animals and people. The best way to reward him was to leave a bowl of rice pudding in the stable on Christmas night, which also may have served as a way of including the tomte in the festivities.

If the tomte was not treated with courtesy or the farm folk mistreated the animals, the tomte would become furious. And if he was mocked, he would see that some misfortune befell the mocker. This punishment varied from something relatively mild, such as tying the cows' tails into knots, to the more serious penalty of causing the harvest to fail or the cows' milk to go sour. The tomte even might abandon the farm altogether, leaving the farm folks to regret losing their helper.

The Christmas rice pudding tradition and an 1881 painting of a tomte by the Swedish illustrator Jenny Nystrom have led people to relate the tomte to Santa Claus. Santa sometimes is said to be helped not by elves but by tomten.

See also: Brownies.

Sources

Blecher, Lone Thygesen, and George Blecher. *Swedish Folktales and Legends.* New York: Pantheon, 1993.
Braekstad, H.L., trans. *Swedish Folk Tales.* New York: Hippocrene, 1998.
Miles, Clement A. *Christmas Customs and Traditions: Their History and Significance.* Mineola, NY: Dover, 1976.

Tongue Twisters

Tongue twisters are alliterative rhymes or sentences that are difficult to say without making a mistake and are perfect for audience participation during a storytelling session. Tongue twisters are a multilingual phenomenon that can be found in almost all languages.

The point of a tongue twister, as every child knows, is to say it as quickly and as accurately as possible. A tongue twister may sound like a real sentence, such as "She sells seashells by the seashore." But it also may be a combination of words put together just to make the sentence difficult to say, such as "How much wood could a woodchuck chuck, if a woodchuck could chuck wood?"

Tongue twisters are often used in speech therapy, to help those with speech problems or those who are trying to diminish an accent. Creating tongue twisters is a common and enjoyable exercise that also can teach word skills.

Above all, tongue twisters have the primary purpose of being fun. Here are some samples from around the world:

France: Tongue twister in French is *virelangues.*
Je suis ce que je suis et si je suis ce que je suis, qu'est-ce que je suis? (I am what I am and if I am what I am, what am I?)

Spain: The Spanish word for tongue twister is *trabalenguas.*
¡Usted no nada nada? No, no traje traje. (Don't you swim? No, no swimming suit.)

Germany: The German word for tongue twister is *zungenbrecher.*
Kluge kleine Katzen kratzen keine Krokodile. (Clever little cats don't scratch crocodiles.)

China: The Mandarin for tongue twister is *jao k'ou ling.*
Ma ma qi ma, ma man, ma ma ma ma. (Mother is riding a horse. The horse moves slowly. Mother chides the horse.)

Indonesia: The words in Indonesian for tongue twister are *pelincah lidah.*
Kuku kaki kakekku kaku. (My grandfather's toenail is stiff.)

See also: Nonsense Rhymes.

Sources

Reck, Michael. *First International Collection of Tongue Twisters*. www.uebersetzung.at/twister/.

Rosenbloom, Joseph. *World's Toughest Tongue Twisters*. New York: Sterling, 1987.

Schwartz, Alvin. *A Twister of Twists, a Tangler of Tongues*. Philadelphia: Lippincott, 1972.

Tree Spirits

Many of the world's cultures have believed that trees had spirits. Among the earliest known spirits of this type were the dryads of Greek mythology. Dryads were nymphs, or nature spirits, who inhabited trees and presided over woodlands.

The word *dryad* means "oak spirit." The Greeks had other names for inhabitants of different types of trees, but they have fallen out of use. The name dryad currently refers to any tree spirit.

Hamadryads were a subset of tree nymphs. They were so closely bound to their trees that they lived only as long as their trees stood, dying when their trees fell or were cut down.

Female Tree Spirits

Usually appearing as beautiful young women, dryads and other nymphs often were pursued by satyrs and the nature god Pan. They were said to entrance humans as well. Eurydice, the doomed bride of Orpheus, was a dryad.

The mortal lovers Baucis and Philemon prayed to never be parted, even in death. Zeus answered their prayers and turned them into trees upon their deaths.

The god Apollo pursued the reluctant nymph Daphne, who transformed into a laurel tree to escape his attentions. Apollo consoled himself by claiming the laurel as his tree and weaving her leaves into a wreath. Laurel wreathes, real or symbolic, are still used as a prize for athletic prowess.

There are several examples of spirits and other beings that were trapped in trees. In some versions of the King Arthur myths, the sorceress Nimue locked Merlin inside a tree after he finished teaching her the secrets of his magic.

In Shakespeare's play *The Tempest* (c. 1611), the magician Prospero speaks of having rescued Ariel from a "cloven pine," where the spirit had been imprisoned by a witch. He then threatens to shut Ariel in an oak, presumably a more uncomfortable prison, if she does not submit to serving him.

The Green Man

In medieval Europe, the tree spirit appeared in the form of the Green Man (called *ghille-dhu* in Scotland). The Green Man has worn many guises.

In Arthurian legend, the terrifying Green Knight let Sir Gawain cut off his head, then put it back on and rode away, challenging Gawain to accept an axe blow from him in a year's time. Fertility figures, such as England's John Barleycorn, were sacrificed each year so the crops would grow.

Many Polynesian cultures include tales of a vegetable god who dies and is buried so food plants can grow from his body for a starving village. To the American Indians, all living things have a spirit, though they usually do not manifest as a separate being.

Evidence of the Green Man can be found in architecture around the world. Buildings in America and Europe are often decorated with faces sprouting leaves, vines, and flowers. Surprisingly, these images often appear on churches. It is unclear whether they were holdovers from pre-Christian traditions or were meant to represent Jesus's incarnation.

Sculptures from the Indian Jain tradition, which teaches kindness and reverence for all forms of life, including plants, depict human figures so entwined with vegetation that it is difficult to tell where one ends and the other begins.

The English author C.S. Lewis included dryads in his fantasy world of Narnia. J.R.R. Tolkien described sentient and often malevolent trees that were shepherded by the giant, treelike Ents in his *Lord of the Rings*

(1954–1955). More recently, little white *kodama,* tree-dwelling nature spirits, played a small but crucial role in Hayao Miyazaki's animated film *Princess Mononoke* (1997).

Like animal spirits, dryads and other tree spirits remind us that there are more voices in the world than our own and that it is important to listen to them all.

Shanti Fader

See also: Adroanzi; Lutin.

Sources

Grant, Michael. *Myths of the Greeks and Romans.* Cleveland, OH: World, 1962.

Mercatante, Anthony S. *The Magic Garden: The Myth and Folklore of Flowers, Plants, Trees and Herbs.* New York: Harper and Row, 1976.

Tricksters

Tricksters are archetypical figures—basic images in the world's folklore, mythology, and popular culture. They may be divine or mortal, but they always exist as agents of pure change, characters who breaks taboos and laws without a thought and who lack the ordinary concept of human morality. The tricksters' greatest weapons are their quick wits.

Although a trickster may be the hero or heroine of a story, he or she is very different from the traditional hero of folktale, fairy tale, or myth. Traditional heroes are fearless, while tricksters often are cowards who trick or bribe others into fighting for them. Heroes are compassionate and loving, but tricksters usually are selfish, or at least appear to be so. And heroes seek to restore order, while tricksters do everything in their power to overturn it—as long as they can profit from the resulting chaos.

General Characteristics

One important function of the trickster in story is to teach the difference between right and wrong by pointing out correct and incorrect behaviors. Native American trickster tales, with a few exceptions, teach this way, through negative example: The outrageous behavior, stupid-ity, or unchecked appetite of characters such as Coyote, Rabbit, Turtle, and Inktomi shows an audience exactly what becomes of people who conduct themselves in similar ways.

Tricksters sometimes turn their attention and energy toward fighting against monsters or ridding a place of a corrupt leader. In these stories, a trickster's quick wit and silver tongue can be held up as an example of how to deal with adversity or extract oneself from a difficult situation.

A trickster also can succeed where traditional methods and wisdom fail. Since they are unpredictable, they are that much harder to foil. One Hindu tale tells of a compassionate Brahman who freed a tiger from a cage. The tiger tried to eat his benefactor (despite having promised while still in the cage that it would not) as the Brahman begged for his life. Grudgingly, the tiger agreed to spare the Brahman if he could find three creatures who agreed that it would be wrong to eat him. The Brahman tried in vain to find three advocates, but he did encounter a jackal who tricked the tiger back into its cage. Trickery succeeded where appealing to virtue had failed.

Tricksters often act as heroes for the underprivileged. While some tricksters are gods, kings, and queens, most are simple people—farmers, peasant girls, animals, thieves, gypsies, and wanderers. They represent the poor and oppressed, give power to those who are traditionally powerless, and help those who generally have no way to protect themselves when their rulers are corrupt.

Tricksters pit themselves against those who try to cheat the honest poor or who wield tyrannical power. One such corrupt official was the plantation master in the American folktales of High John the Conqueror. High John scored numerous victories against his master, some trivial, some not, on behalf of all the slaves who had to bend their heads and obey.

Female Tricksters

While female trickster figures are less common than male tricksters, they are far from absent in world myth and folklore. Female tricksters tend to fall into one of two categories: clever wives or daughters who use their wits to save their family, or wronged wives who must resort to trickery to prove their innocence and win back their beloved.

Clever wife or daughter tricksters can answer difficult questions that stump their husbands or fathers. In one tale that appears in many different cultures, a king threatened to take a poor family's home and land unless one of them appeared before him neither dressed nor naked, neither riding nor walking, and bringing him a gift that was not a gift. The clever daughter wrapped herself in a fishnet, appeared on the back of a goat with her feet brushing the ground, and offered the king a bird that flew away when released from its basket. The king was so impressed that he not only returned the land but also married the clever daughter.

The character of the wronged wife generally turns to trickery out of necessity. The husband brags about his wife's fidelity, or decides to test it, and a friend tries in vain to seduce her. The friend then bribes someone, often an elderly woman, to gain the faithful wife's confidence and learn some intimate secret about her—a description of her bedroom, or a mark on her body. The friend then presents this information to the husband as proof of his conquest. The husband believes the man and throws his wife out of their home, despite her protests of innocence. The wronged wife often disguises herself as a man, taking on the role of warrior, judge, or sage in order to learn how she was tricked. She then returns to set up an elaborate show that reveals the would-be seducer's falsehood and proves her chastity.

A third type of female trickster is the unfaithful wife. This character resorts to trickery to hide her infidelity from her husband. In most cases, this woman is tricked in return, and both she and her lover are punished.

One of the most famous female tricksters is Scheherazade, the central character in *The Thousand and One Nights* or *The Arabian Nights*. Scheherazade was married to a jealous and embittered man, King Shahryar, who had killed each of his previous wives the morning after their wedding. Scheherazade managed to stay alive by telling a story each night that ended on a dramatic cliffhanger. The king was so eager to learn what happened next that he let her live another night to finish the story, and so on for the thousand and one nights.

It is interesting to note that while most traditional stories involving love end with a wedding, stories featuring female tricksters sometimes go further and portray married life, with its compromises and strife. Perhaps the lesson here is that the spirit of the trickster is needed in life beyond the wedding day.

Western Tradition

The Greek god Hermes was a trickster. Within days of his birth, Hermes stole a flock of cattle from his brother, Apollo, and reversed his footprints to hide the deed. When the angry Apollo eventually found his little brother and demanded that he return the cattle, Hermes made peace by giving Apollo the lyre, or harp, that he had fashioned from a turtle shell. Hermes was allowed to keep the cattle.

The Norse pantheon also had a trickster, called Loki. But while Hermes eventually learned to behave himself and became the messenger of Olympus, Loki was a more malevolent force. Loki gladly cheated the giants who built Midgard, the home of the gods, out of their payment. He also tricked the blind god, Höd, into killing his half brother, Balder, who was the most beloved of the gods. Loki eventually was punished by the other gods, who bound him under the earth, but it was too late—he already had sired the monsters that would eventually bring about the gods' destruction.

In Europe, perhaps the most famous trickster is the ubiquitous Jack. He is best known for planting a magic beanstalk and then robbing the giant who lived at the beanstalk's top. The Flemish trickster-fool Till Eulenspiegel told fortunes and wandered around playing pranks on the rich and pompous.

Somewhat nastier is the Danish trickster Little Claus, who was a character in the Hans Christian Andersen story "Little Claus and Big Claus." Little Claus convinced his neighbor Big Claus to slaughter all his cattle and murder his old grandmother. Little Claus then persuaded Big Claus to throw himself into a river by describing the fabulous city that lay at the bottom.

Eastern Tricksters

Hindu mythology has the trickster god, Krishna, who was the eighth incarnation of the compassionate preserver god, Vishnu. As a child, Krishna stole butter from his mother and neighbors. When he was a young man, he stole the clothing of the village cowherd women, called *gopis,* while they bathed in the river. At night, he would play his flute, and the gopis would rise from their husbands' beds and run into the forest to dance in a holy frenzy around him.

In the Chinese legend of Monkey, an audacious warrior and magician tried to leap to the end of the earth. He succeeded only in leaping to the edge of the Buddha's hand, where he marked his supposed triumph by urinating on the Buddha's finger.

Japanese tricksters often are more malicious. Examples include the shape-shifting fox and *tenuki* (badger) spirits, who play tricks on humans.

In the Middle East, there are a number of stories of Jewish tricksters. The great Hebrew King Solomon appeared in a trickster's role in some stories, as in the famous tale of the child claimed by two women. By offering to cut the child in half and watching the reactions of the two women, Solomon was able to determine who the real mother was.

From Africa to America

One of the best-known African tricksters is Anansi, the spider. Though tiny and weak, Anansi is clever enough to trick the powerful tiger into giving up his box of stories, thus making Anansi the keeper of wisdom. To win the box of stories, Anansi had to accomplish three impossible tasks. Instead of seeking supernatural help, Anansi used his wits.

Downtrodden and utterly without rights or liberty, African slaves in early America loved trickster tales and wove them into the culture they shaped for themselves. Many of their stories were animal tales, often modeled after African or Native American stories. These included the fearless and inventive Brer Rabbit, who could talk his way out of any trouble. The Brer Rabbit story, in which the rabbit is caught and tricks his captor into throwing him into a briar patch, is based on a Cherokee rabbit tale.

Many Native American tricksters are animals: Raven, in the Pacific Northwest; Inktomi, the spider trickster of the Sioux; Rabbit, among the Cherokee; and perhaps the best-known trickster of all, Coyote. Coyote appears in the stories of many Native American tribes, including the Navajo, Hopi, Zuni, and Nez Percé.

Some of these tribes honor Coyote as a creator with the power to sing and unsing the entire world, as well as a protector who destroys monsters using his wits and magic. Others paint Coyote as a bumbling fool whose plans consistently backfire, or as amoral, greedy, and lecherous, forever undone by his boundless appetites. Many books and collections of stories are devoted to the exploits of Coyote. He is portrayed either as the trickster or as the tricked one, and sometimes he shifts between the two roles, even within the same story.

Tricksters cross boundaries and ignore what is proper. They dance outside the lines of what is acceptable. In doing so, they shatter our dull routines and our preconceptions. Perhaps most important, tricksters can make us laugh at our own foolishness. It is no wonder that they are such popular and enduring figures.

Shanti Fader

See also: Anansasem; Archetype; Gremlins; Hermes; Lange Wapper; Leprechauns; Leshy, Leshiye; Lutin; Maui; Ravens and Crows; Reynard the Fox.

Sources

Chinen, Allan B. *Beyond the Hero: Classic Stories of Men in Search of Soul.* New York: Putnam, 1993.
———. *In the Ever After: Fairy Tales and the Second Half of Life.* Wilmette, IL: Chiron, 1989.
Jurich, Marilyn. *Scheherazade's Sisters: Trickster Heroines and Their Stories in World Literature.* Westport, CT: Greenwood, 1998.
Ramsey, Jarold, comp. *Coyote Was Going There: Indian Literature of the Oregon Country.* Seattle: University of Washington Press, 1977.

Tristan and Isolde

(Celtic)

In the story of Tristan and Isolde, a pair of star-crossed lovers, Sir Tristan (also Tristram or Tristrem) was sent to Ireland to bring Isolde the Fair (also Yseult or Iseult) back with him to Cornwall to wed his uncle, King Mark.

A magic potion that Tristan and Isolde unwittingly swallowed bound them together in eternal love. After many trysts and difficulties, not the least of which was the anger of King Mark, the lovers separated, or were forced apart. In some versions, Tristan married another Isolde, Isolde of the White Hands.

In all versions, Tristan later lay dying of a battle wound. He sent for Isolde the Fair. Deceived into believing she would not come, or after she deliberately delayed her coming, Tristran died of despair. Isolde, finding her lover dead, died of grief beside him.

There are versions of this medieval romance from many countries, including England, France, and Germany. The earliest existing written version is in Anglo-Norman French verse, authored by Thomas of Britain in about 1185. Gottfried von Strassburg wrote a German version of the story in about 1210. The story was originally not part of the Arthurian cycle but somehow entered that legend. In the fifteenth century, Sir Thomas Malory included a version of Tristan and Isolde in his classic *Morte d'Arthur*.

The story is mainly Irish in origin. It bears a strong resemblance to the Irish tales of Deirdre, in which the lovers Deirdre and Naoise flee from King Concobar. It is also similar to stories of the lovers Grainne and Diarmid, who fled from Fionn McCumhail.

There are numerous modern versions of the story, including Matthew Arnold's *Tristram and Iseult* (1852), A.C. Swinburne's *Tristram of Lyonesse* (1882), and Joseph Bédier's retelling, *Tristan and Iseult* (1900). Richard Wagner's opera *Tristan und Isolde* premiered in 1865.

See also: King Arthur; Tale Types.

Sources

Bedier, Joseph. *The Romance of Tristan and Iseult.* 1900. Trans. Hilaire Belloc. New York: Pantheon, 1965.
Grimbert, Joan T., ed. *Tristan and Isolde: A Casebook.* New York: Garland, 1995.
Malory, Sir Thomas. *Le Morte d'Arthur: The Winchester Manuscript.* Ed. Helen Cooper. New York: Oxford University Press, 1998.

Trojan War

(Greek)

The Trojan War was a conflict between the united forces of ancient Greece and the powerful Anatolian trading city of Troy. Legend places the war at about 1200 B.C.E. It is not known whether the events actually took place as written, were purely mythological, or were partially based on a real war.

According to Greek mythology, the war began with an insult to a goddess. At the wedding of mortal King Peleus of Phthia and the sea nymph Thetis, all the gods and goddesses were invited—except one, Eris, goddess of discord. Eris was insulted by the omission and plotted to cause trouble. She created a beautiful golden apple and inscribed on it, "For the most beautiful." She then sent the lovely apple to the feast, sat back, and watched.

As Eris had expected, three of the goddesses, Hera, queen of the gods, Athena, goddess of wisdom, and Aphrodite, goddess of love and beauty, promptly claimed the apple. They quarreled over it without coming to a resolution. Before matters got out of hand, they called upon Paris, a son of King Priam of Troy,

This fifteenth-century painting on wood shows a scene from the Trojan War in which the Trojans drag the great horse into their city, never guessing that it is full of Greek warriors. *(Réunion des Musées Nationaux/Art Resource, NY)*

to judge the impromptu beauty contest. Paris was in a dangerous position, but he boldly awarded the apple to Aphrodite because she promised him Helen, the most beautiful woman in the world.

Paris and Helen

Helen was already married to King Menelaus of Sparta. But when Paris arrived in her husband's court, Helen promptly fell in love with him. Helen was either abducted or willingly fled with Paris to Troy. Menelaus and his brother Agamemnon, who was married to Helen's sister, Clytemnestra, organized a large Greek expedition against Troy to win Helen back. The Greek army included the notable heroes Achilles and Odysseus.

The walls of Troy proved to be impenetrable. The Greek army laid siege for ten years without success. Because of this frustrating situation, trouble arose in the Greek camp. The great Achilles refused to fight because he felt that Agamemnon, the Greek commander, had insulted him. Without

Achilles, the Trojans, led by Hector, son of King Priam, were able to attack and drive the Greeks back to their ships. But when Hector slew Achilles's best friend, Patroclus, Achilles returned to combat and killed Hector to avenge Patroclus's death.

The Trojans had received help from their two allies, the Ethiopians and the Amazons. But Achilles demoralized the allies by killing Penthesilea, queen of the Amazons, and Memnon, king of the Ethiopians. But then Paris, aided by the god Apollo, shot an arrow at Achilles, hit his one vulnerable point, his heel, and killed him.

The Trojan Horse

The siege continued. Odysseus, who had not wanted to go to war and desperately wanted to get home, finally came up with a scheme to get the Greeks inside the Trojan walls. The Greeks built a huge wooden horse, now known as the Trojan horse, and placed it outside the walls of Troy. The horse was hollow, and Odysseus and several other warriors hid inside while the rest of the Greek army sailed away, appearing to retreat.

Cassandra, daughter of King Priam, had the gift of prophecy, which she had gained from the god Apollo. But because she had refused Apollo's advances, the god put a curse on her so that no one would believe her prophecies. Cassandra warned the Trojans that they must not take this horse into their city, but no one listened to her. The rejoicing Trojans, sure the horse was a token of the Greek surrender, pulled the horse into Troy.

That night, the Trojans fell asleep after celebrating their apparent victory. Odysseus and the others stole out of the horse and opened the city gates for the rest of the Greek warriors, who had returned from a nearby island.

The Greeks stormed into Troy and massacred the Trojans, killing most of the men and enslaving the women, including Cassandra. They burned the city and took back Helen. The Trojan War was over at last.

Works Inspired by the Trojan War

The story of the Trojan War has inspired storytellers, playwrights, writers, and composers throughout the ages. The plots of the epic works the *Iliad* and the *Odyssey* center around the war, and various Greek playwrights took the war for their subject. Among the plays are Euripides's sympathetic treatment of the victims of war in *Hecuba* (named for King Priam's wife) and *The Trojan Women*. The Roman poet Virgil added a new dimension to the story by inventing another Trojan prince, Aeneus, and writing the *Aeneid* about his adventures.

In the nineteenth century, Hector Berlioz composed an opera, *Les Troyens*. Irish writer James Joyce loosely based his novel *Ulysses* (the Roman name for Odysseus), first published in serial form from 1918 to 1920, on the story of Odysseus.

Historians and archaeologists have yet to find definitive proof of an actual war. Troy existed at a strategic point overlooking the entrance to the Black Sea, but its walls were breached and it was ruined not once, but several times. There may have been several small battles fought against the Greeks, or there actually may have been one large war. If there was a major Trojan War, it was most likely fought over trade, not Helen.

See also: Iliad.

Sources

Allen, Susan Heuck. *Finding the Walls of Troy: Frank Calvert and Heinrich Schliemann at Hisarlik.* Berkeley: University of California Press, 1999.

Grant, Michael. *Myths of the Greeks and Romans.* Cleveland, OH: World, 1962.

Homer. *The Iliad.* Trans. Robert Fagles. New York: Viking, 1990.

Troubadours

(French)

Troubadours were composers and professional singers of medieval Europe. They are believed to have originated in eleventh-century France. The first troubadour may well have been William IX, Duke of Aquitaine, who was known as a songwriter.

The word *troubadour* comes from the French verb *trobar,* meaning "to find" or "to compose." The themes of troubadours' songs ranged from the adventures of gallant knights to romantic ballads of courtly love. Their songs were often, though not always, secular and were sung in the regional vernacular. Since many troubadours created true narrative ballads, they also can be considered storytellers.

The troubadours rarely had fixed residences. They wandered the land, passing along news, songs, and stories as they went. The image of the wandering troubadour has been romanticized over time.

Perhaps the most familiar story about a troubadour is that of Blondel. Jean de Nesle, whose nickname, Blondel, referred to someone with flowing blond hair, was either a troubadour at the court of King Richard I of England or the monarch's personal friend. The stories claim that when Richard returned from the Crusades, he was taken prisoner in what is now Germany. Blondel went in search of him, singing a song only the two of them knew. When Blondel finally heard Richard's voice singing the song from a barred tower window, Blondel knew he had found his king and returned to England with the news. This tale is almost certainly fiction, but it is true that Richard ceded land to someone named Blondel; whether or not this was the troubadour is unknown.

Another troubadour has earned a footnote in modern musical history. In the thirteenth century, Adam de la Halle became the first of the troubadours known to compose only secular music. He was the author of the first musical comedy, *Le Jeu de Robin et Marion* (*The Play of Robin and Marion*). This light tale tells of a girl who chooses her true love over a wealthy knight. The play and its songs still can be found in print and recently have been recorded.

See also: Jongleurs; Minstrels.

Sources

Press, Alan R., comp. *Anthology of Troubadour Lyric Poetry.* Austin: University of Texas Press, 1971.
Smythe, Barbara, trans. *Troubadour Poets.* New York: Duffield, 1911.

Truth and Falsehood, The Tale of

(Egyptian)

The Tale of Truth and Falsehood, an allegorical Egyptian tale, dates to the nineteenth dynasty (c. 1315–1201 B.C.E.).

In the lost opening to the story, Falsehood complained to the Great Ennead of Heliopolis (the nine gods of Heliopolis) that his elder brother, Truth, had stolen a marvelous dagger from him. According to Falsehood, all the copper from Mount Yal and all the trees in the forest of Coptus had gone into the creation of this dagger. At the behest of Falsehood, the nine gods blinded Truth and assigned him to act as his brother's doorkeeper.

Falsehood soon grew tired of seeing his virtuous brother sitting at his threshold. He ordered two servants to cast him out where lions would eat him. Truth asked the men to spare him, and, through adventures that have not been preserved, he succeeded in avoiding this fate. A lady whose servants had found Truth lying in the brush was struck by his handsome appearance. She made him her doorkeeper and slept with him one night.

The lady gave birth to a godlike son. The boy excelled at writing, as well as at the art of war, arousing the envy of the older schoolboys. They taunted him, saying "You don't have a father!"

So the young man went to his mother demanding to know who his father was. When he discovered that his father was none other than their blind doorkeeper, he was enraged. He brought Truth into the house and promised vengeance on whoever had blinded him. Truth told his son that Falsehood was responsible, so the young man formulated a plan.

Truth's son paid Falsehood's herdsman to guard an exceptionally beautiful ox. Some months later, Falsehood noticed the fine ox in his herd and decided to eat it, although the herdsman warned him that it belonged to someone else. When word of Falsehood's deed reached Truth's son, the youth took his case before the ennead.

"My ox," he said, "was so big that the horns stretched from the eastern mountain to the western mountain. The Nile was its bed, and sixty calves were born to it each day." The ennead did not believe that such a creature existed. Truth's son then asked Falsehood if there had ever been a dagger so big that all the copper of a mountain and all the trees in a forest went into its manufacture. The gods again were charged with judging between Truth and Falsehood.

Believing that his brother had been eaten by lions long ago, Falsehood vowed that if Truth were still alive, then he should be blinded and made to serve his older brother. Shown by the boy that Truth was still alive, the gods blinded Falsehood and appointed him Truth's doorkeeper.

Noreen Doyle

See also: Tale Types.

Sources

Griffiths, J. Gwyn. *The Conflict of Horus and Seth from Egyptian and Classical Sources.* Liverpool, UK: Liverpool University Press, 1960.

Lichtheim, Miriam. *Ancient Egyptian Literature: A Book of Readings.* New ed. Vol. 2. Berkeley: University of California Press, 2006.

Twin Brothers

The "twin brothers" is a world folktale type in which the basic elements are the same from culture to culture, but the details can differ widely.

Twin sets of boys, hounds, and horses were born. This was usually the result of magic, whether accidental, as in their mothers eating magic fruit, or deliberate. In some cases, it was the result of a magic fish that was caught three times. Upon being caught a third time, the fish told the fisherman to divide it in three and feed it to his wife, his hound, and his mare.

The boys grew up, either normally or with miraculous speed, and were given twin swords. The two young men set out to find adventure on separate paths after exchanging tokens or learning signs that would tell either brother if the other was in trouble. The tokens or signs ranged from a knife blade that would turn black or rusty to tracks suddenly filling with blood.

The first brother rescued and married a princess. He was then lured away from her side by a witch or demon, who either imprisoned him or turned him to stone.

The second brother saw from the token or learning sign that his twin was in deadly danger and went hunting for him. He met his brother's wife, who took this twin for her husband, but he was too honorable to take advantage of her. Instead, he went on to disenchant his brother.

But that brother, smitten by jealousy, instantly thought he had been betrayed. In many versions, he killed his twin. Then, learning the truth a bit too late, the surviving twin killed the witch (or demon), and his brother was returned to life. In an alternate ending, the brother was returned to life through a magic potion.

Variations of this basic story have been found throughout Europe and in Greece, Turkey, India, and Indonesia. The story is also known in North America and the Caribbean, having been brought to the New World by immigrants.

See also: Motifs.

Sources

Aarne, Antti, and Stith Thompson. *The Types of the Folktale: A Classification and Bibliography.* 2nd rev. ed. Helsinski, Finland: Academia Scientiarum Fennica, 1987.

Grimm, Jacob, and Wilhelm Grimm. *The Complete Fairy Tales of the Brothers Grimm.* Trans. Jack Zipes. New York: Bantam, 2003.

Mercatante, Anthony S. *The Facts on File Encyclopedia of World Mythology and Legend.* New York: Facts on File, 1998.

Thompson, Stith. *The Folktale.* Berkeley: University of California Press, 1977.

Two Brothers, Tale of the

(Egyptian)

The ancient Egyptian source for the *Tale of the Two Brothers,* commonly referred to as "the oldest fairy tale in the world," was written at the end of the nineteenth dynasty (early thirteenth century B.C.E.). This tale of two brothers and their wives is an early incarnation of the poor-boy-becomes-prosperous motif that became popular in later European folktales.

The characters are identifiable with one or more of the Egyptian deities: The elder brother, Anpu, can be identified with Anubis; the younger brother, Bata, with Osiris, an older funerary deity named Bata, or Seth; and the unnamed two wives with forms of Hathor.

A parallel with the biblical tale of Samson and Delilah also can be drawn.

The Betrayal

Anpu, Bata, and Anpu's wife lived together in Anpu's house. Bata was exceptionally handsome and strong and understood the language of cattle. One day, while fetching seed grain, Bata encountered his brother's wife braiding her hair. His ability to carry five sacks greatly impressed Anpu's wife, who offered herself to him. This repulsed Bata, who thought of this woman as his mother. He promised to keep her attempted adultery a secret.

While the two brothers were sowing in the fields, Anpu's wife applied fat and grease to her body to give the appearance of bruises. Arriving home, Anpu found his wife lying in the darkened house, vomiting and injured. She claimed that Bata had made unwanted advances toward her and beat her into silence. If Anpu refused to kill him, she would die.

Infuriated by these allegations, Anpu took a spear and waited for his brother in the stable. When Bata brought the cows in from the fields, the animals saw Anpu hiding behind the door and warned Bata of the danger. Bata fled, with Anpu in pursuit. The god Re-Horakhty heard Bata's prayers and separated the brothers with a body of crocodile-infested water.

Bata explained to his brother what had really transpired. He was deeply hurt that Anpu would take the word of a "filthy whore" above that of his own brother. To demonstrate his grief, Bata cuts off his penis. He threw his member into the water, where it was eaten by a fish. Anpu was consumed with sorrow, but Bata told him to go home to take care of the cattle.

Bata announced that he would go to the Valley of the Pine, where he would place his heart on the blossom of a pine tree. If that tree was ever felled, Bata would die. Anpu would receive a sign on Bata's death: A jug of beer in Anpu's hand would begin to foam. On receiving this sign, Anpu should seek Bata's heart and, upon finding it, put the heart into a bowl of cool water so that Bata might live again.

Bata's Wife

The brothers went their separate ways. Bata settled down in the Valley of the Pine, initially dwelling under the pine tree that bore his heart but eventually building a house.

The Great Ennead of Heliopolis (nine gods of Heliopolis) visited Bata with news that Anpu had slain his wife and thrown her corpse to the dogs. They also provided Bata with a wife, made by the god Khnum, and told Bata that his wife's fate was to die by the knife. Bata provided for his new wife and told her the secret of his heart. He also warned her not to leave the house, because the sea might seize her, and Bata, castrated, was unable to fight the sea.

But Bata's wife did leave the house, and the sea did attempt to catch her. She escaped back into the house, but not before the pine, at the sea's request, snagged a lock of her hair. The sea brought the hair to the place where the royal laundrymen washed the king's linens, and a marvelous odor impregnated the clothes. The king, who was told that the scented hair must come from a daughter of Re-Horakhty, dispatched messengers abroad to seek out this woman.

Bata killed all but one of the messengers. This last messenger returned to Egypt and told the king that Bata had killed the others. The king sent an army to the valley. The army returned with the woman, Bata's wife, and the people rejoiced. She instructed the king to have the pine felled and destroyed. When this was done, Bata fell dead.

Recognizing the sign of his brother's death, Anpu armed himself and set off for the valley, where he found Bata lying dead in the house. For three years, Anpu sought Bata's heart. Just as he was about to give up and return to Egypt, he discovered it. Anpu placed the heart in water, and Bata's body trembled. He drank the water and recovered. Bata enlisted Anpu in a plan for revenge against his traitorous wife.

The Brothers Unite

Bata transformed into a beautiful bull. Anpu rode him to the palace, where the king and all the people praised the fine animal. The king rewarded Anpu with silver and gold, and Anpu became a close friend of the king.

One day, Bata the bull entered the kitchen, where he met the noble lady who had been his wife. "See, I live again," he told her, making her greatly afraid. She tricked the king into promising to give her anything she wished. Then, she asked to eat the liver of the bull.

Although he was deeply upset by this request, the king sacrificed the bull. Two drops of the bull's blood fell beside the palace gate. Overnight, two trees, called persea trees, grew up, which caused great rejoicing throughout Egypt.

One day, when the king and the noblewoman were honoring the persea trees, Bata again announced himself to his former wife. Yet again the noblewoman tricked the king into granting her wish. This time, the two persea trees were cut down to be made into furniture.

As the noblewoman watched the felling, a splinter flew into her mouth. As a result, she was impregnated and gave birth to a son, and again the king and Egypt rejoiced. The king loved the boy greatly and appointed him viceroy of Nubia and, later, crown prince.

After many years the king died, and his son became king.

The newly crowned king made known all that had happened to him. He passed judgment on the noblewoman and appointed Anpu crown prince. He reigned for thirty years. On the day of his death, Anpu became king.

Noreen Doyle

See also: Tale Types.

Sources

Hollis, Susan Tower. *The Ancient Egyptian "Tale of Two Brothers," the Oldest Fairy Tale in the World.* Norman: University of Oklahoma Press, 1990.

Lichtheim, Miriam. *Ancient Egyptian Literature: A Book of Readings.* Vol. 2. New ed. Berkeley: University of California Press, 2006.

Velde, Herman te. *Seth, God of Confusion.* 2nd ed. Leiden, The Netherlands: E.J. Brill, 1977.

Typhon

(Greek)

In Greek mythology, Typhon was a dragon-like monster that tried to wrest control of the heavens from Zeus, king of the gods.

In Greek mythology, the monstrous Typhon tried unsuccessfully to steal power from Zeus, chief of the gods. This illustration shows Zeus and Typhon in combat. Zeus appears poised to win. *(Foto Marburg/Art Resource, NY)*

Typhon was a massive creature, winged and breathing fire, with a man's body from the head to the thighs, and coils of vipers for legs. He was the offspring of Gaia, the earth, and Tartarus, the lowest realm of being.

Typhon attacked heaven with roars, hurling blazing rocks and breathing great blasts of fire. When the gods on Mount Olympus saw him rushing at them, they fled in the shapes of animals.

Only Zeus stood his ground, hurling thunderbolts at the monster and then attacking him with a sickle. It was a savage fight that covered all the land that now is Greece. At times, it seemed as though Typhon would win.

But at last, Zeus cast Mount Etna down upon Typhon, trapping him forever. To this day, the blasts of fire that shoot up from Mount Etna are said to be the remnants of Zeus's thunderbolts and Typhon's fire.

See also: Dragons.

Sources

Evslin, Bernard. *Gods, Demigods and Demons: An Encyclopedia of Greek Mythology.* Reissue ed. New York: Scholastic, 1988.

Grant, Michael. *Myths of the Greeks and Romans.* Cleveland, OH: World, 1962.

South, Malcolm, ed. *Mythical and Fabulous Creatures: A Source Book and Research Guide.* New York: Greenwood, 1987.

Ugly Baby

Every mother thinks her child is beautiful, even if everyone else disagrees. This truism can be found in stories and folktales from around the world, as well as in various folk jokes. Storytellers can share these jokes and tales from either a sympathetic or cynical point of view, depending on the situation.

The sixth-century Greek fabulist Aesop told the story of Zeus and the monkey, in which the god offered a prize to the mother with the most beautiful offspring. Among the other animals came the monkey, with her hairless, flat-nosed, ugly baby in her arms. When they saw it, the gods all laughed. But the monkey hugged her little one to her and said, "Zeus may give the prize to whomever he likes. But I shall always think my baby the most beautiful of them all."

Haitian folklore agrees with Aesop. A Haitian proverb states, "*Makak pa janm kwe petit-li led,*" or "A monkey never thinks her baby is ugly."

European Fables and Folktales

French fabulist Jean de La Fontaine told of a rather tragic misunderstanding between an eagle and an owl. The eagle agreed not to eat the owl's babies if the owl would only describe them. The owl spoke of the most beautiful babies in the world, and the eagle agreed not to eat them. But the eagle did eat the owlets. When confronted by the owl, the eagle could not understand the fuss: To him, the babies had been truly ugly.

In a Norwegian folktale, a hunter agrees not to kill a snipe's "beautiful" babies. After the hunter kills the ugly babies, the snipe mourns, as every child is beautiful to its mother.

A Romanian folktale has a happier ending, in which God sees the crow's babies and wonders how he could have created such ugly things. The mother crow defends them. God agrees that every mother sees her babies as beautiful and blesses the crows.

Ugly Baby Jokes

There are also several related folk jokes about ugly babies.

Woman, crying: Everyone thinks my baby is ugly!
Man: Aw, he isn't. And here's a banana for your monkey.

A minister schooled himself not to react to ugly babies but to smile at them and say innocuously, "Now, *that's* a baby!" But one day, confronted by a truly hideous baby, he heard himself say, to his horror, "*Now, that's a baby?*"

A woman got on a bus holding a baby. The bus driver said, "That's the ugliest baby I've ever seen!"

In a huff, the woman slammed her fare into the fare box and took an aisle seat near the rear of the bus. She fumed for a few stops and started getting really worked up. The man seated next to her sensed she was agitated and asked her what was wrong.

"The bus driver insulted me!" she fumed.

The man sympathized and said, "Hey! He's a public servant, and he shouldn't say things to insult the passengers."

"You're right!" said the mother. "I think I'll go back up there and give him a piece of my mind."

"That's a good idea," the man said. "Here, let me hold your monkey!"

Every so often a baby is born that is so horrifyingly ugly, the father screams, "Put it back, put it back, put it back!"

Of course, anyone using ugly baby jokes in his or her repertoire had better first make sure that no one in the audience is holding an ugly baby.

See also: Tall Tales; Urban Legends.

Sources

Asbjornsen, Peter Christen. *Popular Tales from the Norse, by George Webbe Dasent.* 3rd ed. Edinburgh, UK: Douglas, 1888.

Gaster, Moses. *Rumanian Bird and Beast Stories Rendered into English.* London: Sidgwick and Jackson, 1915.

Ullikummi

(Hittite)

In Hittite mythology, Ullikummi was born from the mating of the god Kumarbi with the Rock, a sentient boulder. Ullikummi, made entirely of diorite, a type of dark, coarse-grained rock, had been created as a weapon to defeat the storm god and his allies. To hide him from the storm god, the sun god, and Ishtar, the goddess of fertility, Kumarbi placed him on the shoulder of Upelluri, the dreaming god, where he grew an acre in a month.

After fifteen days, Ullikummi had grown enough to stand waist deep in the sea, which is where the sun god first spotted him. Warned by the sun god, the storm god fought Ullikummi on Mount Imgarra, but the battle had no clear victor. Then, Ullikummi drove the goddess Hebat out of her temple. An army of seventy gods attacked him, and they all plunged off the mountain, falling down into the sea.

Ullikummi rose out of the sea, a huge 31,000 miles (about 9,000 leagues) tall. He towered over the city of Kummiya. Ea, god of the sky, cut off Ullikummi's feet with the copper knife that had separated the heavens from the earth. Despite his wounds, Ullikummi still boasted that he would take the kingship of heaven.

Although no complete text remains, it seems clear that despite his boasts, Ullikummi was defeated.

Ira Spar

See also: Giants.

Sources

Gurney, O.R. *The Hittites.* Rev. ed. New York: Penguin, 1990.

Hoffner, Harry A. *Hittite Myths.* 2nd ed. Atlanta, GA: Scholars, 1991.

Hooke, S.H. *Middle Eastern Mythology.* Mineola, NY: Dover, 2004.

Unicorns

Unicorns are fabulous creatures, beautiful symbols of immortality, power, justice, and purity. They are said to resemble a horse, goat, or deer with a long, shining horn in the center of the forehead.

Usually depicted as pure white in the West and multicolored in the East, unicorns were once believed to be native to India. However, folklore about unicorns, as well as reputed physical sightings, can be found throughout the world.

The Unicorn in the Classical World

In 416 B.C.E., the Greek physician Ctesias left his native Cnidus to tend to the ailing Persian King Darius II. After eighteen years in Persia, Ctesias returned to Cnidus and wrote a book describing his travels. Of the unicorn, which he had not actually seen, Ctesias wrote,

> There are in India certain wild asses which are as large as horses, and larger. Their bodies are white, their heads are dark red, and their eyes dark blue. They have a horn on the forehead which is about eighteen inches in length. The dust filed from this horn is administered in a potion as a protection against deadly drugs.

About a century later, the Ionian historian Megasthenes visited India. The four books of his work *Indika* offered educated Greeks the most complete account of India available. This work is now lost, and only extracts remain, cited in writings of other scholars. Megasthenes described an Indian unicorn, called a *cartazoon*, even though, like Ctesias, he had never actually seen one. He stated that the cartazoon, which kept to itself in the mountains, had a black, spiral horn and excellent hooves. Megasthenes described the unicorn as gentle toward other species of animals, yet likely to engage in battles to the death with other unicorns.

Another notable Greek historian who wrote about the existence of unicorns was Herodotus. Writing in the third century B.C.E., he commented on the "horned ass" of Africa.

Although the philosopher Aristotle criticized Ctesias's writing, he never denied the existence of one-horned creatures. Aristotle characterized the different types of unicorns by the kind of hooves they possessed, and mentioned, in particular, two types of one-horned animals. The first was a sort of antelope, while the second, the so-called Indian ass, more closely resembled a horse. It is possible that, given Aristotle's authority, subsequent generations of naturalists and mythographers conflated his descriptions of two different one-horned creatures into the figure we now know as the unicorn.

Aristotle's student Alexander the Great once boasted that he rode a unicorn into battle.

The Unicorn in the Roman Empire

Julius Caesar, the Roman ruler and general, who lived during the first-century B.C.E., claimed in his work *De Bello Gallico* (*The Gallic War*) that unicorns could be found in the Hercynian Forest in southwestern Germany. Apollonius of Tyana, a Greek writer who lived close to the time of Caesar, claimed to have seen a unicorn in India.

The Roman naturalist Pliny the Elder, who died during the eruption of Mount Etna in 79 C.E., gave the description that has influenced most subsequent portrayals of unicorns in the West. According to Pliny, the unicorn, or monoceros, was a very ferocious beast, similar "in the rest of its body to a horse, with the head of a deer, the feet of an elephant, the tail of a boar, a deep, bellowing voice, and a single black horn, two cubits in length, standing out in the middle of its forehead." He added that it could not be taken alive. Pliny very possibly may have been confusing his monoceros with the rhinoceros.

The Roman natural philosopher Aelian wrote about unicorns several times. In one passage, he described a creature resembling a wild ass. It was about the size of a horse, with a white body, red head, and blue eyes. He elaborated on Ctesias's description of the unicorn's horn, saying that the horn was white at the base, crimson at the top, and black in the middle. Aelian also claimed that the Indians used the horns as drinking cups, which they believed kept them safe from convulsions and the holy disease, epilepsy, as well as from poisons. Like Ctesias, Aelian claimed that the unicorns lived in the mountains of the Indian interior that were inaccessible to men.

The Unicorn in the Bible and in Biblical Folklore

The King James Version of the Bible includes six specific references to unicorns.

> Numbers 23:22: "hath as it were the strength of an unicorn."
>
> Numbers 24:8: "the strength of an unicorn: he shall eat up"
>
> Job 39:9: "Will the unicorn be willing to serve thee?"
>
> Job 39:10: "Canst thou bind the unicorn with his band?"
>
> Psalm 29:6: "a calf; Lebanon and Sirion like a young unicorn."
>
> Psalm 92:10: "with the horn of an unicorn: I shall be anointed"

These biblical references to *unicornis* reflect the Latin translation of the Hebrew word *re'em,* which was used as a metaphor for strength. Later versions of the Bible have no references to unicorns, although the goat with a prominent horn between his eyes in the book of Daniel does seem distinctly unicorn-like. In the later versions, the word *re'em* has been translated to mean wild ox, as in Numbers 23:22, "He has as it were the strength of the wild ox."

Nevertheless, the unicorn seems to have left its tracks in Judeo-Christian tradition. Jewish folklore calls the unicorn the fiercest of all animals, able to kill an elephant with a single thrust from its horn. Certain stories claim that the unicorn was the first animal named and that it accompanied Adam and Eve into exile.

Some stories say that the unicorn did not make it onto Noah's ark and thus perished in the flood waters. Others versions say that Noah brought the unicorns onto the ark, but they demanded so much space and attention that he banished them. Their fate upon leaving the ark differs from story to story, from

A unicorn often is pictured as a white horse with a single horn, sometimes with cloven hooves. The three-toed unicorn in this illustration resembles a cross between a horned horse and a lion. This representation is from the thirteenth-century Harleian Bestiary. *(© British Library/HIP/Art Resource, NY)*

drowning, to surviving as unicorns, to transforming into narwhals.

The Unicorn and the Narwhal

In the West, medieval sightings of narwhals added to the body of written work and oral tales about unicorns. The narwhal (*Monodon monoceros*) is an arctic whale that is conspicuous for the long, fluted, single tusk that protrudes from its upper lip.

For centuries, such "unicorn" horns were brought back to Europe by sailors and were regarded as great treasures. Queen Elizabeth I of England owned one of these so-called unicorn horns, which was said to be worth 10,000 pounds.

The Unicorn in the Middle Ages

Mentions of unicorns continued through the Middle Ages. Prester John, the fabled twelfth-century priest-king of a vast realm in Asia, supposedly possessed a number of tame unicorns. The medieval polymath Hildegarde of Bingen thought that unicorns could heal illness.

An early-thirteenth-century story holds that Genghis Khan encountered a unicorn as he prepared to take India and turned back, convinced that this was a sign from heaven not to attack. And in the late thirteenth century, Marco Polo reported seeing a large unicorn. This sighting, like so many others, was most likely of a rhinoceros.

The work known as the *Physiologus,* which was written by an unknown author in Alexandria during the second century C.E., not only described every beast in Christendom, but also provided allegories that linked them to their rightful place in creation. The *Physiologus* says this of the unicorn:

> He is a small animal, like a kid, but surprisingly fierce for his size, with one very sharp horn on his head, and no hunter is able to catch him by force. Yet there is a trick by which he is taken. Men lead a virgin to the place where he most resorts and leave her there alone. As soon as he sees this virgin, he runs and lays his head in her lap. She fondles him and he falls asleep. The hunters then approach and capture him and lead him to the palace of the king.

The Medieval church equated the unicorn with Christ, and its horn to the unity of Christ and the Father. That no hunter could capture him alone reminded readers that the will of the Messiah was not subject to earthly authority. The unicorn's small stature became a metaphor for Christ's humility, and its likeness to a kid was a reference to Christ's association with sinful men. The virgin in this description represented the Virgin Mary.

Probably the most familiar depiction of the Christian unicorn allegory is found in the sixteenth-century *Dame a la Licorne* (*Lady with a Unicorn*) tapestries, which are thought to have been designed in France and woven in Brussels. This series of textile artworks is now housed in the Cloisters, a branch of the Metropolitan Museum of Art in New York City.

In the central tapestry, a lady is accompanied by a unicorn, set on a background of exquisitely woven flowers. The other tapestries in the series show the unicorn in the forest. It is accompanied by various animals that wait by a stream until the unicorn dips its horn into the water to purify it. The unicorn is subsequently snared by a pure maiden and places its head in her lap. The unicorn is then captured and killed by hunters. The tapestries depict the triumph of the unicorn's purity, as it is restored to life in the final scene, where it is shown with a collar and chain in a garden.

Unicorns in Heraldry

During the reign of Scotland's King Robert III, the Scottish royal arms were designed with two unicorns supporting the royal shield.

Upon the ascension of King James VI of Scotland to the throne of England, which effectively united Scotland and England, James retained the lion on the left of the new royal arms of England and added a unicorn on the right. Unicorns had long been held to be deadly enemies to lions, so this new configuration signified the reconciliation between the Scottish unicorn and the English lion.

The Unicorn in Astronomy

Western astronomers placed a unicorn in the heavens. The first historical reference to a constellation named for a unicorn is a seventeenth-century star chart. The chart was drawn by Jakob Bartsch, the son-in-law of the German astronomer Johannes Kepler. A constellation is marked *Unicornu,* which is Latin for the constellation Monoceros (One-Horn).

Unicorns in China

Unicorns have been loved and venerated in China for thousands of years. It was said that two unicorns lived during the reign of the Emperor Yao, fourth of the mythic five emperors who shaped the world 4,000 years ago. Indeed, along with the dragon, the phoenix, and the tortoise, the unicorn is supposed to have helped to create the world.

Other emperors also associated with unicorns were the Emperor Fu Hsi, to whom the unicorn gave the secret of written language, and the first emperor, Huang Di, who took his sighting of a unicorn as an indication that his reign would be long and peaceful.

Unicorn stories are associated with the sage Confucius, including several accounts of Confucius's mother. In one story, she is said to have met a unicorn while on her pilgrimage to ask for a child. The unicorn spoke to her, predicting the birth of a "king without a crown." In another story, while Confucius's mother was pregnant, she encountered a unicorn in the woods. It gave her a piece of jade, told her that her child-to-be would possess great wisdom, and placed its head in her lap. When Confucius was an old man, he is said to have seen a unicorn, which he believed meant that he would soon die.

The Chinese unicorn is said to have the body of a deer, the tail of an ox, and the hooves of a horse. Its horn is short and grows out of the middle of its forehead. This unicorn is called the *ki lin,* a combination of the *ki,* which is male, and the *lin,* which is female. The Chinese unicorn is a brightly colored creature. The hair on its back represents the five sacred Chinese colors—red, yellow, blue, white, and black—and it has a yellow belly. Some accounts claim that the Chinese unicorn has green scales like another magical and auspicious Chinese creature, the dragon.

Another Chinese unicorn is the *zhi,* a goatlike animal that points out the guilty and punishes them. Because the zhi was a mythic creature that served to ward off evil and evildoers, it was considered a guardian, second only to the dragon and the tiger in power. Logically enough, the zhi became associated with Chinese courts. In ancient China, unicorns were painted on the doors of courthouses and government buildings. This led to the use of the zhi as a symbol of the government's incorruptibility.

In Japan, the name for unicorn is *kirin,* an image preserved on the label of a popular exported beer. Like the ki lin, the kirin is associated with justice. It has been said to appear at courts to free the innocent and kill the guilty, by piercing them through the heart with its horn. The Japanese also have another unicorn-like creature, called the *sin-you.*

Stories of unicorns also appear in Mongolia, Tibet, and Arabia. The horn of the *karkadann* (probably an oryx) is supposed to be good luck against scorpions, and eating its meat is said to rid one of demons.

Unicorns in Popular Culture

Today, images of unicorns are almost as popular as those of teddy bears. They show up on T-shirts, as stuffed or sculptured ornaments, and on wall hangings.

There have been attempts to create flesh-and-blood unicorns. One such creature was recently exhibited at Ringling Bros. and Barnum & Bailey circus, which was duly picketed by animal-rights activists. Unicorn fiction has become a veritable subgenre of fantasy, and sooner or later most writers of genre fantasy include a unicorn in one of their books.

Although unicorns are mentioned in Lewis Carroll's *Through the Looking Glass* (1872) and T.H. White's novel *The Once and Future King* (1958), probably the most beloved story of a unicorn in the past few decades is Peter S. Beagle's *The Last Unicorn* (1968). This tender, wry story tells of Schmendrick the Magician and his quest to free the unicorns from King Haggard.

In Patrick O'Brian's novel *The Hundred Days* (1998), the naturalist Dr. Stephen Maturin brings a narwhal's horn on board the HMS *Surprise* about the time that Napoleon returned from Elba and attempted to regain power. The horn, however, was broken, and the superstitious crew believed that their ship was afflicted by bad luck until the horn was repaired.

In *Harry Potter and the Sorcerer's Stone* (1997), by J.K. Rowling, the wicked Voldemort drinks the silver blood of a unicorn to sustain his own life.

Perhaps the most astonishing thing about unicorns in western culture is that they have managed to survive as untameable figures of wonder and power. Unicorns continue to be symbols of strength and purity in a skeptical world.

Susan M. Shwartz and Josepha Sherman

See also: Bestiary.

Sources
Beagle, Peter. *The Last Unicorn*. New York: Roc, 1991.
Gotfredsen, Lise. *The Unicorn*. New York: Abbeville, 1999.
Nigg, Joseph. *The Book of Fabulous Beasts: A Treasury of Writings from Ancient Times to the Present*. New York: Oxford University Press, 1999.
Shepard, Odell. *The Lore of the Unicorn*. Mineola, NY: Dover, 1993.

Upelluri/Ubelluris

(Hittite)

The Hittite gods built the earth and heaven upon the powerful sleeping giant Upelluri. But he did not notice, even when heaven and Earth were separated with a copper knife.

Kumarbi's messenger, Imbaluri, commanded the Issira deities to place Ullikummi, the giant made of rock, on Upelluri's right shoulder. Ea, the sky god, questioned Upelluri in his search for Ullikummi. Upelluri admitted that there was a small pain in his shoulder, although he could not identify which god was causing it.

In his world-carrying aspect, Upelluri can be seen as related to, and possibly even the ancestor of, Atlas, who also carried the world on his shoulders.

Ira Spar

See also: Atlas; Giants.

Sources
Gurney, O.R. *The Hittites*. Rev. ed. New York: Penguin, 1990.
Hoffner, Harry A. *Hittite Myths*. 2nd ed. Atlanta, GA: Scholars, 1991.
Hooke, S.H. *Middle Eastern Mythology*. Mineola, NY: Dover, 2004.

Urban Legends

Urban legends, also known as urban folklore, are fantastic stories that are believed (or at least claimed) to be true. They concern recent events that involved people and places that are fairly familiar to the teller and members of the audience.

In both their fantastic elements and the insistence that they are true, urban legends differ from myths and folktales. Myths are sacred stories believed by members of a particular culture. Folktales may take place in the actual world but are not taken to be true.

Urban legends are an important resource for storytellers because they express modern concerns in urban societies and are told and believed by individuals in all segments of those societies. These legends are not the exclusive domain of any single age, race, profession, or socioeconomic group.

Unlike traditional folklore, urban legends are formulated and transmitted not only by the general population but by the mass media as well. They may be transmitted orally or spread electronically via e-mail. They are the subject of numerous Web sites and online discussions and are retold visually in film, television, and comic book formats. Urban legends also have been the inspiration for short stories, poems, plays, and other literary works.

Feelings of unease about strange places, unfamiliar people, and bewildering situations and innovations are related through these legends. Urban legends often are cyclical, resurfacing to help articulate new fears about universal issues. There are legends about topics as diverse as animals, both strange and familiar, car culture, contaminated food, other threats to our children and our own personal safety, famous celebrities, and various horrifying incidents.

Elements

Urban legend narratives share many features with other traditional folk stories. They usually are anonymous, are primarily communicated face-to-face, and often exist in multiple versions, as they are adapted and re-created with each retelling and circulated among members of certain economic, familial, occupational, or cultural groups. But what sets urban legends apart from their more traditional counterparts are two elements: authentication of content and film-noir tone.

Authentication, which corroborates the truth of the story, is handled in three basic ways. The most frequent form of authentication is the use of the "friend-of-a-friend" (or FOAF) motif, "My grandmother's neighbor's cousin" and the like as the source of the tale. Because these sources are supposedly known to the teller, they are perceived as reliable.

A second method of authentication is the use of actual names, dates, and events to ground the stories in reality. This often works so well that urban legends are printed in newspapers as actual news items. These concrete details change over time and space, usually by tellers who refresh the relevance of the tales for each particular audience and situation.

The third common methodology is to attribute the story to the mass media. For example, "I heard it on *Oprah*" or "I read it in the newspaper."

The setting in an urban legend also must appear authentic. The lover's lane of "the boyfriend's death" may be generic, but the teller still must take the listener there to visualize the action. Details such as the moonlight or the make of the car are added for further validation.

Film noir refers to a film genre that provides steamy, dark, urban landscapes and ordinary characters facing unexpected twists and turns throughout the plot. Urban legends, for the most part, reflect this dark, steamy tone. They feature black comedy derived from the ill fortune of their characters and habitually depend on twisted endings and ambiguous characters and situations for effect.

Presentation

Even the grimmest tale of warning or the most sincere testimony of belief has to be told effectively if it is to impress its audience. Setting plays an important role in the communication process. If the legends are being told around campfires or at slumber parties, rather than in the course of regular conversation, they are being told for effect, and therefore will reflect that purpose. Stories told in such a setting will generally be much lengthier and usually will be polished for maximum effect.

Urban legends usually are conveyed in informal, face-to-face conversations, generally are brief, and often are constructed and told communally rather than by a single teller. Questions are encouraged, and comments from the listener during and at the end of the telling help to move the story along and develop its shape.

Because the legends serve diverse functions, their format is flexible and is influenced by the teller's purpose in relating the legend, the situation in which it is being told, and the people who are interacting in the telling. When transferred to the storyteller's repertoire, these stories become much more formalized, but some audience interjection—"That is not the way I heard/read/saw it"—is still anticipated.

The audience for urban legends generally is teenaged and older. The tales are generally too dark and frightening or simply too sophisticated for a younger audience, which may not have the necessary background to fully appreciate these cautionary tales.

Gail de Vos

See also: Hook, The; Ugly Baby; Vanishing Hitchhiker.

Sources

Brunvand, Jan Harold. *Encyclopedia of Urban Legends.* New York: W.W. Norton, 1979.
———. *Readings in American Folklore.* New York: W.W. Norton, 1979.

Utu/Shamash

(Sumerian)

In the ancient Middle East, the god Utu, known as Shamash in Akkadian, was a Sumerian sun deity. As the personification of the sun, whose light illuminates darkness, the god Utu sought justice for both gods and mankind.

In Sumerian myths, Utu was the son of Nanna, the moon god. He was also the twin brother of Inanna, the goddess of heaven. In later Akkadian traditions, he was the son either of the sky god, An, or of Enlil, a god of creation.

Utu's consort was Sherida (Akkadian, Aya), the goddess of light. In narrative tales of the land of Aratta, the hero Lugalbanda was called the son of Utu.

Utu is depicted in examples dating from the twenty-fourth century B.C.E. as a bearded deity with rays emanating from his shoulders. He usually is shown with his emblem, a serrated saw, which probably referred to his role as the guardian of justice. A Babylonian hymn indicates that the saw was used to punish criminals. Some images show Utu emerging from the eastern mountains in the morning, as two deified attendants open the gates of heaven.

Utu was also believed to have an attachment to humans. Meshkiagasher, a legendary king of the city of Uruk, was said to have been an offspring of the god. Utu is also a character in the Sumerian poem "Dumuzi's Dream," which describes how Dumuzi, husband of Inanna and brother-in-law of Utu, prayed to Utu for help.

In the Sumerian tale of the enmity between Enmerkar and Ensuhgirana, the lord of Aratta, Utu responded to the cries of the cowherd and shepherd whose animals had been bewitched by a sorcerer.

In the Babylon legend of Etana, Utu, here called Shamash, helped a trapped eagle to escape from a pit. The legendary King Etana had no heir and prayed to Shamash to grant him one. In a dream, Etana heard the voice of the god of justice, who told him to go to the aid of the eagle. In return for his assistance, the bird would help him find the mythical plant of fertility. Etana freed the eagle, which carried him to heaven in search of the "Plant of Giving Birth."

In the *Epic of Gilgamesh,* Shamash (again, the name used for Utu), upon the request of the goddess Ninsun, the mother of Gilgamesh, protected and assisted the hero in his battle with the Humbaba monster. In a later episode, after Gilgamesh and Enkidu subdued and killed the Bull of Heaven, the two heroes ripped out its heart, prostrated themselves before the god Shamash, and presented the heart to him.

Ira Spar

Sources

Alster, Bendt. *Dumuzi's Dream: Aspects of Oral Poetry in a Sumerian Myth.* Copenhagen, Denmark: Copenhagen Studies in Assyriology 1, 1972.

Black, Jeremy A., and Anthony Green. *Gods, Demons and Symbols of Ancient Mesopotamia.* Austin: University of Texas Press, 1992.

Black, J.A., G. Cunningham, J. Ebeling, E. Flückiger-Hawker, E. Robson, J. Taylor, and G. Zólyomi. *The Electronic Text Corpus of Sumerian Literature.* http://www-etcsl.orient.ox.ac.uk/.

Vainamoinen

(Finnish)

Vainamoinen was the wise wizard and adventurer of the Finnish epic the *Kalevala*.

Vainamoinen was the son of the heavenly maiden, the demigoddess Ilmatar. Trapped in her womb for more than 700 years, he grew to adulthood and then finally escaped into the world as an active, white-bearded old man.

In the land that would become Finland, Vainamoinen brought the world such gifts as agriculture and fire. He also invented the *kantele*, a type of harp or lyre, from the bones of a giant pike.

Among Vainamoinen's adventures was an encounter with the young, brash Joukahainen, who challenged him to a duel of magic. Vainamoinen literally sang the younger man into the ground, and Joukahainen escaped only because he promised Vainamoinen that Joukahainen's sister, Aino, would marry him. Vainamoinen agreed, but Aino threw herself into the sea to avoid marrying the old man.

Joukahainen sought revenge, shooting Vainamoinen's horse and sending the wizard tumbling into the sea. Vainamoinen was rescued by a large eagle and was carried to the land of Pohjola. The mistress of Pohjola, Louhi, tended to Vainamoinen until he recovered. She then refused to let him go until he promised

that Ilmarinen, the master smith, would forge a magical artifact, called a *sampo,* for Pohjola.

On his way home, Vainamoinen met Louhi's daughter, the Maiden of Pohjola, and asked her to marry him. She agreed on the condition that Vainamoinen would carry out certain seemingly impossible tasks. While Vainamoinen carved a wooden boat, however, his axe slipped, wounding his knee so he was unable to complete the tasks. He searched for an expert blood stauncher and found an old man who stopped the flow of blood by using magic incantations.

The Maiden of Pohjola chose to marry Ilmarinen, the forger of the sampo, as he performed the three tasks she set before him: He plowed a field full of vipers, hunted down the bear of Tuonela and the wolf of Manala, and fished the Great Pike out of the Tuonela River. Vainamoinen held no ill will toward the couple and entertained the wedding guests with his singing.

Now, Vainamoinen and other heroes set out to steal back the sampo from Pohjola. Vainamoinen put the people of Pohjola to sleep with his kantele playing, and the sampo was taken away. Louhi set off in pursuit in the form of a giant bird of prey. In the ensuing battle, the sampo was smashed and fell into the sea. There, it continued to grind and turned the sea to salt water.

Louhi sent diseases to destroy the people of Kalevala, but Vainamoinen cured the sick.

Louhi sent a bear to attack the Kalevala cattle, but Vainamoinen slew the bear. The mistress of Pohjola, Louhi, hid the Sun and the Moon inside a hill and stole the fire as well. Vainamoinen and Ilmarinen freed the fire and forged keys needed to release the Sun and Moon.

In his final adventure, Vainamoinen set sail in a copper boat. He planned to return when he was needed.

J.R.R. Tolkien, author of *The Lord of the Rings* (1954–1955), was familiar with the *Kalevala*. Tolkein's wizard adventurer, Gandalf, was almost certainly inspired by the wise wizard Vainamoinen.

See also: Kalevala; Wizards; *Retelling: Vainamoinen.*

Sources

Lönnrot, Elias. *The Kalevala: An Epic Poem After Oral Tradition.* Trans. Keith Bosley. New York: Oxford University Press, 1999.

Pentikäinen, Juha Y. *Kalevala Mythology.* Trans. and ed. Ritva Poom. Bloomington: Indiana University Press, 1999.

Valhalla

(Norse)

Valhalla was the great hall, or palace, that stood in the Grove of Glesir in Asgard, the realm of the Norse gods. It was presided over by the head god of the Norse pantheon, Odin. The name *Valhalla* means hall of the slain.

Valhalla was said to be truly enormous, with 540 doors. Each door was large enough for 800 warriors to pass through at once. The walls were made of spears, the benches of breastplates, and the roof of shining shields. The hall held countless warriors, all of whom were former mortals. A wolf guarded Valhalla's main door, and an eagle flew watch over it.

Valhalla was home to the Norse heroes called the *einherjar,* who had died bravely and honorably in battle. Those who came to Valhalla were chosen for this honor by the Valkyries, the nine warrior daughters of Odin. Each day, these warriors rode out to take part in military games and mock battles. Every night, they returned to the hall to feast. Any wounds sustained during the day healed instantly, and the fine roasted boar and intoxicating mead never ran out. The warriors waited in Valhalla for the final battle, called Ragnarok, at which time they would march forth into a doomed but glorious fight against the giants, the enemies of the gods.

Valhalla was the ideal afterlife for Norse Viking warriors. They could think of no worse fate for themselves than losing their fighting abilities through crippling injuries or old age and gradually becoming useless in a warrior society. It was far better for true warriors to die in glorious combat at the peak of their powers, assured of a true and honorable warrior's afterlife in Valhalla.

There was also a place at Valhalla for women in the hall of Frigga, Odin's wife. Women who died in childbirth were welcomed as warriors. Couples who died when they were fervently in love with each other also were permitted to enter.

Warriors who did not get to Valhalla, whether through cowardice, dying in bed, or some other shameful end, went to the dark home of the dead. This was ruled over by the grim goddess Hel in a realm deep within the underworld. The Vikings considered such an end to be literally a fate worse than mere death.

See also: Norse Mythology; Odin/Odhinn; Valkyries.

Sources

Crossley-Holland, Kevin. *The Norse Myths.* New York: Pantheon, 1981.

Hollander, Lee M., trans. *The Poetic Edda.* Austin: University of Texas Press, 1928.

Lindow, John. *Norse Mythology: A Guide to the Gods, Heroes, Rituals, and Beliefs.* New York: Oxford University Press, 2002.

Sturluson, Snorri. *The Prose Edda: Tales from Norse Mythology.* Trans. Jean I. Young. Berkeley: University of California Press, 2001.

Valkyries

(Norse)

The Valkyries were the daughters of Odin, chief god of the Norse pantheon. They escorted the spirits of the bravest slain warriors, the *einherjar*, to Valhalla, Odin's great hall. The name *Valkyrie* means choosers of the slain.

The einherjar were taken to Valhalla to prepare for the final battle, called Ragnarok. This battle would mark the end of the gods and change the fate of everything.

The Valkyries' names were Brynhild, Göll, Göndul, Gudr, Gunn, Herfjoturr, Hildr, Hladgunnr, Hlokk, Hrist, Sigrdrifa, Sigrún, and Svafa. They were portrayed as beautiful young women armed with helmets and spears, and they rode winged horses.

"The Ride of the Valkyries," an oil painting by British artist William T. Maud (1865–1903), shows the Valkyries, accompanied by one of Odin's two ravens, riding out to find those who had died honorably in battle. The chosen men will be carried to Valhalla, Odin's great hall. *(Snark/Art Resource, NY)*

The Valkyries also often acted as Odin's messengers. According to the myth, when they rode forth on their errands, their bright, glinting armor caused the strange lights of the aurora borealis.

Some scholars have speculated that originally the Valkyries were priestesses. These were not beautiful young maidens in armor but old women who selected victims for human sacrifice. But the image of beautiful women taking the brave warriors up to Valhalla replaced this less pleasant image.

The nineteenth-century German composer Richard Wagner included the Valkyries in his operatic work *Der Ring des Nibelungen* (*The Ring of the Nibelung*, 1869–1876), commonly known as "The Ring Cycle," which is based on Norse mythology. One of the most familiar melodies from that work is the orchestral overture, commonly known as "Ride of the Valkyries."

See also: Brunhilde/Brynhild/Brunnehilde; Norse Mythology; Odin/Odhinn.

Sources

Crossley-Holland, Kevin. *Norse Myths*. New York: Pantheon, 1981.

Davidson, H.R. Ellis. *Myths and Symbols in Pagan Europe: Early Scandinavian and Celtic Religions*. Syracuse, NY: Syracuse University Press, 1988.

Lindow, John. *Norse Mythology: A Guide to the Gods, Heroes, Rituals, and Beliefs*. New York: Oxford University Press, 2002.

Vampires

Vampires are undead beings who feed off the blood and life of the living. They have existed in the folklore of many cultures for thousands of years.

The fear that the dead can return to spread disease or sap the vitality of the living has caused many superstitions and beliefs to spring up concerning how vampires are made, detected, and destroyed. Legends of vampires are most common in Eastern Europe but also occur in China.

Although the vampire in recent fiction is often depicted as lanky, tall, and pale, the most common of the folkloric vampire are bloated and ruddy. In Greece, vampires sometimes are thought to have dark blue or black faces. This may be due to the practice of burying people who were suspected of being vampires face-down. The blood in the corpse would pool in the face rather than the back; if the corpse was exhumed at a later date to determine if it had become a vampire, the face would be dark rather than pale.

The word *vampire* first appeared in English in 1679, but there is no agreement as to the ultimate origin of the word. One theory is that the word comes from the Slavic *upior,* or *upyr,* which are in turn derived from the Turkish *uber.* Others think it may come from the Greek *pi,* Serbo-Croatian *pirati,* or Lithuanian *wempti.* The theory that is most widely accepted is that the word derives from the Serbian *bamiiup,* which essentially means "vampire."

In Hungary and Romania, where legends of vampires are very common, the word was introduced fairly recently. In Hungary, the earliest evidence of the word occurred in 1786. In Romania, the word first appeared around 1815, but the more common terms are *strigoi* and *moroi.* While the term *vampire* has become widely accepted in Hungary, the older, more common terms still are preferred in Romania. In Transylvania, home of the historical Count Dracula, the term is *şişcoi.*

Vampires in Folklore

The modern concept of vampires is that they are created when a person is bitten by another vampire, but folkloric vampires were created in a number of different ways. The following individuals might become vampires:

A person born with a caul, a membrane that covers the head.

A person born with teeth.

Someone who lived an immoral life or was an alcoholic.

Someone who committed suicide.

A murder victim whose murder was not avenged.

Someone who died while under a curse.

Someone who died while excommunicated from their religion.

A convert to Islam.

A priest who celebrated Mass while living with an unconfessed mortal sin.

A person born or conceived on a Church holy day.

Someone whose godparents stumbled while reciting the Apostle's Creed at his or her baptism.

A person also might be doomed to become a vampire after death if a cat or dog jumped across the corpse or if the shadow of a man fell on it. Consequently, the danger of becoming a vampire was very real and of great concern to people living with these beliefs, so precautions were often taken with every corpse to attempt to protect the dead.

Protecting the Dead

Since piercing a vampire with a sharp object was one way to destroy it, placing a sharp implement, often a sickle, in the coffin with the recently dead was a custom designed to keep the dead from rising at all. In some areas, the sickle was placed on the abdomen of the deceased; in others, the sickle was placed across the neck so that if the vampire tried to rise from the grave it would cut off its own head. In Morocco, knives were placed on the body for the same purpose.

Binding the deceased's limbs was another way to keep the dead from rising, though local variations determined whether the dead could be bound inside the coffin. Sometimes, the dead had their ankles or knees bound for a time, but the knots were removed prior to burial so that they would not bind the soul to the body.

People in other districts left the knots in the coffin, as the vampire would be forced to untie them before it could escape. In some practices, nets were placed in the coffin in the belief that the vampire would be forced to undo each knot in the net at the rate of one per year. Poppy seeds could also be spread on the ground, as the vampire would be obsessed with finding every single one before it could move beyond its grave.

In Greek folklore, binding the corpse was thought to keep a vampire from returning from the dead. This may be why, in Greek mythology, the infant Oedipus had his ankles tied together when he was abandoned as an infant by his parents. This practice was not to keep the newborn from crawling away, but to keep the infant from returning from the dead.

Protecting oneself and one's family from wandering vampires was a constant concern. As it was believed a vampire could only return to its home the same way it had left, corpses were sometimes removed from homes feet first, via a window.

Turning the items in one's home upside down would prevent a vampire from asking these items to open the door. People slept with their feet at the head of the bed to keep a vampire from finding them if one did enter the home.

Destroying a Vampire

Once someone was suspected of vampirism, his or her corpse was exhumed and examined. If the corpse was bloated and had bloody lips, it was presumed to be a vampire. The vampire could be dispatched by piercing its abdomen with a stake of ash or hawthorn, or a sickle, or another sharp object such as a needle, depending on the particular beliefs of the village. Sometimes, a hide was placed on the vampire before staking it to control blood splatter, as being touched by the vampire's blood could drive someone mad or even turn that person into a vampire.

In some traditions, staking was sufficient to destroy a vampire. In others, the corpse had to be beheaded and cremated. The heart had to be burned entirely to ash or the vampire might return. Sometimes, corpses simply were buried deeper than usual, buried face-down, thrown into swiftly flowing water, or buried at a crossroads.

During plagues, stories of vampires were extremely common. Since the manner in which the disease was transmitted was unknown, it was not unusual to blame outbreaks on vampire activity. When a plague killed great numbers of people, many remained unburied or were buried improperly. The misunderstood processes of decomposition were readily observable. Those who were improperly buried often were dug up by wolves or dogs, or simply "rose" out of the ground due to the bloating of the body and the shallowness of the grave. This may be where beliefs that wolves and dogs were the enemies of vampires originated, as well as the belief that the earth might reject the unholy corpse.

Eastern Europe

Serbian vampires were active and out of their graves every day but Saturday. Romanian vampires were active at all times, but most particularly on Saint Andrew's Eve and Saint George's Eve. In Romania, a vampire that remained undestroyed for seven years could pass into another country, become a man again, marry, and have children. But he and his children would become vampires upon death and ravage the wife's family and her village.

Since it was widely believed in many parts of Eastern Europe that nearly anyone could become a vampire, identifying those who had become vampires was extremely important. If a village had some bad luck, such as terrible weather, a plague, or a string of unusual deaths, it could be blamed on a vampire.

The villagers looked for a vampire by checking recent graves. They would check to see if there were holes by which the vampire might have escaped. Or they might lead a white (or, in some cases, a black) horse over fresh graves. The horse would refuse to walk over the grave of a vampire. Many traditions held that it would take either nine days or forty days for a vampire to rise, so anyone who had not yet been dead for the specified time would not be suspect.

In Russia, a woman who made a pact with the devil was believed to rise from her grave as an *eretica*. These undead creatures would be most active in spring and autumn, when they would spread death and disease via the evil eye.

In Poland, a child born with teeth or a caul was destined to become a kind of vampire called an *ohyn*. The ohyn did not leave its grave, but it did chew on its own flesh and thereby magically brought death to its family.

The *liougat* of Albania rose from its grave armed with huge fingernails. It killed and devoured anything it found. The liougat could be thwarted by wolves, which tore off its legs. The maimed vampire then had to return to its grave, defeated, and remain there forever.

Germany

In Germany, the *Neuntöter,* which means "ninekiller," would rise nine days after burial to spread plague. But a lemon placed in its mouth would keep it in its grave.

The *nachzehrer* of northern Germany chewed on its burial shroud and its extremities, so its appearance was often quite tattered. In fact, it was supposed to make so much noise while chewing on itself and its shroud that it could be located in its grave by sound alone.

A person could become a nachzehrer if his or her name was not removed from his or her clothing before burial. If the nachzehrer rang the church bells, whoever heard them was doomed to die soon thereafter. A nachzehrer could be destroyed through decapitation, as long as the head and body were reburied separately.

China

The Chinese *xiang shi* was often greenish in color and sometimes glowed. The xiang shi was animated by the *po,* or inferior soul of a person, and was created by a sudden or violent death or an improper burial.

Modern Vampires

A new kind of vampire was created in the nineteenth century by authors such as J. Sheridan Le Fanu and Bram Stoker. Le Fanu's *Carmilla: A Vampyre Tale* (1872) and Stoker's *Dracula* (1897) combined the horror of the revenant with eroticism and spawned an industry that equated the vampire with seduction. Though Bram Stoker named his vampire after a historical fifteenth-century Wallachian prince, the name of Dracula is not associated with vampires in Romania.

Since the publication of Stoker's *Dracula,* vampires have developed into something completely separate from their folkloric antecedents. Modern fictional vampires cannot see themselves in a mirror, are afraid of crosses, and are friends with wolves. They create other vampires by drinking victims' blood, then forcing the victims to drink their blood. The stake driven through the vampire must be through the heart rather than the abdomen. And the vampire cannot enter a private residence without an invitation.

These vampires often rise from the grave after three days, rather than the more traditional nine or forty days. They possess a hypnotic gaze, and their overall appearance and demeanor can be quite sensual. They bear no resemblance to a bloated corpse. They can turn into mist or shape-shift into a bat. Often, vampires cannot cross running water, and their coffins must contain a quantity of their home earth. The modern vampire is difficult to find and harder to kill.

More than a century since Bram Stoker brought the sensual vampire to life, the character of the vampire has been molded into many different forms in film. He has been a thing of horror (*Nosferatu,* 1922; *Dracula,* 1931), the subject of jokes (*Love at First Bite,* 1979), a misunderstood antihero (*Dracula,* 1979; *Bram Stoker's Dracula,* 1992), a mentor (*My Best Friend Is a Vampire,* 1988), and even a disaffected teenager (*The Lost Boys,* 1987). In China, the xiang shi has been transformed into the hopping vampire of Hong Kong kung fu films.

Writers such as Anne Rice, P.N. Elrod, Fred Saberhagen, Chelsea Quinn Yarbro, Barbara Hambly, and Laurell K. Hamilton each have their own take on the modern vampire. The concept of the vampire has proved malleable enough to be re-created again and again.

Marella Sands

See also: Bats; Liderc; Shape-Shifters.

Sources

Barber, Paul. *Vampires, Burial and Death: Folklore and Reality.* New Haven, CT: Yale University Press, 1988.

Dundes, Alan, ed. *The Vampire: A Casebook.* Madison: University of Wisconsin Press, 1998.

Hoyt, Olga. *Lust for Blood: The Consuming Story of Vampires.* New York: Stein and Day, 1984.

Jackson, Nigel. *Compleat Vampyre.* Chieveley, UK: Capall Bann, 1995.

Vanishing Hitchhiker

The tale of the vanishing hitchhiker may be the most widespread and popular folktale of all. It has been collected by folklorists in, among other countries, the United States, Canada, Great Britain, Malaysia, China, and the Philippines.

The vanishing hitchhiker is the ghost of a victim, usually female, of an automobile accident. The ghost is trying to get home and is picked up by a Good Samaritan. When the Good Samaritan arrives at the ghost's house, the ghost vanishes. The bewildered Good Samaritan then learns from the still-grieving family that yes, this was a ghost that had been trying to get home for days, weeks, or years. Some variants add the detail of the ghost being cold, and the Good Samaritan lending her a sweater. When the ghost vanishes, the sweater is left behind, or, in a neat twist, is found draped over her tombstone.

One of the earlier recorded versions of the story is in the New Testament. An Ethiopian driving a chariot picked up the Apostle Philip, who baptized him, and then disappeared.

Other versions of the basic story include a tale from Hawaii. An old woman was given a

lift by a Good Samaritan. She asked to be driven near Mount Kilauea and then disappeared, leaving the Good Samaritan to realize he had just given a ride to the volcano goddess, Madame Pele.

Another version, from Appalachia, involves a vanishing hitchhiker who turned out to be John the Baptist. He told the Good Samaritan that Jesus Christ would return and then disappeared.

The vanishing hitchhiker also turns up in movies, such as Orson Welles's *Return to Glennascaul* (1951), in which both a mother and daughter are hitchhiking ghosts who vanish after they are taken by a Good Samaritan back to their home.

See also: Urban Legends.

Sources

Brunvand, Jan Harold. *The Study of American Folklore.* New York: W.W. Norton, 1988.

———. *The Vanishing Hitchhiker: American Urban Legends and Their Meanings.* New York: W.W. Norton, 1981.

Vegetable Sheep/Lamb

(European)

Plant-animal hybrids, vegetable sheep and vegetable lambs, were believed to produce cotton as sheep produce wool and are depicted in the bestiaries, the medieval collections of fact and folklore about real and imaginary animals. Also known as the lambs of Tartary, these creatures were believed to live in the Asian land of Tartary, which is part of present-day Eastern Europe and Russia.

The origins of this odd belief are almost certainly connected to the arrival of cotton bolls from the East into Western Europe. Since no one in Western Europe had ever seen cotton in its unspun, natural form, they assumed that the bolls were a form of wool. So, the reasoning went, these strange little fleeces probably came from a miniature plant-animal that produced tiny sheep-fruit that ate the grass under the main plant until the bolls ripened and dropped off.

Further "proof" was found in the root—or rhizome, to be accurate—of the fern species *Cibotium barometz,* which does vaguely resemble a lamb, complete with a body and four legs, especially when all extraneous material is pared away. Seen together with a cotton boll by someone who had never before seen either one, the leap could be made to the belief that these items were the body and fleece of a vegetable lamb.

Surprisingly enough, belief in the vegetable lamb lasted well past the Middle Ages. Sir Hans Sloan, member and secretary of Britain's preeminent organization of scientists, the Royal Society of England, and the founder of the English Natural History Museum, had in his possession a "vegetable lamb of Tartary." But Sloan lived in an age of scientific investigation—Sir Isaac Newton was president of the Royal Society at the time—and so the "lamb" was studied. It turned out to be a carefully pared example of the *Cibotium barometz* rhizome.

See also: Bestiary.

Sources
Barber, Richard. *Bestiary: Being an English Version of the Bodleian Library.* Woodbridge, UK: Boydell, 1993.
Baxter, Ron. *Bestiaries and Their Users in the Middle Ages.* London: Courtauld Institute, 1998.
White, T.H. *The Book of Beasts: Being a Translation from a Latin Bestiary of the Twelfth Century.* Mineola, NY: Dover, 1984.

Verse Stories

Verse stories are short dramatic tales for children that are told in verse. These stories are related to nursery rhymes and have an equally long history. Verse stories often are longer than other types of rhymes, have simple plots and melodies, and usually lack magical or tragic elements.

One example of a very popular verse story, the anonymous "The Queen of Hearts," dates back several centuries. It was used by Lewis Carroll (the pseudonym of Charles Lutwidge Dodgson) in his famous fantasy, *Alice's Adventures in Wonderland* (1865).

> The Queen of Hearts,
> She made some tarts,
> All on a summer's day;
> The Knave of Hearts,
> He stole those tarts,
> And took them clean away.
> The King of Hearts
> Called for the tarts,
> And beat the knave full sore;
> The Knave of Hearts
> Brought back the tarts,
> And vowed he'd steal no more.

As this example shows, a verse story can be relatively short, but verse stories also may be long and quite complicated. Storytellers may adjust the length, depending on what will suit the audience.

See also: Ballads.

Sources
Carroll, Lewis. *The Annotated Alice.* New York: W.W. Norton, 2000.
"The Hive: A Collection of Scraps." *European Magazine,* 1782.
Lamb, Charles. *The King and Queen of Hearts: With the Rogueries of the Knave Who Stole the Queen's Pies.* London: M.J. Godwin, 1809.

Vietnamese Storytelling

Vietnam is made up of more than fifty ethnic groups, each one with its own oral traditions.

Folktales and storytelling are both still popular throughout Vietnam. But storytelling generally takes place on a smaller scale in the cities than it does in the more isolated mountain areas because large gatherings are still discouraged by the government. However, the Vietnamese government has worked with the Association of Vietnamese Folklorists to conserve as much as possible of the country's oral tradition. Many stories have been collected and are compiled in massive volumes of Vietnamese tales and legends.

In addition to standard storytelling, each ethnic group has its own type of epic songs about mythical or legendary heroes. One type of epic singing performance is called the *h'mon.*

The h'mon generally takes place at night, with the audience sitting outside, listening in the darkness. The epic is recited in a mixture of spoken word and song and can take anywhere from three to twenty nights to complete. In addition to local epics, the Indian *Ramayana* is also known and performed in Vietnam.

The thousand-year-old tradition of *ca dao* is still popular in rural Vietnam. These songs and ballads, which are sung without any instrumental accompaniment, are a form of Vietnamese folk poetry that covers a wide range of subjects, from romance to children's themes.

A unique form of Vietnamese storytelling theater is *mua roi nuoc,* or water-puppet theater. Performances of mua roi nuoc take place at the edge of a river or pond, with the audience sitting along the shore facing a large screen that stands up out of the water. The water's surface forms the stage floor. Puppeteers stand in the water behind the screen and manipulate colorfully painted wooden puppets using rods held underwater.

The mua roi nuoc puppet characters represent everything from humans and animals to fairies and dragons, and there may be as many as fifteen different puppet characters in use at the same time. As the puppeteers perform, an accompanying ensemble plays background music.

Sources

Jamieson, Neil L. *Understanding Vietnam.* Berkeley: University of California Press, 1993.

Nguyên, Huy Hông. *Water Puppetry of Vietnam.* Hanoi, Vietnam: Foreign Language Publishing House, 1986.

Thang, Vo Van, and Jun Lawson. *Vietnamese Folktales.* DaNang, Vietnam: DaNang Publishing House, 2001.

Vodianoi

(Slavic)

In Slavic myth and folklore, the *vodianoi* is the unpredictable, dangerous king or spirit of water, particularly of freshwater.

As a water spirit, the vodianoi needed no clothes. He generally was seen by humans as a being that was half fish and half human, or as an old man covered in scales and mud. His hair and beard were green, and his hands were webbed. When he chose to have a tail, he looked something like a heavyset merman. When he decided to take a two-legged shape, his long toes helped him to propel himself underwater.

The vodianoi was not actively evil, but he lacked all concept of human morality. He sometimes willfully drowned humans out of sheer dislike, but more often he dragged them underwater to provide entertainment for himself and his wife, the *vodianikha.* Those humans who were foolish enough to bathe at twilight were at greatest risk of being snatched.

When he became truly angry with humanity, the vodianoi was said to cause floods that destroyed dams and mills. Wise millers and fishermen made him offerings to keep him docile. The vodianoi was considered to be wealthy due both to these offerings and to the bounty he had taken from sunken ships.

In the Christian era, the vodianoi was often confused with the Christian devil, as both were believed to live underwater and to look alike, except, of course, that the devil had horns.

See also: Slavic Mythology.

Sources

Afanaseyev, Alexandre. *Russian Fairy Tales.* New York: Pantheon, 1980.

Simonov, Pyotr. *Essential Russian Mythology: Stories That Change the World.* London: Thorsons, 1997.

Vol'ka

(Slavic)

Prince Vol'ka is portrayed in Slavic epic folk poems, called *bylini,* as a heroic warrior. He protects the residents of his isolated, forest-bound principality by performing such traditional deeds of heroism as defeating an enemy in single combat. He is also the only hero of a *bylina* who is a magician and shape-shifter.

Vol'ka's fictional world is based on regions of Russia and Ukraine in the twelfth century. These regions were divided into principalities, the most important of which was ruled by Prince Vladimir of Kiev. Much of the land was heavily forested, and traveling between the principalities, or even between villages, was difficult. A local prince in the twelfth century could technically be a vassal of Vladimir yet, because of the forests and lack of decent roads, might never see him.

This is the setting for the Kievan cycle of tales. It is a domain of myth and folktale in which historical figures, like Prince Vladimir, mingle with folkloric creatures, such as dragons and magic-wielding princes.

Russian folklorists have collected Prince Vol'ka's bylina in manuscript form at least seventeen times in the last 200 years. The epic is usually included in the Kievan cycle. However, it is not known whether Vol'ka was one of the knights, called *bogatyri.* Vol'ka is not a member of Prince Vladimir's court. His character is unique in that generally the bogatyri were featured in each other's bylini, but Vol'ka is mentioned in only one bylina besides his own. In this other bylina, he appears not as a bogatyr but as a secondary character. It is possible that the bylina of Prince Vol'ka does not actually belong to the Kievan cycle.

Some scholars have tried to find a link between Prince Vol'ka and various historical characters, such as the tenth-century Prince Vseslav of Polovsk. But the only evidence to support the claim that Vol'ka is based on Vseslav is the fact that Prince Vseslav was born with a caul, which is a traditional sign of someone born to be a sorcerer.

Vol'ka's Birth and Childhood

Vol'ka's family background differs from that of the other bylini protagonists. While the other bylini heroes are born into noble or common human families, Vol'ka does not have a human father. One story variant does not mention a father at all. In the more common version, Vol'ka's mother, Princess Marfa, was strolling in the garden when a snake suddenly coiled around her leg and slapped her thigh with its tail. Soon after this incident, she discovered she was pregnant.

As one might expect after that strange engendering, the baby Vol'ka was hardly ordinary. His birth was announced by an earthquake and a storm. Birds, fish, and wild beasts flew, swam, and ran wildly in all directions.

Vol'ka quickly displayed the common traits of a culture hero: miraculous growth and the supernaturally rapid gaining of wisdom. Able to speak at birth, the one-day-old baby looked as large and well developed as a child of one year. He told his mother "in a voice like thunder" to put away childish toys and instead prepare a warrior's proper gear and arms for him. In a request that separates Vol'ka from most culture heroes, he also asked for books of wisdom.

Vol'ka became as sage as any man by the time that he was five. The bylina makes a clear distinction between true wisdom and sly wisdom. The latter includes tricks such as the art of shape shifting. Vol'ka swiftly learns and masters both types.

In traditional Christian Slavic folklore, the *kolduni* are sorcerers of human and demonic ancestry who are feared for their dark powers. But Vol'ka is never characterized in any of the folklore as a *koldun,* and his powers are never portrayed as dark. Vol'ka more closely resembles the heroes found in world folktales and myths that are born of two worlds, the human and the animal.

Vol'ka and the Animal World

The hero's ties to the animal world indicate that his tale predates Christianity's arrival in Slavic lands. Christianity and its antimagic bias reached the area in the twelfth century. Vol'ka's name may derive from *volkhv,* an ancient Slavic word for "sorcerer." However, some linguists think that the name may have ties with the ancient Slavic word for wolf, *volk.* The latter seems fitting, given Vol'ka's shape-shifting abilities. Apparently without needing any special rituals or preparation, he can become a falcon, fish, wolf, or bull.

Vol'ka's subjects calmly accepted their prince's magic. At one point, Vol'ka, in the form of a hunted animal, teased his hunters, asking who among them was able to shape-shift to hunt. They answered matter-of-factly that no one could do this but their prince.

Vol'ka the Warrior

Vol'ka is also a great warrior. In the only complete tale about this character, word reached the prince that the tsar of India (or in some versions Turkey or Central Asia) was planning an attack. Vol'ka instantly mustered his *druzhina,* or war band, and led them to battle. The druzhina was, as befitted a folk hero, far larger than any in the real world. Rather than the standard thirty men, Vol'ka's band consisted of 7,000. When so large an army was unable to find enough food during their march, their magician-prince changed roles from warrior to hunter. He shape-shifted into a wolf and then a falcon to capture game for his men.

The prince's shape-shifting ability also allowed him to gather information from behind enemy lines. As an aurochs, a type of bison, he leapt toward India with magical swiftness. Then, as a falcon, the princely spy perched on the tsar's window sill. While within enemy walls, the tireless Vol'ka turned himself into an ermine and destroyed as many of the royal armaments as he could by chewing through bowstrings, separating arrowheads from shafts, and, in one anachronistic variant, destroying flintlock muskets.

When Vol'ka's army arrived at the royal fortress, however, his men despaired. The walls were too tall and solid for any army to scale or pierce. The men said only an ant could get under them. So Vol'ka turned himself and the entire army into ants. They tunneled under the walls, were turned back into men, and proceeded with the attack.

At this point, Vol'ka proved he was an honorable twelfth-century hero. Rather than blasting the enemy with magic, he fought the foe in hand-to-hand combat. Vol'ka hurled the tsar down with great force and killed him. The Indian threat ended, and Vol'ka and his men were married to the lovely Indian maidens.

And so ends this tale, a curious combination of medieval folk epic and ancient folkloric elements with the unique hero-warrior Vol'ka at its center.

See also: Bylina/Bylini; Kievan Cycle; Slavic Mythology.

Sources

Magnus, L.A. *The Heroic Ballads of Russia.* Port Washington, NY: Kennikat, 1967.
Pronin, Alexander. *Byliny: Heroic Tales of Old Russia.* Frankfurt, Germany: Possev, 1971.

Völva

(Norse)

In Norse and Teutonic mythology a *völva* was a female prophet, a type of priest or shaman. Generally, this figure was an older woman who was not bound to a single family or clan and could wander freely.

The völva might travel alone or have a retinue of apprentices. She performed a craft called *seidr,* which was either shamanistic ritual or true sorcery. Völvas were held in high regard. Men could be völvas as well but were not revered as the women were. True seidr was considered a woman's craft.

A völva is described in the *Saga of Erik,* dressed in a blue-black gem-studded cloak, a necklace of glass beads, and a hat trimmed with white catskin. A pouch containing her magical tools hung from a belt around her waist. She wore calfskin shoes ornamented with brass and catskin gloves, with the white fur on the inside. She carried a distaff decorated with brass and gems, which was said to create a spell of forgetfulness on anyone she tapped with it three times on the cheek.

The völva would sit on a small platform and make her predictions after slipping into a trance. In the *Saga of Hrolf Kraki,* the völva located two missing boys this way, chanting out the information.

It was said that the völva was so important a figure that even Odin, one of the chief Norse deities, consulted a völva about the future of the gods.

See also: Norse Mythology.

Sources

Byock, Jesse L., trans. *The Saga of King Hrolf Kraki.* London: Penguin, 1998.

Lindow, John. *Norse Mythology: A Guide to the Gods, Heroes, Rituals, and Beliefs.* New York: Oxford University Press, 2002.

Magnusson, Magnus, and Hermann Palsson, trans. *The Vinland Sagas: The Norse Discovery of America.* Baltimore: Penguin, 1965.

Sturluson, Snorri. *The Prose Edda of Snorri Sturluson: Tales from the Norse Mythology.* Trans. Jean I. Young. Berkeley: University of California Press, 1964.

Wayang

(Indonesian)

Wayang is an ancient Javanese word meaning "shadow" or "ghost." It is also the name for the traditional sacred dramas of Java and Bali. There are seven main forms of wayang, but *wayang kulit,* or shadow-puppet theater, is the most common. In Java, shadow plays are performed to celebrate public holidays, religious festivals, weddings, birth celebrations, and circumcisions. In Bali, they are staged at all these events, as well as at cremations.

Wayang Kulit

The wayang kulit may have originated in Java thousands of years ago. Wayang kulit stories are told with flat puppets made of leather and cut out in profile. These shadow puppets are beautifully painted and intricately pierced so that their shadows are amazingly detailed. The puppets' arms are moved by manipulating small sticks.

The puppeteer is called the *dalang.* He sits cross-legged behind the screen, which is usually a large white cloth stretched on a wooden frame. An oil lamp hangs above the puppeteer so that as he moves the puppets the lamp casts their shadows onto the screen.

Shadow plays generally are extensive events. In its entirety, a typical wayang kulit may last from sundown until sunrise, about eight or nine hours. Not only must the dalang be a trained performer, but he has to be strong and in excellent health as well. During the full nine hours, he must remain cross-legged, moving only to control the puppets and the *kechrek,* or rattle, which he constantly strikes with his right foot.

The dalang speaks for all the puppets and has to be able to change his voice to portray every type of character. A shadow play is always accompanied by a *gamelan,* a traditional Indonesian orchestra, which is made up mostly of metal percussion instruments. The dalang also acts as conductor, giving hidden cues to the gamelan musicians.

Two Forms of *Wayang Kulit*

There are two subcategories of wayang kulit. The older form is *wayang purwa,* in which stories from the two great Indian epics, the *Mahabharata* and the *Ramayana,* are told. Both of these epics arrived in Java with the influx of Indian influence in the first century C.E. There are about 200 different *lakon,* or stories, based on what are now truly Javanese versions of the tales within those two epics. In Java, the Pendawa cycle was inspired by the *Mahabharata,* and the Rama cycle by the *Ramayana.* Perhaps the most popular stories in the Rama cycle are

This Indonesian cotton fabric, dyed in a technique known as batik, is decorated with a design that depicts wayang puppets. (*© Werner Forman/Art Resource, NY*)

those concerning the marriage of Rama to Sinta (Sita in the *Ramayana*) and Sinta's abduction and rescue.

The second form of wayang kulit is called *wayang gedog*. In this type, stories from the later Hindu era of Java are retold. They feature tales of a mythological hero-prince, Panji. Wayang gedog is rarely performed today.

Puppet shows on nonmythic themes are less common. Those that are performed include *wayang golek,* which uses round puppets carved of wood, and *wayang wong,* dance dramas performed by live actors.

See also: Puppetry and Storytelling.

Sources

Brandon, James R., ed. *On Thrones of Gold: Three Javanese Shadow Plays.* Honolulu: University of Hawaii Press, 1993.

Herbert, Mimi. *Voices of the Puppet Masters: The Wayang Golek Theater of Indonesia.* Honolulu: University of Hawaii Press, 2002.

Keeler, Ward. *Javanese Shadow Plays, Javanese Selves.* Princeton, NJ: Princeton University Press, 1987.

Zurbuchen, Mary Sabina. *The Language of Balinese Shadow Theater.* Princeton, NJ: Princeton University Press, 1987.

Wele

(Kenyan)

Wele is the supreme god of the Kavirondo people of Kenya.

It was Wele who created everything. First, he created the heavens, then the Sun, the Moon, the other celestial bodies, and finally Earth and humanity.

Wele can appear to people in two ways. He can appear as Omuwanga, the benign white god, or as Gumali, the black god who brings misfortune.

See also: An/Anu; Odin/Odhinn; Sius; Zeus.

Sources

Abrahams, Roger D., comp. *African Folktales: Traditional Stories of the Black World.* New York: Pantheon, 1983.

Courlander, Harold. *A Treasury of African Folklore.* New York: Marlowe, 1996.

Radin, Paul. *African Folktales.* New York: Alfred A. Knopf, 1987.

Wenamun, Report of

(Egyptian)

The *Report of Wenamun* literary text recounts events that took place during the reign of Pharaoh Ramses XI, who ruled from about 1104 until 1075 B.C.E. It is not known if this work was derived from a genuine report or is entirely a work of fiction.

Written during the twenty-first dynasty (c. 1081–931 B.C.E.), the tale reflects the political reality of this period, during which Egypt was divided. The northern region was ruled by a king who resided in the city of Tanis. A high priest of Amun ruled the southern region from Thebes. As a result, the government was largely ineffective. This impotence is presented frankly in Wenamun's story.

Wenamun Sails for Byblos

The author of the report calls himself Wenamun, Elder of the Portal of the Temple of Amun. He relates leaving Thebes to fetch the timber needed to build the sacred barque, or boat, of Amun, the supreme god of ancient Egypt.

After paying a call on King Smendes and his wife, Tantemon, in Tanis, Wenamun departed for Byblos (in Syria) on a Syrian ship. Within a month, he arrived at the harbor of Dor, Israel (present-day Tell Dor), where a crewman ran off with his gold and silver.

Wenamun lodged a complaint with the ruler of Dor, who had jurisdiction over incidents at the port. Wenamun reminded the unnamed ruler that the valuables that were stolen belonged to the rulers of Egypt, the ruler of Byblos, and Amun-Re. After nine days, the chief of Dor was unable to find the thief and could only offer Wenamun this advice: He should avoid Tyre on his way to Byblos.

Wenamun sailed safely to Byblos. Before disembarking to meet with Zekerbaal, prince of Byblos, he searched the ship and confiscated thirty *deben* of silver, almost equal to the amount of silver that had been stolen from him. Wenamun took lodging in a tavern, where he set up a shrine to Amun-of-the-Road.

Upon learning of Wenamun's arrival, Zekerbaal ordered him out of the port. For twenty-nine days Wenamun defied Zekerbaal's daily order to leave, saying he would depart only when there was a ship available that was bound for Egypt.

Wenamun and Zekerbaal

Zekerbaal's attitude changed, however, when one of his servants fell into an ecstatic fit. The servant cried out that "the image" of Amun and the Egyptian envoy (Wenamun) should be brought to the palace, because Amun had sent them. And so, just as Wenamun was about to set sail, he was ordered to stay.

The next morning, Wenamun met with Zekerbaal at the palace. The prince asked for his written orders, but Wenamun had already given them to King Smendes. They argued briefly about the nature of Wenamun's ship before getting down to business: Wenamun explained that he had come for the timber, which Zekerbaal's predecessors had always given to Egypt. Zekerbaal agreed that they had given timber to Egypt, but only in exchange for six shiploads of Egyptian goods. Wenamun had brought nothing. Zekerbaal expressed sympathy that Wenamun had been made to undertake this task with no support. Formerly, it would not have been so.

This remark insulted Wenamun. He declared that he did have support—from Amun, lord of all ships and of Lebanon. In the past, those treasures were sent only because the kings could not send life and health. Amun, who was the lord of life and health, granted these instead of mere material goods. If Zeker-baal were to provide the timber, the god would assure his prosperity and that of his people. Nevertheless, Wenamun dispatched a letter to Smendes, who replied with gold, silver, and other valuables.

Satisfied at last, Zekerbaal ordered the timber to be cut. But he was still unhappy with Wenamun's conduct. He warned that if the Egyptian attempted to transport the timber during the stormy season, he would face Zeker-baal's wrath. Wenamun soothed his host by proposing the wording of an inscription that would memorialize Zekerbaal's generosity.

Wenamun's subsequent attempts to obtain ships to return to Egypt were thwarted. Frustrated, he watched helplessly as southbound migratory birds passed by on their way to his homeland. Learning this, Zekerbaal sent wine, a sheep, and an Egyptian songstress to cheer Wenamun until the next day.

At last, Wenamun was able to leave. Once he was on his way, a storm took him to the country of Alashiya (on the island of Cyprus), where the inhabitants attempted to kill him. Wenamun fought his way to the home of Princess Hatiba, who, by means of an interpreter who spoke Egyptian, offered Wenamun safety.

Although we know that Wenamun survived to file his report, any other troubles that assailed him are unknown, as the papyrus is broken at this point.

Noreen Doyle

See also: Fantasy.

Sources

Egberts, Arno. "Wenamun." In *The Oxford Encyclopedia of Ancient Egypt*. Vol. 3. Ed. D.B. Redford. New York: Oxford University Press, 2001.

Goedicke, Hans. *The Report of Wenamun*. Baltimore: Johns Hopkins University Press, 1975.

Lichtheim, Miriam. *Ancient Egyptian Literature: A Book of Readings*. Vol. 2. Berkeley: University of California Press, 2006.

Werewolves

Werewolves are the unfortunate beings that are believed to have the ability to transform into wolves and then back into human beings. The English word *werewolf* is a descendant of the Old English *wer* (man) and *wulf* (wolf).

Indo-European Origins

The concept of the werewolf is common to many Indo-European cultures that can be traced back to Russia and the Ukraine in the fifth to the third millennium B.C.E.

The Indo-European word for wolf has been reconstructed by scholars as *wlkwos*. Many modern words for werewolf can be traced to this Indo-European word for wolf: *vulcolaca* (Old Slavic), *vukodlak* (Slovenian), *wilkolak* (Polish), *vrykolokas* (Greek), *vurvolak* (Albanian), and *varcolac* (Romanian). These words also are used to mean "vampire" in some areas. As most of these terms are a combination of the words *wolf* and *pelt*, they can be loosely translated as wolf-coat.

The Romanian varcolac is sometimes a vampire, and sometimes a wolf that eats the Moon, causing eclipses. In other cases, the var-colac is a person who periodically descends into a deep sleep from which his or her soul wanders forth in the shape of a wolf. This may be a dim recollection of ancient shamanic traditions.

Shamans

The earliest werewolves in Indo-European cultures were probably shamans, or spiritual leaders. A shaman placed himself in a trance to travel to the realm of the dead, and he used his great power to return safely to the realm of the living. He also might seek to be possessed by a creature of great strength to help him in this journey.

That some shamans in Indo-European cultures had a special relationship with the wolf is evident in many cultural traditions. The Magyar shamans of Hungary were said to have been fathered by wolves. Slavic priests were referred to as *volkhvy,* which derived from the word for wolf, *velku.*

These shamans were not only magicians and holy men, but also often warriors. Many warrior societies developed among Indo-European cultures. One of the best known is the so-called berserkers. Though the group's name literally meant "bear-shirt," such warriors also were identified with wolves.

In the poem *Hrafnsmal,* which was composed in Iceland around 900 C.E., the Ulfedhnar, or wolf-warriors of Norway, are described as those who carry swords and participate in slaughter. The only armor worn by the Ulfedhnar was the *vargstakkar,* or wolf-shirt. The warriors, who could become possessed by the spirit of wolves due to their shamanic magic, were outside the realm of ordinary people. Often, they could kill without consequences when they were so possessed.

Other Early Traditions

Those who did not belong to these societies and broke the laws of the tribe also were identified with wolves. In Germanic areas, criminals were referred to as *vargr i veum,* or the "wolf in the temple." These men's lives were forfeited to anyone who caught them.

In the Middle Ages, condemned criminals who had taken to the forest to hide were referred to as wolfsheads. In Saxon, the gallows was called the *varg treo,* or wolf tree. The association with criminality and the wolf appears even in Sanskrit, where *vrka* was the word for a highwayman.

The ability to shape-shift into a wolf is a common element among many folklore traditions. In *Saga of the Volsungs,* composed in thirteenth-century Iceland, Sigmund and his son, Sinfjotli, became wolves. During their time as werewolves, they killed many men in the land of King Siggeir, who was responsible for the death of much of Sigmund's family. Eventually, Sigmund and Sinfjotli removed the coats and burned them. As there were no wolves in Iceland, this story may be a reference to earlier initiation rites of young men into the wolf-warrior cults of Northern Europe.

Another werewolf appears in this saga. When Sigmund and his nine brothers were captured by King Siggeir, they were bound in chains. Each night, a wolf came and devoured one of them. Sigmund, who had been left for last, killed the werewolf, which was believed to be King Siggeir's mother wearing wolf skin.

In 1187, Giraldus Cambrensis, a Welsh writer and historian, related the following werewolf tale from Ireland:

A priest traveling from Ulster to Meath was waylaid on the road at night by a wolf. The wolf spoke to him and pleaded with him not to be afraid. The wolf called upon the almighty God and invoked the Trinity and, in time, convinced the priest that he meant no harm.

When the priest was at last convinced to put aside his fear, the wolf told him that he and a companion had been placed under a curse and that his companion was near death. The priest followed the wolf to where a she-wolf lay and administered extreme unction. The male wolf then ripped open the she-wolf's coat and revealed an old woman who had been trapped inside. The wolf and woman thanked the priest for his kindness, and he went on his way.

Werewolf Trials

Most werewolf legal cases were recorded between 1520 and 1630. In that time, it is estimated that 30,000 people in France were identified as werewolves. Many were tortured into confessions, and many were executed. For those who survived, the stigma of being identified as a werewolf became a lifelong curse.

One of the most famous werewolf cases took place in 1603. Jean Grenier, who was only thirteen years old at the time, was accused of changing into the form of a wolf and killing and eating other local children. Grenier apparently believed he could become a wolf, and at least one witness claimed to have seen him change form. However, the judge in this case ruled that Grenier was not a werewolf, but a boy deluded into believing he could change shape. It was determined that Grenier was mentally deficient and therefore could not be executed for his crimes. He was sentenced to life imprisonment in a monastery, where he died seven years later at age twenty.

Many werewolves were executed in Germany. In 1589, Peter Stubbe was convicted of killing fifteen people when in werewolf form. His lover and his daughter were convicted as accomplices and were burned at the stake. Stubbe was strapped to a cartwheel and had his flesh pulled from his body with red-hot pincers. After his arms and legs were broken, Stubbe was beheaded.

In some stories, it is indeed a man-wolf rather than a true wolf that is encountered. In one tale, a man who had persecuted those he believed to be evil was lost in the woods at night. A werewolf approached him and led him to a house, where the werewolf performed human tasks, such as opening doors and pouring soup into a bowl. This werewolf walked upright and had hands, rather than paws. In the morning, the man discovered that the wolfish visage of his benefactor had disappeared. He learned that this was one of the men whom he had persecuted and whose family he had sent to the executioner. In this case, it was the werewolf that showed compassion and mercy, and the man who was revealed to be the monster.

Real or Imaginary?

The belief that werewolves do not truly exist, but are merely deluded people, is older than the modern practice of psychiatry. In 1590, Henri Boguet, a French judge who presided over many cases involving witches and werewolves, declared that no one could truly change his or her shape. A person could merely be deluded by Satan into believing he or she could change. Anyone who saw the person change was equally deluded by Satan. Boguet also allowed that certain "natural maladies" could cause people to be so deluded, and that Satan might not actively be involved in each and every case.

The belief that a person can change into a wolf has not completely died out, though modern cases consist of individuals who are habitual drug users or who have been diagnosed with a psychiatric disorder, such as schizophrenia. Two cases were reported in the *Canadian Psychiatric Association Journal* in 1975. Another case was presented in the *American Journal of Psychiatry* in 1977. The medical term for this condition is *lycanthrope,* which is Greek for "wolf-man."

By the twentieth century, werewolves had almost completely retreated into the realm of fiction. But as recently as 1993, the Associated Press reported that the *Evenimentul Ziliei,* a daily newspaper in Romania, had urged its readers to use garlic to protect themselves on Saint Andrew's Day against ghosts and werewolves.

The concept of a "beast within" has remained popular with modern readers of fiction and the moviegoing public. From Robert Louis Stevenson's novel *The Strange Case of Dr. Jekyll and Mr. Hyde* (1886) to tales of the Incredible Hulk, people remain fascinated with the idea that animal ferocity, uncivilized and untamable, lurks within us all.

The first movie to feature a werewolf character was *The Werewolf,* an eighteen-minute movie filmed in 1913. In this story, a Navajo girl became a werewolf in order to exact revenge for her father's murder. Since then, werewolves have been the focus of more than fifty movies, including *The Wolf Man* (1941), *The Werewolf* (1956), *I Was a Teenage Werewolf* (1957), *The Curse of the Werewolf* (1960), and *An American Werewolf in London* (1981). And in the 1985 film *Ladyhawke,* a man was cursed to become a werewolf every night and change back into a man during the day.

Werewolves in recent fiction obey different rules than those found in history. Usually, fictional werewolves are created through a gypsy's curse or when a character is bitten by a werewolf. Most of these werewolves transform only during the full moon and must be dispatched with silver bullets.

Marella Sands

See also: Shape-Shifters.

Sources

Byock, Jesse L., trans. *The Saga of the Volsungs: The Norse Epic of Sigurd the Dragon Slayer.* Berkeley: University of California Press, 1990.

Dundes, Alan, ed. *The Vampire: A Casebook.* Madison: University of Wisconsin Press, 1998.

Jackson, Nigel. *Compleat Vampyre.* Chieveley, UK: Capall Bann, 1995.

Otten, Charlotte F., ed. *A Lycanthropy Reader: Werewolves in Western Culture.* Syracuse, NY: Syracuse University Press, 1986.

West African Mythology

The region of West Africa includes many nations, some peaceful and some troubled by civil war or corrupt politics. The list of nations includes Benin, Cameroon, Gabon, Ghana, Guinea, the Ivory Coast, Mali, Nigeria, and Sierra Leone. Each of these countries is home to several ethnic groups, and each group has its own mythology.

The myths of these people are a part of a living religion and should be treated with respect by storytellers.

Benin

The supreme god of the Fon people of Benin is Nana Buluku. He is the father of the twins Lisa and Mawu, deities of the Sun and Moon. The creator god is Mawu. An aid to Mawu was Aido-Hwedo, the great serpent power, a primal force who assisted in the ordering of the cosmos. Above the earth, Aido-Hwedo had 3,500 coils, and the same number below; together, they supported Mawu's creation. Fa is the god of destiny, who provided the personal fate for each human. A son of Mawu and Lisa is Gu, god of iron and war.

Other deities include Age, patron of hunters. Age is in charge of the wilderness, the uninhabited bush, and the animals therein. Legba is a trickster god of language and fate, Minona is a goddess diviner, and Sogbo is the god of thunder, lightning, and fire.

Other interesting characters of Fon traditional beliefs are Honsi and Honsu, a pair of mythical twins with magical powers, and Yehwe Zogbanu, the thirty-horned forest-dwelling giant.

Cameroon

The Bamileke and the Bangwa people recognize one supreme god called Si. But they are more likely to pray to ancestral spirits for help or guidance. Si remains a rather remote figure.

The Efik of Cameroon and Nigeria

Abassi, or Obassi, is the Efik creator god. His wife, Atai, brought death to humankind. Atai convinced her husband to allow their human children, one man and one woman, to live on Earth. The children were not allowed to reproduce or work so that they would not overwhelm Abassi in strength and wisdom.

When the first humans broke those rules, Atai killed them both and caused strife, death, and war between their children. Abassi and Atai were so disgusted that they withdrew from the affairs of their descendants.

Ghana

Nyambe is the creator god of the Asante people. He planted the tree of life in his garden then moved it to heaven when humans failed to appreciate it.

Perhaps the best-known being in the myth and folklore of West Africa is Ananse (also spelled Anansi). He is the trickster spider-being of the Asante and other West African peoples, and a figure in Caribbean folklore. Dubiaku is a culture hero of the Asante people and the only mortal to outwit death. He is known to the Asante people living in Nigeria as well.

Wuni is the creator god of the Dagamba people. One myth says that the people sent a dog to Dagamba to tell him what a terribly hard life they led, but the dog got sidetracked by a juicy bone. So a goat was sent, but its bleating was so difficult to understand that Wuni misunderstood and decided that life would be ended by death.

The Ivory Coast

The supreme deity of the Akan is Nyame, who created all things and from whom lesser gods derive their power. Nyame is not worshiped directly but is approached through intermediaries. These lesser gods, called *abosom,* may inhabit lakes, streams, rivers, or trees. Below them in status are minor deities whose power is invoked through amulets or charms worn for protection. The *samanfo,* or ancestral spirits, are very important to the Akan people, since the ancestors are believed to protect their descendants.

Now predominantly Muslim, the Mande mix elements of Islam with their traditional beliefs. The Mande creation myth, for example, describes the biblical account of creation, but it also includes the creation of two sets of twins from seeds. These twins were commanded to populate the earth and teach their children how to grow crops. The twins created music and prayed for rain. The Niger River is said to have been formed from the resulting floods.

Mali

The majority of Mali's population is Muslim, but some people still practice indigenous religions. Yo is a primeval world spirit in the belief system of the Bambara people. This trickster is made up of both male and female elements. Yo allowed Pemba, the creator god, and Pemba's brother, Faro, god of sky and water, to visit Earth.

Pemba is a vegetation deity, and Faro created humankind. Faro is a remote deity who visits Earth only once every 400 years. Musso-Koroni is the Bambara goddess of disorder. She is the wife of Pemba but dislikes him and prefers to wander, causing sadness and disorder wherever she goes.

Amma is the sky god and the creator of the universe for the Dogon people. Nommo was the first living being created by Amma. Nommo multiplied himself into four sets of twins. One twin rebelled against the others, causing unrest in the world. To restore stability, Amma cut Nommo up and placed the pieces evenly around the world to balance it. Shrines to the ancestral spirits known as Binu commemorate this event.

Lebe is the Dogon earth god, concerned with the agricultural cycle. Tradition claims that Lebe visits the *hogons,* or priests, every night as a serpent who licks their skin to fill them with renewed life force and purity.

Ogo is the trickster god, also known as the Pale Fox or Jackal. Ogo's tricky children are Andumbulu and Yeban, the underworld spirits. Yasigi is the goddess of dancing, beer, and masks.

Nigeria

Nigeria is the home of several different ethnic groups. The culture that is perhaps most familiar to the people of the United States is that of the Yoruba people. Many Yoruba were brought to the New World as slaves, and they brought their beliefs with them.

The Bura and Pabir Peoples

Hyel, or Hyel-Taku, is the supreme god of the Bura and Pabir people. He is worshipped indirectly, through the *haptu,* or personal gods. Some of these personal gods belong to particular clans, and there is no single haptu for a whole tribe.

The Ibo People

The supreme Ibo deity is Chuku, or Chukwu, from whom all good comes. Ala is his daughter, the earth goddess, mother of all things and spirit of fertility.

Igwe is the sky god. Interestingly, the Ibo do not pray to Igwe for rain, because rainmaking is the job of professional tribal rainmakers. Imo Miri is the spirit of rivers. Larger rivers are so holy that it is forbidden for humans to fish in them.

Ekwu, goddess of the hearth, is the women's patron, and Aha Njoku is the goddess of yams, an important crop for the Ibo people, and the patron of the women who care for them. Lesser gods include Mbatuku, spirit of wealth, Agwo, who is always envious of others' wealth, and Ikoro, the spirit of the drum.

The Yoruba People

Olorun is the ruler of the sky and father of the gods Obatala and Odudua (heaven and Earth). He is the deity of peace, harmony, justice, and purity. Obatala is one of the most important Yoruban gods. He created humankind and is the patron of the handicapped. Odudua created the earth. The world began as only water, and Odudua threw soil onto the water. He sent a rooster to scratch at it, which pushed it around and created the dry land.

Yemaja, who is variously described as the daughter of Olorun, Odudua, or Obatala, is the mother goddess of the living ocean. She is the patron of birth and is worshipped primarily by women. Her brother and husband is Aganju. When Orungan, their son, raped Yemaja, her body burst open and fifteen gods were born, including Shango.

Shango, the god of thunder and the ancestor of the Yoruba people, has three wives. The first is Oya, who stole Shango's secrets of magic; the second is Oshun, the river goddess, who is Shango's favorite; and the third is Oba, who was cast away by Shango to become the turbulent Oba River. Oshun, Shango's favorite wife, is the goddess of love, pleasure, beauty, and diplomacy. While she is generous and kind to humankind, Oshun has a fierce temper.

Shakpana is another of Yemaja's sons, an angry god who afflicts humans with disease and madness. Eshu is a trickster god to whom offerings must be made before any magic ritual may be performed. He is the protector of travelers and a teacher who uses tricks to make his point.

Olokun is the sea deity, seen in both male and female versions, who lives in an underwater palace and symbolizes deep wisdom. Olokun is also the patron of those who were carried off in the slave trade.

Aja is a forest goddess who teaches her followers the use of medicinal herbs. Oya is the goddess of fire and wind, a warrior deity whose anger causes hurricanes. She is also the patron of change and guardian of the gates of death.

In addition to the deities, there are other beings in Yoruban mythology. The orishas are the guardian spirits and include Babalu-Aye, the spirit of healing. Egbere always weeps and carries a mat. Whoever steals his mat will become rich.

This sampling of the mythologies of West Africa gives storytellers a hint of the riches to be found by researching them more thoroughly.

See also: Yoruban Storytelling.

Sources
Courlander, Harold. *Tales of Yoruba Gods and Heroes.* New York: Crown, 1973.

Murphy, Joseph M. *Santeria: An African Religion in America.* Boston: Beacon, 1988.

Owomoyela, Oyekan. *Yoruba Trickster Tales.* Lincoln: University of Nebraska Press, 1997.

Parrinder, Geoffrey. *African Mythology.* London: Hamlyn, 1967.

Shaub, Harold. *A Dictionary of African Mythology.* New York: Oxford University Press, 2000.

White Horses of England

The white horses of England are among a number of figures, usually of animals, that are cut into hillsides. The turf has been cut away, revealing the figures in the chalk underneath. Several white horses appear in Wiltshire, where there are nine large equine images. It is impossible to accurately date these figures, but they are estimated to have been carved anywhere from 4,000 to 2,000 years ago. The reason for the carvings is unknown.

The white horse with the greatest number of folk beliefs attached to it is the Uffington horse, the most stylized, least naturalistic, of the horses. The Uffington horse is said to be able to grant the wish of anyone who stands on its eye and turns around three times clockwise. This belief can no longer be tested, however. So many people walked on the horse that they began to damage it, and it is no longer accessible to the public.

Once every hundred years, the Uffington horse is said to gallop across the sky to be reshod by Wayland, the wonder-smith of Anglo-Saxon mythology. Wayland's smithy is said to have stood near where the Uffington horse was carved. It is also said that when King Arthur awakes from his magical sleep, as some believe he will, the Uffington horse will rise up and dance on nearby Dragon Hill.

In other local folk beliefs, the Uffington white horse is said to be a mare with an invisible foal on the hill beside her. Every night, the mare and foal come down the hill to graze at the slope known as the manger. They drink at nearby Woolstone Wells, which is believed to have been formed by the mare's hoofprint.

White horse figures in other locations also are said to come to life and go to drink. The Tan Hill horse is supposed to come to life when the church clock of All Cannings strikes midnight. It then goes down to a pond to drink. The Westbury white horse is also a thirsty one. It wakes when the Bratton church clock strikes midnight and goes down to Briddle Springs to drink.

See also: Motifs.

Sources

Bergamar, Kate. *Discovering Hill Figures*. Buckinghamshire, UK: Shire, 1968.

Bord, Janet, and Colin Bord. *The Secret Country: Interpretation of the Folklore of Ancient Sites in the British Isles*. New York: Walker, 1977.

Plenderleath, William Charles. *The White Horses of the West of England: With Notices of Some Other Ancient Turf-Monuments*. London: Allen and Storr, 1892.

White Magic

White magic is used solely for beneficial purposes. It can be used toward the personal well-being of the magician or with the intention of helping or healing another. White magic traditionally is said to draw its power from heavenly forces. White magic spells are the essence of good, the very opposite of those used in black magic.

White magic spells are never used for personal gain or to harm others. They are used to protect, bless, and heal those in need. White magic also can hold off black magic and break ill wishes and curses.

White magic is found in folktales and fantasy stories around the world. Merlin, the powerful magician of Arthurian lore, practices white magic. Merlin is part demon (or part fairy), yet he chooses to stay on the side of right. The magician Michael Scott of Scottish folklore kept his soul safe from the devil by never straying from white magic.

Perhaps the most familiar practitioners of white magic are the fairy godmothers found in more than 700 versions of the "Cinderella" story. These benevolent fairies cast spells to help the protagonists of their stories to live happily ever after.

Magicians are extremely popular in modern fantasy fiction, more so than in the fiction of earlier eras. Gandalf, in J.R.R. Tolkien's *Lord of the Rings* series (1954–1955), is a powerful white wizard who refuses to use his magic for ill, even when tempted by the One Ring. And, in J.K. Rowling's more recent fictional series about the adventures of Harry Potter (1997–2007), Harry is a powerful wizard who uses his powers for good.

It is important to note that Harry Potter is a rare exception to the norm. Magicians generally are not the heroes of the stories in which they appear. In works with a magic user as protagonist, the author must include some check on the power of that character. It is for good reason that Gandalf disappears for a significant portion of the *Lord of the Rings* series—if he remained, there would be little worry for the other characters, which would make for a rather dull plot.

See also: Black Magic.

Sources

Ahlquist, Diane. *White Light: The Complete Guide to Spells and Rituals for Psychic Protection.* New York: Citadel, 2002.

Bias, Clifford. *A Manual of White Magic: Rituals, Spells, and Incantations.* Van Nuys, CA: Newcastle, 1985.

Zipes, Jack, ed. *The Oxford Companion to Fairy Tales.* New York: Oxford University Press, 2000.

Wicked Stepmothers

The character of the wicked or evil stepmother is common in the world's folklore. Scholars and storytellers have long debated the reason for the existence of this character type.

Stepmothers were common in societies where women were likely to die in childbirth or shortly afterward. A man often would take a second wife to replace his children's deceased biological mother. The motif continues today as a result of modern-day patterns of divorce and remarriage.

Stepmothers in folklore are almost always wicked. This is probably due to two issues: the psychology of the child, who sees the stepmother as an intruder who has done away with the birth mother, and inheritance laws. A second wife rarely felt that the first wife's child, rather than her own offspring, should inherit everything, and a first child would not wish to share an inheritance with interlopers, such as stepsisters.

Some of the most familiar wicked stepmothers appear in the many "Cinderella" variants, in which the wicked stepmother is often accompanied by wicked stepsisters. In most of these stories, protection of the stepmother's own children is the most common motivation for her wickedness. This is, perhaps, more understandable than the truly evil nature of the "Snow White" stories, in which the stepmother is consumed by jealousy of the heroine.

There are several odd variants to the wicked stepmother theme. In the English tale of "Kate Crackernuts," the story's heroine is not the first daughter but the stepdaughter. The stepdaughter is a lively, active character, and the first daughter is more passive. In the German tale "The Juniper Tree," the stepmother murders and eats her stepson. She is then slain by the stepson in the form of a bird-spirit, and he is restored to life.

In the Grimm Brothers' version of "Hansel and Gretel," it is the stepmother who cast the children away. In earlier versions, it was their own mother.

See also: Motifs.

Sources

Jacoby, Mario, Verena Kast, and Ingrid Riedel. *Witches, Ogres, and the Devil's Daughter: Encounters with Evil in Fairy Tales.* Trans. Michael H. Kohn. Boston: Shambala, 1992.

Leach, Maria, ed. *Funk & Wagnalls Standard Dictionary of Folklore, Mythology and Legend.* San Francisco: Harper and Row, 1984.

Tatar, Maria, ed. *The Annotated Classic Fairy Tales.* New York: W.W. Norton, 2002.

Thompson, Stith. *The Folktale.* New York: Dryden, 1946.

William Tell

(Swiss)

Few medieval heroes are as widely known as William Tell. His exploits have been celebrated by poets, playwrights, and composers.

The Story of William Tell

A cruel Austrian official called Gessler was assigned to Switzerland. Gessler arranged to have a pole planted in the square of Altdorf with a hat at the top in Austrian colors. All those who passed had to bow to the hat in order to show their respect. William Tell and his son passed through the square and did not salute the hat.

Tell was arrested and brought before Gessler. His punishment for this disrespect was to shoot an apple off his son's head. Tell, a famous marksman, accomplished this, but he had hidden a second arrow under his quiver. He told Gessler, "It was to pierce your heart if my first arrow killed my son."

In spite of his vast reputation, it is very likely that William Tell never existed, and it is certain that the story of the apple is pure fiction. Even so, the Swiss proudly recognize the legend, and the marksman's image is on the back of the five-franc coin.

Truth Versus Fiction

Details have been added to the story over time in an attempt to make it seem true.

The earliest work that makes any allusion to the adventures of William Tell is the chronicle of the younger Melchior Russ, written in 1482. As the shooting of the apple was supposed to have taken place in 1296, this leaves an interval of 186 years between the event and the written account. In the interim, neither a Tell nor a William, nor the apple, nor the cruelty of Gessler received any mention in historic records. Also, the charters of Kussnach (the village where the events supposedly took place) have been examined and show that no man by the name of Gessler ever ruled there.

Contemporary chroniclers described in detail the tyrannical acts of the Duke of Austria that goaded the Swiss to rebellion. Yet they do not once mention Tell's name or betray the slightest acquaintance with his exploits or with his existence. These painstaking medieval chroniclers would never have kept silent about the adventures of this character if they had known about them.

William Tell, the crossbow-wielding hero of Swiss folktales, prepares to shoot an apple off his son's head. This colored print, or acquantinta, was made around 1820. *(Bildarchiv Preussischer Kulturbesitz/Art Resource, NY)*

The greatest proof that William Tell's story is not historical comes from an almost identical earlier tale recorded by the medieval Danish author Saxo Grammaticus. He tells of a skilled archer named Palnatoki, one of King Harold's bodyguards, who was envied by the others. Once, when Palnatoki had drunk too much, he boasted about his skill, saying that he could hit the smallest apple placed a long way off at the first shot.

The envious warriors turned the mind of the king against Palnatoki. Harold declared that Palnatoki must prove the truth of his boast by shooting an apple off his son's head. Like Tell, Palnatoki did so, and like Tell, he hid another arrow. He told the king the reason: If he had accidentally killed his son, he would then have killed Harold.

Versions of the same story also appear in Central Asia, Finland, Norway, Persia, and Russia.

See also: Culture Heroes.

Sources

Buff, Mary, and Conrad Buff. *The Apple and the Arrow.* Boston: Houghton Mifflin, 1951.

Florian, Chevalier de (Jean Pierre Claris). *William Tell; the Hero of Switzerland. A Posthumous Work. To Which Is Prefixed, the Life of the Author, by Jauffret.* Philadelphia: Snider, 1830.

Newton, J.J. *William Tell, the Hero of Switzerland.* London: George Peirce, 1841.

Schiller, Freidrich. *William Tell.* Chicago: University of Chicago Press, 1973.

Wise Man or Woman

They stand in the shadows of kings, point the way to questing heroes, and shelter the dispossessed and help them regain their birthright. They teach valuable lessons to those willing to learn, and inflict punishment upon the stubborn and steadfastly ignorant. Sometimes, they are gods or fairies in disguise. They are the wise man and wise woman, and the importance of their role in story cannot be overlooked.

Every hero or heroine setting forth on a quest needs guidance. Most traditional heroes step out into the world with only a vague idea of their goals and an even less distinct notion of how to attain them. A prince seeks the water of life for his dying father or a young wife must travel to the ends of the earth to find her vanished husband. Sometimes, they are thrust out into the world with no goal other than survival.

These heroes are armed with courage, optimism, beauty (usually), and the strength of a noble heart. Yet they cannot accomplish their goals without specific knowledge about their quests and the obstacles that must be overcome.

Help for the Hero

The source of this crucial knowledge is often the archetypal wise man or woman. The wise man or woman appears to the hero early in the quest, often just as the hero rides forth or when his or her plight seems hopeless. The wise man or woman may be in the guise of an animal, elderly beggar, dwarf, or crone.

The wise man or woman asks the hero where he or she is headed or pleads for a bit of food. How the questing hero responds to the wretched figure by the path often determines whether the journey will succeed or end in disaster. The wise man or woman knows the hero's goal and can offer specific instructions on what to avoid, what signs to look for, what tasks will be required, and the one hidden weakness of the demon, monster, or evil king that stands in the hero's way.

The young prince in "The Water of Life" shares his meager meal with a dwarf. In return, he is given detailed instructions on how to find the precious water.

The abandoned wife who seeks her husband in the Norwegian fairy tale "East of the Sun, West of the Moon" encounters three old women in succession; none of them helps her directly, but each gives her a token that eventually proves useful and then sends her on to the next helper. Step by step the young woman makes her way to the place where her husband lies hidden.

In the tale "Eros and Psyche," also known in the Roman form as "Cupid and Psyche," a jealous Aphrodite gives the mortal girl Psyche the seemingly impossible task of descending to the underworld and bringing back a box of Persephone's beauty. Psyche is about to give up in despair, when she is given instructions on how to safely pass through the underworld by, of all things, a sentient tower. In some versions, the nature deity Pan instructs Psyche.

Heroes often receive help from completely unexpected sources. Many of the terrible giants, ogres, and demons that menace fairy tale heroes have mothers and wives who are much more sympathetic. Explanation is never given as to why the female companions of these monsters are sympathetic to the heroes.

The wife of Grandfather Wisdom, in the Czech tale "The Ogre with the Three Golden Hairs," not only hides the hero from her man-eating spouse, but actually plucks out the three golden hairs the hero needs from her spouse's head or chin. She teases out of Grandfather Wisdom the answers to the three puzzles the hero had promised to solve and sends the young man on his way while her husband is safely asleep. In other variants, Grandfather Wisdom is a giant, a man-eating ogre, or the devil himself.

Testing the Hero

Sometimes there is no quest, and the role of the wise man or woman is simply to test the protagonist and offer a reward or punishment.

One of the most familiar of these morality tales is the Grimm Brothers' "Toads and Diamonds." A typically abused and overworked stepdaughter is fetching water for her ungrateful family when an elderly woman asks her for a drink. Unhesitatingly, the girl fills the old woman's cup and gives it to her with a gracious word. The old lady, who is a fairy in disguise, rewards the girl by causing a flower or gemstone to drop from her lips with every word she speaks.

When the stepmother discovers the girl's newfound treasure, she sends her own daughter to the well with strict instructions to be nice to any old woman she might meet there. Unfortunately for the daughter, the fairy is disguised not as a hag but as an elegant lady. She asks for a drink. The daughter, who had only been instructed to be kind to old hags (the girl being apparently as dim as she is rude and ugly), insolently tells her she can fetch her own drink. Displeased, the fairy curses the girl to spit out a toad or serpent with every word.

In another Grimm Brothers fairy tale, "Mother Holle," the eponymous wise woman is a powerful earth spirit who controls the weather. She is able to send snowstorms across the world with a shake of her featherbed. The virtuous girl who works for Mother Holle diligently and without complaint for an entire season is rewarded with a shower of gold. Her lazy stepsister is sent home covered in sticky black tar.

Fairy Godmothers

The figure of the fairy godmother has been made famous by the many versions of the Cinderella story. She is either the spirit of the heroine's dead mother or a kindly fairy.

The fairy godmother is less a tester of virtue than a supernatural matchmaker. She magically erases the worst obstacles between the heroine and her prince. She even attempts to act as a chaperone by setting up the spells so that all the magical implements she has provided will vanish at midnight.

Mythic Figures

Some wise figures wield great power. The myths of ancient Greece, Rome, and India are filled with gods that wander in the guise of helpless old mortals.

Hera, the Greek queen of the gods, approached the hero Jason in disguise as an old crone who was unable to cross a river. Jason carried her over, losing one of his sandals in the process. Hera blessed him in his quest to regain his kingdom and continued to watch over his journeys.

In the great Hindu epic the *Mahabharata,* the god Krishna offered Prince Arjuna spiritual advice along with his services as charioteer.

Hags and Wizards

In British fairy tales, handsome young knights were often approached by hideous hags. These repulsive creatures demanded a kiss, lovemaking, or marriage. The rare knight of quality who accepted this challenge received an unexpected reward when the crone turned into a beautiful maiden and, in some cases, conferred kingship upon him.

This tale was told in the late fourteenth century by Geoffrey Chaucer in "The Wife of Bath," one of the stories in *The Canterbury Tales* (c. 1387–1400). The Arthurian story of Sir Gawain and Dame Ragnell has a similar plot. In some of the oldest, pre-Christian versions, joining with the hag symbolized the king's marriage to his land, and the crone's transformation into a maiden represented the rejuvenation of the earth in the wake of this divine marriage.

Wizards, powerful magic users of folklore and fiction, sometimes appear in the role of the wise old man. The most famous of these helper wizards, at least in the West, is King Arthur's aide, Merlin. Another well-known wizard is J.R.R. Tolkien's Gandalf, who is both a hero and a wise helper.

A common theme in fiction that utilizes wise characters such as wizards is the realization that there is more to the universe than what is obvious. This theme also encompasses the idea that the desire for power is not enough for an individual to become part of this otherworld. Ambition must be tempered with wisdom. In the role-playing game "Mage: The Ascension," for example, the potential for magic and a greater understanding of the universe lies sleeping in every human.

Wisdom in the Modern Age

In many ways, but not universally, modern Western culture values youth and vitality over age and wisdom. Nevertheless, wise elders still are considered by many to be people of authority whose insight is sought in solving community problems. Native American tribal elders; the shamans still found in a few tribal cultures, particularly in South America and parts of Russia; the patriarchs and matriarchs of extended Asian and European families; and even, in a more humorous form, the imperious Jewish mothers and grandmothers of folklore are treated with deference and respect.

It is also true that age and wisdom are not always connected. Wisdom can also be found in the young, and the aged do not always possess it.

Shanti Fader

See also: Archetype.

Sources

Campbell, Joseph. *The Hero with a Thousand Faces.* Princeton, NJ: Princeton University Press, 1968.
———. *The Masks of God.* New York: Arkana, 1991.
Doniger, Wendy. *The Implied Spider: Politics and Theology in Myth.* New York: Columbia University Press, 1998.
White, T.H. *The Once and Future King.* 1958. New York: Berkeley, 1979.

Wise Men of Chelm

(Polish)

The townspeople of Chelm, Poland, have been made famous for their bizarre wisdom through Jewish folktales.

As the saying goes, "It's not that the people of Chelm are fools; it's just that foolish things keep happening to them." Of course, another saying announces that when two angels were delivering souls, the bag ripped open, and all the foolish souls landed in Chelm.

Tracing the age of the tales about the wise men of Chelm is difficult. A comprehensive collection has never been compiled, and there is no solid proof of their origin. Scholars guess that some of the tales date from the late

Middle Ages, while others are almost certainly more recent. And since new tales are constantly being added to the repertory, it has become almost impossible to separate the old tales from the new.

A few examples of the wise men of Chelm's way of thinking follow:

The wise men of Chelm began to worry about how much they were worrying. So they decided to each pay a man one ruble to do the worrying for them. But, they thought, if he had all that money, why would he worry?

One of the wise men of Chelm went to his doctor, worried because he talked to himself. The doctor told him it was no real problem. After all, he was only talking to himself. The man complained, "But I'm such a bore!"

When the wise men of Chelm appointed one among them as chief sage, they decided he must have golden shoes to wear to show how special he was. But the first time he wore them, mud covered the gold. So the wise men made leather shoes to cover the golden shoes. But now the golden shoes could not be seen. So the wise men cut holes in the leather shoes to let the gold show through. But now mud seeped into the holes! So the wise men stuffed straw into the holes. Now the gold could not be seen. At last they came up with a solution. To show how special he was, the chief sage wore his golden shoes on his hands.

A house caught fire in Chelm on a dark, moonless night. Everyone agreed that it was fortunate that the fire was burning so brightly, or they would never have been able to see to put it out. Fortunate, indeed: If nothing else, the wise men of Chelm are eternally optimistic.

See also: Fools; Wise (or Foolish, or Mad) Men of Gotham.

Sources

Sherman, Josepha. *A Sampler of Jewish-American Folklore.* Little Rock, AR: August House, 1990.

Simon, Solomon. *The Wise Men of Helm and Their Merry Tales.* West Orange, NJ: Behrman House, 1996.

Tenenbaum, Samuel. *The Wise Men of Chelm.* New York: Collier, 1975.

Wise (or Foolish, or Mad) Men of Gotham

(English)

Gotham is a real city in Nottinghamshire, England, but it has become known as the site of the folktales about the wise men of Gotham. Also known as the foolish men of Gotham or even the madmen of Gotham, they sometimes seem more wise than foolish.

According to a story from the late twelfth century, the people of Gotham heard that King John was going to visit them. They did not want him there, as he and his retinue and retainers would be far too expensive a group of visitors for their town. So they deliberately started acting in foolish or even wildly insane ways. They did stunts, such as trying to drown a fish or cage a bird (fittingly enough, a cuckoo) by joining hands. King John heard of this behavior and decided to stay elsewhere. The villagers were said to have remarked, presumably smirking as they did so, that more fools passed through Gotham than remained in it. There is no historical evidence to prove this story.

In 1540, a collection of twenty tales of Gotham was published. A number of towns claim to be the village of origin. A town in Sussex, as well as almost fifty other villages in England and Wales, maintain that the silly tales belong to them. Even Mother Goose stepped into the fray:

Three wise men of Gotham went to sea
in a bowl.
If the bowl had been stronger,
My song had been longer.

In 1807, the American author Washington Irving dubbed New York City "Gotham," since he considered it a city of fools. The name stuck. For instance, the comic book character Batman, the caped crusader and avenger, lives in none other than Gotham City.

See also: Fools; Wise Men of Chelm.

Sources

Anonymous. *The Merry Tales of the Wise Men of Gotham.* Portland, OR: Richard Abel, 1970.

Carrick, Malcolm. *The Wise Men of Gotham.* New York: Viking, 1975.

Elias, Gillian. *The Tales of the Wise Men of Gotham.* West Bridgford, UK: Nottinghamshire County Council Leisure Services, 1991.

Wizards

In world folklore, a wizard is a usually male, often aged figure of immense magical power. In Western folk tradition, wizards are usually portrayed with flowing robes, a pointed hat, and a long white beard. A wizard can be on the side of either good or evil.

Wizards are found in many fantasy tales as well, sometimes as heroic figures and sometimes as frauds.

Merlin

Merlin, the wizard of Arthurian legend, appears in numerous and varied forms. Authors have portrayed him as a magician, a conjurer, a student of alchemy, and a prophet.

T.H. White, in *The Once and Future King* (1958), described Merlin as living backward in time, which meant that he could remember the future. Marion Zimmer Bradley's feminist retelling of Arthur's story, *The Mists of Avalon* (1982), makes Merlin a title that is held by high-ranking Druid priests, rather than the name of a single man. Sometimes, Merlin directs and influences the events of the Arthurian tales (including the birth of the king). In other versions, he is swept along by events, helplessly able to foresee but not prevent them. Often, Merlin is too wise to try, and he merely passes along his visions, knowing that what will happen is what is meant to be.

Merlin arranged the tryst between Uther Pendragon and Igraine of Cornwall (in some versions using magical means) that resulted in Arthur's conception. After the child's birth, Merlin hid him away in Sir Ector's court to grow up in anonymous safety until it was time

Merlin, the great wizard of Arthurian lore, counseled the young King Arthur. This illustration is from about 1350; it now resides in the British Library in London. *(Art Resource, NY)*

for him to claim the throne. *The Once and Future King* begins with Merlin overseeing the education of the young Arthur, whom he nicknames Wart.

Long before Arthur's time, Merlin had helped the warlord Vortigern discover why the castle he was building was continually unbuilt each night. Merlin directed Vortigern to dig underneath the foundation. When he did so, a pair of dragons was discovered fighting in an underground cavern. Released, the dragons streaked off into the sky, symbolizing Uther and Arthur, the great kings to come. Vortigern finally was able to complete his fortress.

At the end of his life (or the beginning, in White's version), Merlin was seduced by the sorceress Nimue (sometimes called Viviane). She cajoled the wizard into teaching her the secrets of his magic, and then trapped him inside a tree, a cave, or a hollow hill. In some retellings, Merlin was killed and sealed inside this tomb. In others, he lives on and will emerge upon King Arthur's return.

It is difficult to understand why someone as wise and powerful as Merlin could not prevent such an untimely and undignified fate. The Nimue story could be interpreted as a warning against the treacherous wiles of women, but it seems unlikely that Merlin actually would let himself be tricked and imprisoned in this way. Far more probable is the idea that he foresaw Nimue's intentions, and either he resigned himself to retirement (knowing what was coming and that he could not avert it) or he actually was looking forward to getting some rest after centuries of advising the kings of Britain. Unfortunately for King Arthur, Merlin's wisdom was not available during the darkest hours of Arthur's reign.

Tolkien's Wizards

In *The Lord of the Rings* (1954–1955), British author J.R.R. Tolkien created a race of wizards, the Istari, for his world of Middle Earth. The Istari were a subgroup of demigod-like beings known as Maiar. The Maiar could take on human form and interact with living creatures. Their task was to defeat the evil Maia Sauron.

The two most important Istari are Saruman the White, whose task was to gather knowledge and whose name derives from the Old English word for knowledge, and Gandalf the Grey, whose task was the seeking of wisdom and whose name likewise derives from the Old English word for wisdom. Aficionados of *The Lord of the Rings* know the fate that befalls each of the two wizards and which path Tolkien clearly preferred. That Tolkien was influenced, especially in the character of Gandalf, by the Finnish *Kalevala* can be seen through comparisons between Gandalf and the Finnish wizard Vainamoinen.

The Wizard of Oz

Created by American author L. Frank Baum and first introduced in his *Wonderful Wizard of Oz* (1900), the Wizard of Oz was the ruler of the land of Oz. He lived in the Emerald City.

Dorothy Gale and her three friends went to ask the wizard for help; he responded that they must first complete a dangerous mission, bring him an evil witch's broom, before he would grant their requests.

Upon the friends' successful completion of the task, they returned to the Emerald City. There, they discovered that Oz was not a wizard at all. He was just an ordinary man who had been using tricks to fool everyone into thinking he was "great and powerful."

Modern Wizards

A number of contemporary authors have envisioned entire worlds full of witches and wizards. In Diane Duane's *Young Wizard* series (1983–), wizards can be cats, whales, and even humans; J.K. Rowling's popular Harry Potter books (1997–2007) describe a huge and intricate wizard world just out of sight of the mundane, with its own schools, government, and sports. Terry Pratchett's *Discworld* series (1983–) features a university of wizards who are as arrogant, human, and bumbling as equivalent university professors.

Today, the term *wizard* does not necessarily imply magic. It is more often applied to someone particularly clever in a specific field, such as a computer or gaming wizard, or, as in Pete Townsend's rock opera *Tommy* (1969), a pinball wizard. But, judging from the success of Harry Potter and his kind, the magic-wielding wizard is likely to be with us for some time.

See also: Vainamoinen; Wise Man or Woman; *Retelling: A Story of Gwydion.*

Sources

Hahn, Thomas, ed. *Sir Gawain: Eleven Romances and Tales.* Kalamazoo, MI: Medieval Institute Publications, Western Michigan University, 1995.

Tolkien, J.R.R. *The Lord of the Rings.* 1954–1955. Boston: Houghton Mifflin, 2003.

———. *The Silmarillion.* Ed. Christopher Tolkien. Boston: Houghton Mifflin, 1977.

Wonder Woman

(American)

Wonder Woman was the first strong, female, comic-book character. William Moulton Marston created the Wonder Woman character in 1941, under the pen name of Charles Moulton.

Wonder Woman provides storytellers with an opportunity to tell about a powerful female protagonist and to make a connection to strong female characters of folklore and history. Examples of other such characters are the Irish mythic figure Scathach, the woman warrior who trained the Irish heroes; the Irishwoman Grace O'Malley of the sixteenth century, the warrior pirate who battled and won against the English forces of Queen Elizabeth I; and the Amazons, the mythic warrior women of ancient Greece.

Wonder Woman was an Amazon princess whose real name was Diana. The goddess Aphrodite had created the Amazon women, who were women of superior strength, in her fight against Mars, the god of war. Mars set Hercules upon the Amazonian women and Aphrodite intervened to save them from enslavement. The women were banished from Greece to reside on Paradise Island, where no man set foot.

Eventually, a man, Steve Trevor, crashed on the shores of Paradise Island. A contest was held among the Amazons to determine who would go with Trevor as ambassador to the world of men. Diana entered the contest and won. She was given special powers, an invisible jet, bracelets that could deflect bullets, and a magic lasso forged from the girdle of Gaea, which would cause people ensnared in it to tell the truth.

So armed, she went forth into the world of men, obtaining a position in the military. Going by the name of Diana Prince, she battled villains of all types. Wonder Woman frequently battled Mars and other foes that he sent to harm her. Norse gods such as Odin and Loki also made appearances in the comic books as villains.

In the 1970s, the American actress Lynda Carter brought Wonder Woman to life on television. The character has also appeared in several animated cartoons. Wonder Woman still remains an icon for young girls who are learning to combine strength with femininity.

See also: Culture Heroes.

Sources

Daniels, Les. *Wonder Woman: A Complete History.* San Francisco: Chronicle, 2004.

Robinson, Lillia. *Wonder Women: Feminism and Superheroes.* London: Routledge, 2004.

Wilde, Lyn Webster. *On the Trail of the Women Warriors: The Amazons in Myth and History.* London: Thomas Dunne, 2000.

World Tree

The World Tree is an unimaginably mighty tree with branches and roots that connect the many realms of existence. Its roots spread into the underworld, its trunk is in the mortal world, and its branches reach up into the heavens. The World Tree, also known as the Tree of Knowledge or the Tree of Life, is a common theme in the world's mythology.

A sampling of the many examples of the World Tree from around the world follow:

- In Babylonian mythology, the World Tree was known as Kuluppu, and it stood on the bank of the Euphrates River. Its wood was said to be medicinal.

- In Hindu mythology, as related in the *Bhagavad Gita,* the World Tree was a great fig tree called Asvattha. Its roots reached down into the underworld, and its branches reached up into the heavens. On its leaves were inscribed the holy words of the Vedas.

- In ancient Persian mythology, the World Tree was also the first tree, the Saena Tree, which grew in the middle of the primal ocean, Vourukasha. From the Saena, also known as the Tree of Life or the Tree of All Remedies, came all the world's plants.

- In the Hebrew Kabbalah, the Sephirothal Tree of Life has been pictured as a palm, its ten branches spreading outward from the lowest world up to the heavens. Another image portrays tree upon tree, reaching up to the heavens.

- For the Norse, the World Tree was known as Yggdrasil, from which the chief god, Odin, hung himself for nine days to gain his knowledge of the runes.

- To the Buryat people of Siberia, the World Tree is a great birch or willow. It has no name, but it connects the underneath realm, the present, and the sky, and the point where the tree meets the earth is the center of the world and of all time and space. The Yakut people, also of Siberia, have a similar concept, although they see all trees as sacred.

- The World Tree in Mayan mythology was the Yax Imix Che, the "first green ceiba" tree, with its roots in the underworld and its branches in the heavens. It is also the Wakah Chan, the "raised-up sky," which is symbolized by the Milky Way.

Because the World Tree concept relates to the image of the family tree as well—the linked "world" of a specific family and its generations is often depicted as the image of a tree—the World Tree is clearly a living mythic concept.

See also: Yggdrasil.

Sources

Martin, Laura C. *The Folklore of Trees and Shrubs.* Chester, CT: Globe Pequot, 1992.

Philpot, J.H. *The Sacred Tree in Religion and Myth.* Mineola, NY: Dover, 2004.

Porteous, Alexander. *The Forest in Folklore and Mythology.* Mineola, NY: Dover, 2002.

Wurusemu

(Hittite)

Wurusemu was a Hittite goddess, later known as the goddess Hebat.

Wurusemu was the primary goddess in the region of Arrina, where she bore the titles of sun goddess of Arrina, mistress of the Hatti lands, the queen of heaven and Earth, and mistress of the kings and queens of Hatti. It was believed that she directed the government of Hatti.

One of Wurusemu's aspects was as a creator who had made the cedars and the land on which they grew. In another aspect, she was a goddess of battle and was associated with Hittite military victories.

In some myths, Wurusemu was said to be the mother of the storm god.

Ira Spar

See also: Mother Goddess/Earth Mother.

Sources

Beckman, Gary M., ed. *Hittite Myths.* Trans. Harry A. Hoffner. Atlanta: Society of Biblical Literature, 1991.

Gastner, Theodore H., trans. *The Oldest Stories in the World.* New York: Viking, 1952.

Yeti

(Tibetan)

Yeti is the name for a large, apelike creature said to live in the Himalayan mountain range of Nepal and Tibet. While similar to the Sasquatch, or Bigfoot, of North America, the yeti is a hardier creature. It is able to live at high altitudes and in cold, inhospitable conditions in which most humans could not survive.

The creature allegedly walks upright, like a hunched-over person. It is roughly the size of a man, but much broader and with oversized feet. Pale brown or snow-white hair covers most of its body.

The first legends of the yeti appeared in Tibetan mythology long before Western explorers arrived in that country. The word yeti may derive from the words *yah* and *teh,* which mean "rock-animal," or from similar-sounding words that mean "magical creature." Another name given to the creature was *metch-kangmi,* or "repugnant snowman." It is from this moniker that the term *Abominable Snowman* was derived.

Stories about the yeti all agree on the basic facts. It is large and hairy, with a particularly pungent body odor. The yeti is solitary and shy, and it rarely comes into contact with human beings. The occasional traveler or goatherd might encounter huge footprints in the snow or lose a goat from his or her flock under suspicious circumstances, but for the most part the yeti avoids confrontation.

Part of the mystique of the yeti is that the local people believe them to be more than mere animals. According to the Sherpa, a local people best known for guiding Western explorers through the Himalayas, the yeti are supernatural creatures, standing between mankind and the demon-spirits who live on the mountain peaks.

Buddhist religious figures called lamas claim to have relics that came from yeti, including fingers, toes, and skulls, in their lamaseries, or homes. These relics are used to remind Buddhists of their connection to the world around them.

Reported Sightings

The first reporting of a yeti by an outsider was in 1832, when British explorer B.H. Hodson reported an attack on his native guides by creatures he calls *rakshas,* or demons. In 1889, a British soldier, Major L.A. Wadell, reported finding large, bearlike footprints in the snow well above the elevation at which any bear should be living. His guides told him it was a *yeh-tih.*

Over the next fifty years, such reports become more common. But because of the combination of extreme weather conditions and awkward political situations in Tibet and Nepal, no scientific expeditions were mounted to determine the truth. The stories grew and spread with every new sighting.

With the development of cameras and other equipment that could withstand the cold, and the easing of political restrictions between Tibet and the West, the rumors proved irresistible. The first modern sighting of the yeti was made in 1951. Explorer Eric Shipton tracked a yeti along the slopes of the Menlung glacier until it disappeared into an ice field. The photographs taken on that trip of huge footprints, the clearest one measuring 12 inches (30 centimeters) long by 6 inches (15 centimeters) wide, are often held up as the best evidence of the existence of the yeti.

A year later, a British newspaper funded the first scientific survey of the yeti, sending trained scientists and cameramen into the mountains with some of the best guides available. They found more tracks, a scalp of coarse hair, and droppings that they claimed came from a yeti. The team was allowed to take one hair from that scalp out of the country, but testing proved inconclusive. Several other expeditions came back with similar evidence, which also was deemed questionable.

In 1956, a Texas oilman and millionaire named Thomas Slick mounted a large, government-backed expedition to Tibet. He and his team had up-to-date scientific equipment, weapons, and trained bloodhounds. They returned with photos, footprint castings, and two fingers of a mummified hand they claimed was that of a yeti. The fingers later disappeared, and the Slick expedition was thrown into doubt by Sir Edmund Hillary (of Everest fame) and Marlin Perkins (later known for the television series *Wild Kingdom*), who did not believe that the yeti existed.

For a short time, the debate raged fiercely in scientific journals. By the 1970s, however, science moved on, and the search for the yeti, like the pursuit of the Loch Ness monster and other unlikely creatures, became the province of fringe scientists and explorers.

Current Theories

In contrast to theories about other such creatures, perhaps because of its potential relationship to humans, theories about the yeti's origin are still popular topics. Some researchers claim that the yeti and its kin around the world are wild men, perhaps direct descendents of the first primates to come out of Africa, which evolved to possess intelligence almost equal to that of humans. Others believe that the yeti is a modern but not yet identified ape, a close relative to the gorilla.

One theory traces the yeti back to the primate *Gigantopithecus*. This giant ape lived during the Pleistocene era, 1.8 million to 10,000 years ago, in the region that is now China and Southeast Asia. *Gigantopithecus* became extinct, but a branch of its family still may survive in the yeti. A related idea suggests that the yeti is descended from our own ancestor, the Neanderthal. Both of these theories fail to account for the fact that *Gigantopithecus* was last seen in the fossil record at 500,000 B.C.E. and the last Neanderthal dates to 40,000 B.C.E.

The most recent explanation, formulated in 1999, suggests that the human family tree is older and has more branches than previously thought. It has been theorized that the yeti is an unidentified branch, a distant cousin of modern *Homo sapiens* that has adapted to the colder climate.

There have been no reputable reports of face-to-face encounters, and the few photos that are believed to exist were taken from too great a distance to provide positive identification. No one has ever captured a live yeti or discovered a skeleton or other remnant that can be conclusively proven to have come from one. So all theories are pure conjecture.

Laura Anne Gilman

See also: Tibetan Storytelling.

Sources

Coleman, Loren, and Patrick Huyghe. *The Field Guide to Bigfoot, Yeti, and Other Mystery Primates Worldwide.* New York: Avon, 1999.

Gilman, Laura Anne. *The Abominable Snowman.* New York: Rosen, 2002.

Yggdrasil

(Norse)

Yggdrasil is the Norse name of the World Tree, the cosmic tree that links three realms in Norse mythology. Said to be a gigantic ash tree, its name literally means "Ygg's horse." Ygg, which means "terrible" or "dreadful," is one of the names of the chief Norse god, Odin, who hung from the tree for nine days as a willing self-sacrifice to gain the wisdom of the runes.

Three roots support Yggdrasil's mighty trunk. Each root passes through a different world so that Yggdrasil's branches spread out over all worlds.

In one version of the myth, the three worlds are Asgard, home of the gods; Midgard, home of the humans; and Hel, the underworld. Another version of the myth describes the three roots as passing through Asgard; Jotenheim, the world of the frost giants; and Niflheim, the world of the dwarves.

Beneath one of the roots, usually mentioned in texts as the Asgard root, lies the sacred Urdarbrunnr, the well of fate. It is here that the three Norns, or Nornor, live. These are the three Fates of Norse mythology. The Norns hold the destinies of all that live, and not even the gods have power over them. The Norns water the tree every day to keep its bark white and its leaves green.

Beneath the two other roots lie Mimisbrunnr, the well of wisdom, guarded by the giant Mimir, and the Hvergelmir, or roaring kettle, which is said to be the source of many of the Midgard rivers.

Near the Hvergelmir, the great serpent Nidhogg gnaws at one of Yggdrasil's roots. An eagle sits in Yggdrasil's branches, and between its eyes a falcon perches. The beat of the eagle's powerful wings stirs the Midgard winds. The goat Heidrun lives up there, too, and eats Yggdrasil's leaves, while four stags, Dain, Duneyr, Durathror, and Dvalin, feed on Yggdrasil's bark.

A squirrel, Ratatosk, scurries up and down Yggdrasil's trunk. It carries messages back and forth between the eagle and the serpent Nidhogg.

The myths state that someday, when the final battle of Ragnarok arrives, Nidhogg will finish its gnawing and bring down Yggdrasil. Then Yggdrasil will then expire in flames set by the giants.

See also: Norse Mythology; Odin/Odhinn; World Tree.

Sources

Davidson, H.R. Ellis. *Gods and Myths of Northern Europe.* New York: Penguin, 1964.

Lindow, John. *Norse Mythology: A Guide to the Gods, Heroes, Rituals and Beliefs.* New York: Oxford University Press, 2002.

Sturluson, Snorri. *Edda.* New York: Everyman's Library, 1995.

Yggdrasil was the Norse version of the world tree, a widespread motif representing the center of the world. This intricate carving, which shows Yggdrasil being gnawed on by a deer, can be found on the side of a historic church in Umes, Norway. (© *Werner Forman/Art Resource, NY*)

Ymir

(Norse)

In Norse mythology, Ymir is the primordial giant and the progenitor of the race of frost giants.

Ymir was created when there was little else in the world. He was brought forth when ice from Niflheim, realm of eternal cold, was touched by hot air from Muspellheim, realm of eternal fire. The ice began to melt, releasing drops of *eitr* (ether, a substance once believed to be the essence of life). The drops slowly congealed and became the giant's body. The fires of Muspellheim sparked him to life.

But Ymir merely slept. From Ymir's sleeping body came the first giants, creeping out from his legs and from under his arms.

The frost slowly melted. From the drops that fell and congealed, the huge, primal cow, Audhumla, came into being. From her vast udder flowed four rivers of milk, on which Ymir fed whenever he woke. The cow, in turn, got her nourishment by licking hoarfrost and salt from the eternal ice.

On the evening of the first day, as Audhumla licked the ice, the hair of a man appeared. On the second day, the whole head was freed. On the third day, a figure rose up. This was Buri, the first god. From his line came three grandsons, Odin, Ve, and Vili.

There was no world yet, nor a heaven. There was only the ice, Ymir, and his ever-growing number of frost-giant offspring. Odin, Ve, and Vili disliked Ymir and hated the giants. They killed Ymir, and all but two of the giants drowned in the rivers of blood that flowed from Ymir's body. From these two who remained, all other giants descended.

From Ymir's body, the brother gods created the world. Ymir's flesh became the land, and his blood became the rivers, lakes, and oceans. His bones became the mountains, and his teeth the rocks and stones. His hair became the trees and all other plant life, and his brain became the clouds. The maggots that crawled in Ymir's carcass became the race of dwarves. Ymir's skull became the overturned bowl of the sky, which was forever held aloft by four dwarves (the four directions).

In astronomy, Ymir is the name of one of the planet Saturn's moons, a fitting name for an icy moon.

See also: Giants; Norse Mythology.

Sources

Crossley-Howard, Kevin. *The Norse Myths*. New York: Pantheon, 1980.

Hollander, Lee M., trans. *The Poetic Edda*. Austin: University of Texas Press, 1928.

Lindow, John. *Norse Mythology: A Guide to the Gods, Heroes, Rituals and Beliefs*. New York: Oxford University Press, 2002.

Sturluson, Snorri. *The Prose Edda: Tales from Norse Mythology*. Trans. Jean I. Young. Berkeley: University of California Press, 2001.

Yoruban Storytelling

(West African)

The Yoruba people of Nigeria and neighboring Benin in West Africa are primarily farmers who also have a fine tradition of woodcraft and metalworking.

Yoruban stories and histories are primarily passed down orally from generation to generation. Storytelling is still a favorite activity among the Yoruba people, but in the twenty-first century it competes with television and written works, including works by Yoruban authors.

Storytelling in the Yoruban style is a very active art. It involves taking on the voices and personas of the various characters, as well as performing music and dancing. The audience also takes an active role in the story. Listeners are expected to get involved by beating drums or singing along.

Storytelling sessions generally occur after the evening meal. Yoruban folktales always begin with a call-and-response chorus called the *alo* chorus (*alo* means riddle). One of the young men will begin by asking the other young men two or three riddles to determine whether everyone in the group is awake and alert. Then, the tale begins.

The types of stories are similar to those found in other cultures, such as myths, legends, fables, poetry, family or society histories, and folktales. Hero tales, how-and-why tales (also known as *pourquoi* tales), and trickster tales are also popular. Tortoise and Ananse the Spider are the major trickster figures in West African folktales.

Yoruban stories often center on the theme of fertility to a greater degree than is usually found in world folktales. This is due, in part, to a high infant mortality rate in the region.

See also: West African Mythology.

Sources
Courlander, Harold. *Tales of Yoruba Gods and Heroes*. New York: Crown, 1973.
Drewal, Margaret T. *Yoruba Ritual: Performers, Play, Agency*. Bloomington: Indiana University Press, 1992.
Walker, Barbara, and Warren S. Walker. *Nigerian Folk Tales, As Told by Olawale Idewu and Omotayo Adu*. New Brunswick, NJ: Rutgers University Press, 1961.

Yoshitsune

(Japanese)

The historical samurai Yoshitsune (1159–1189 C.E.) was a son of Minamoto Yoshitomo (1123–1160). When Minamoto was assassinated by a rival samurai, Taira Kiyomori, Minamoto's wife and their children were found and brought to Kiyomori, who spared them. Yoritomo, the second eldest, was sent off to Izu, while Yoshitsune was sent to a temple on Kuramayama, north of Kyoto.

Little is know about Yoshitsune's boyhood, but Japanese storytellers have assigned a series of fantastic adventures to him. He was said to have escaped into the woods to be instructed in all the martial arts by the king of the Tengu demons. When Yoshitsune returned to the world of men, he single-handedly exterminated the entire Taira clan.

The factual battles, of course, were less romantic and more complicated, although Yoshitsune did avenge his father and become a famous samurai. The stories of Yoshitsune, which are part history and part legend, are good examples of the folklore that can be spun from true stories of historical figures.

See also: Culture Heroes.

Sources
Davis, F. Hadland. *Myths and Legends of Japan*. Mineola, NY: Dover, 1992.
Hyoe, Murakami, and Thomas J. Harper, eds. *Great Historical Figures of Japan*. Tokyo: Japan Culture Institute, 1978.
Kamachi, Noriko. *Culture and Customs of Japan*. Westport, CT: Greenwood, 1999.

Ys/Ker-Ys

(Breton/French)

In French and Breton folklore, Ys, also known as Ker-Ys, was said to be a great and powerful city. It lay below sea level on the Breton coast and was guarded by a series of seawalls. Ys was ruled by King Gradlon and was eventually submerged in a flood.

The folklore tells that the king was a mighty sea warrior before the city was created. King Gradlon and Malgven, queen of the North, slew Malgven's husband and escaped on a magical horse that could gallop over the waves. From the union of Gradlon and Malgven came a daughter, Dahut. Malgven died during childbirth.

Dahut asked her father to build Ys near the water. Gradlon agreed, and the city was built. Since it was below sea level, Ys was surrounded by a high wall and powerful sluice gates. Only King Gradlon held the key to these gates.

Ys soon became a prosperous city. This may have been because Dahut, who had grown into a beautiful woman, sang to the sea. She called herself its betrothed and promised herself to the sea if it brought ships and handsome fishermen to Ys. The city was rich and lively, but its inhabitants had many vices.

Dahut was among the sinners. She stole the keys to the sluice gates and gave them to her treacherous lover. He opened the gates and destroyed the glittering city of Ys. According to folk belief, if the weather is very still, the bells of Ys can be heard ringing far under the waves.

Another folk belief claims that the name Paris actually means "Par Ys" in Breton, or "Like Ys." Two proverbs speak of the two cities. The first proverb says, "Since the city of Ys was drowned, no equal in Paris has been found." The second proverb predicts that "When Paris is engulfed by the sea, then from the sea Ys returned will be."

It is unlikely, however, that Ys will ever rise again, even if Paris were to be engulfed by the sea.

See also: Sunken Cities.

Source

McNeill, James. *The Sunken City and Other Tales from Round the World*. Oxford, UK: Oxford University Press, 1966.

Spence, Lewis. *Legends and Romances of Brittany*. Mineola, NY: Dover, 1997.

Zeus

(Greek)

In Greek mythology, Zeus was the supreme ruler of Mount Olympus and of the pantheon of gods who resided there. He upheld law, justice, and morals.

The Titans, an ancient race of giants, were ruled by Cronos. It was foretold that one of Cronos's sons would dethrone him. In an attempt to prevent this, Cronos swallowed his children at birth.

Before Cronos could swallow his last child, his wife, Rhea, fled to a cave on the Isle of Crete. She secretly gave birth to Zeus and left him to be raised by nymphs. When Rhea returned to Cronos, she gave him a disguised stone to swallow in place of the last child.

Zeus Gains Control

When Zeus was grown, he asked the goddess Metis for help against his father. She gave Cronos a drug that made him disgorge all the children he had swallowed.

Zeus was able to overthrow Cronos and the rest of the Titans with the help of his brothers and sisters—Demeter, Hades, Hera, Hestia, and Poseidon. Zeus became the ruler of heaven and banished the Titans to Tartarus, the lowest level of existence, below the underworld.

Once Zeus had control, he and his siblings divided the universe among them: Zeus took the heavens, Poseidon took the sea, and Hades claimed the underworld. Demeter took fertility, Hera took marriage, and Hestia claimed the home and hearth.

Not long after he took the throne of the heavens, Zeus had to defend it. Three separate attacks were mounted from among the offspring of Gaia, the living earth. First were the Gigantes, which were giants, as their name implies; then came the monstrous Typhon; and finally the giant twin brothers called the Aloadae attacked. As he had done with the Titans, Zeus banished them all to Tartarus.

The Unfaithful Zeus

Zeus's first marriage, or in some versions, his first love affair, was with Metis. The prophecy that a son would eventually overthrow Zeus led him to swallow both Metis and her unborn child. The child, Athena, was released from Zeus's head.

Zeus's next wife was his sister Hera. Their children were Ares, Eileithyia, Hebe, and Hephaestus. But Zeus was rarely faithful to his wife. He had many affairs, with both gods and mortals.

By Leto, Zeus fathered the divine twins Apollo and Artemis. Zeus took the shape of a swan to seduce the Spartan queen Leda. From

A Hellenic Greek statue of Zeus from the first century B.C.E. The chief god is portrayed as a wise, noble figure, a characterization he did not always live up to in myths. *(Scala/Art Resource, NY)*

the egg that Leda produced came two sets of twins, Castor and Polydeuces and Clytemnestra and Helen of Troy.

Disguised as a bull, Zeus carried off the Phoenician princess Europa to the island of Crete, where she bore three sons: Minos, Rhadamanthys, and Sarpedon. He visited Princess Danae as a shower of gold, and from this union came the hero Perseus.

Zeus also took as a lover the young Trojan prince Ganymede. The prince was carried up to Mount Olympus by an eagle, where he became Zeus's cupbearer.

When Zeus wanted to seduce the mortal Semele, she insisted on seeing Zeus in all his glory. He agreed. Their union produced Dionysus, but the sight of Zeus in all of his splendor, too much for any mortal, destroyed Semele.

The two sides of Zeus—heroic leader of the gods and philanderer—make him a most

unusual deity. In many ways, Zeus seems more human than divine.

Shanti Fader

See also: An/Anu; Hera; Odin/Odhinn; Sius; Wele.

Sources
Evlin, Bernard. *The Greek Gods.* New York: Scholastic, 1995.
Rose, H.J. *Gods and Heroes of the Greeks: An Introduction to Greek Mythology.* New York: Meridian, 1958.
Rouse, W.H.D. *Gods, Heroes and Men of Ancient Greece.* New York: New American Library, 2001.

Ziusudra

(Sumerian)

Ziusudra, whose name means "life of distant days," is the epic hero in the Sumerian version of the flood myth.

In a later Akkadian poem about the creation of humankind, he is called Atra-hasis (exceedingly wise). In the *Epic of Gilgamesh,* Ziusudra is known as Uta-napishti, which means "I found life." The story of Noah in the biblical version of the flood myth contains many similarities to stories about Ziusudra.

In a Sumerian composition called *The Instructions of Shuruppak,* a wise mythological father named Shuruppak, son of Ubar-Tutu, described a Sumerian view of proper conduct to his son, Ziusudra. According to another composition, known as the Sumerian king list, Ubar-Tutu was ruler of the city of Shuruppak, which was the scene of the great flood.

The story of Ziusudra and his father is set in days long past. Shuruppak gave Ziusudra instructions that defined the ideals of proper duty and conduct for a respected landowning citizen of Sumer. Shuruppak's precepts contained proverbs regarding daily life and rules that were presented in an absolute, imperative manner—"do not steal," "do not break into a house," and "do not murder" were some of his directives.

The text described a society in which the canny individual maintained a low profile.

Self-restraint and levelheadedness were right, and hotheadedness, arrogance, impulsive action, and laziness were wrong. Shuruppak warned, "My son, do not sit [alone] in a chamber with someone's wife." On the subject of violence, he said, "Do not throw down a man," and "Do not commit rape upon a man's daughter."

Shuruppak also explained to Ziusudra that one should strive to make rational decisions, pay attention to the words of one's king, abide by the law, and listen to one's parents. A wise individual also should not be fooled by appearances. A man should not choose a wife at a festival, but should seek lasting values rather than superficial qualities that a woman might affect in public. Finally, one should always worship the gods, for "words of prayer bring abundance."

Much of the story of Ziusudra as hero has been lost. This text of advice that was given to him by his father may be the advice that made Ziusudra a hero.

Ira Spar

See also: Culture Heroes; Flood, The.

Sources

Alster, Brendt. *The Instructions of Suruppak*. Copenhagen, Denmark: Copenhagen Studies in Assyriology 2, 1974.

Black, J.A., G. Cunningham, J. Ebeling, E. Flückiger-Hawker, E. Robson, J. Taylor, and G. Zólyomi. *The Electronic Text Corpus of Sumerian Literature*. http://www-etcsl.orient.ox.ac.uk/.

Zmeys and Zmeyitsas

(Bulgarian)

The Bulgarian *zmey*, or dragon, is part snake, part bird, and part human. Usually portrayed as a benign creature, it guarded the fertility of the land and had the ability to change into human form. As a human the zmey could walk among people unrecognized, except by the pure in heart. With serpentine body, legs, wings, a tail, and a human face, the zmey lived in caves, lakes, or mountain palaces and glowed as it flew.

Each village had its own guardian zmey, which fought against the evil forces that caused drought and hail. The ferocity of these battles gave rise to thunderstorms and lightning, a belief that was linked with the mythology of the Slavic thunder god, Perun, and his Christian successor, Saint Ilya.

Zmeys were able to summon whirlwinds or become invisible at will. They were shape-shifters that could take on different forms, from alluring humans to dogs, flower garlands, or even necklaces. *Zmeyitsas,* the females of the species, could shape-shift into bears. Conversely, humans could become zmeys, either through magic or by taking certain herbs.

Zmeys often fell in love with humans, who might then grow pale and sicken. The only way to repulse an unwanted dragon suitor was to take a potion brewed with special herbs such as gentian, tansy, or wormwood.

Zmeys were attracted by music and sometimes seduced maidens with the beauty of their playing on the *kaval,* a kind of flute. They might trick a vain or arrogant maiden and carry her off.

If humans married zmeys, their offspring looked human except for wings growing under their arms. When such a child was born, twelve maidens were called, and under oaths of silence and secrecy, they wove a shirt for the child to hide its wings. The dragon-child could then safely enter the human world, and no one except for the pure of heart would know the child's true nature.

Zmeys should not be confused with their evil relatives, the *lamias,* although zmeyitsas sometimes bear this name.

See also: Dragons.

Sources

Georgieva, Ivanichka. *Bulgarian Mythology*. Sofia, Bulgaria: Svyat, 1985.

MacDermott, Mercia. *Bulgarian Folk Customs*. Philadelphia: Jessica Kingsley, 1998.

Zulu Mythology

In the Zulu religion, the world of the gods can be contacted only by first invoking the ancestors through a diviner, an important person in daily affairs. All bad things are believed to be the result of offended spirit beings or sorcery.

Cleanliness is paramount in Zulu belief. All people are expected to bathe at least once a day and sometimes two or three times. The rules about cleanliness apply to meals as well, as separate dishes are used for separate foods.

Ukqili, "the wise one," is the chief god of the Zulu pantheon. He controls the lightning. When lightning strikes a cow, it is assumed that Ukqili is hungry, and the dead animal becomes a sacrifice. Umvelinqangi is the all-present Zulu creator god, who manifests himself as thunder and earthquakes. He created the primeval reeds from which the supreme god Unkulunkulu emerged. Unkulunkulu, which means "ancestor," is the primary creator god. He grew on a reed in the mythical swamp of Uthlanga.

Three other major deities are Inkosazana, a goddess who makes the crops grow and is venerated in springtime; Mamlambo, who is the mother goddess and goddess of rivers; and Mbaba Mwana Waresa, the goddess of rain and the rainbow, agriculture, and the harvest. It is she who gave humans the gift of beer.

The Amadlozi are the ancestors of the Zulus. Humans can invoke the help of the spirit world by calling upon them. Other ancestral spirits are the *imilozi,* or whistlers, who whistle as they speak.

There are also dangerous supernatural beings that are hostile to humans. Tikdoshe is a malevolent dwarf with only one arm, one leg, and one side. He takes delight in fighting humans. Those whom Tikdoshe defeats die, but those who defeat him are rewarded with magic. The Tokelosh is a small but deadly creature that will strangle any human who sleeps on the ground. Another mythical, malevolent dwarf is Uhlakanyana.

Finally, there is Unwaba. This mythical chameleon was sent to tell the people that they had eternal life. Because the creature was so slow, humans and other species became mortal after all.

See also: Abatwa.

Sources

Du Toit, Brian M. *Content and Context of Zulu Folk-Narratives.* Gainesville: University Press of Florida, 1976.

Lawson, E. Thomas. *Religions of Africa: Traditions in Transformation.* San Francisco: Harper and Row, 1984.

Mutwa, Vusamazulu Credo. *Indaba, My Children.* New York: Grove, 1999.

Zwarte Madam

(Flemish)

The Zwarte Madam is a supernatural and presumably immortal witch being from Flemish folktales.

The word *zwarte* means "black," and *madam* is a courtesy title, so in strict English translation, the Zwarte Madam is the Black Lady. Black refers to her deeds and allegiance, not her appearance. No matter how she is described in the various Flemish folktales, she is always an evil being who works in the service of the devil to help collect mortal souls. But she does not always work actively to corrupt mortals. The Zwarte Madam sometimes appears beside those who are already doomed to hell, presumably as a sort of advance warning.

Fortunately the Zwarte Madam can be warded off with prayer, the utterance of sacred names, or the sign of the cross.

Since good and evil generally balance each other out in folklore, some folk traditions say that there is a direct opposite to the Zwarte Madam, a good figure known as de Witte Madam or the White Lady. The latter character plays only a small role in folktales and does not seem to be an active participant in the saving or protecting of souls.

See also: Black Magic.

Sources

Lindhal, Carl. *Medieval Folklore: A Guide to Myths, Legends, Tales, Beliefs, and Customs.* New York: Oxford University Press, 2002.

Maekelberghe, August, comp. *Flemish Folktales.* Grosse Pointe Farms, MI: Detroit Publication Consultants, 1977.

Retellings

The Ramayana

A Great Mythic Epic from India

The *Ramayana,* loosely translated as "the travels of Rama," is the story of King Rama, avatar of the god Vishnu, and his wife, Sita, who is an avatar of the goddess Lakshmi. Originally written in Sanskrit, and dated somewhere between 500 B.C.E. and 100 B.C.E., it is one of the two great epics of India (the other is the *Mahabharata*). The *Ramayana* can be read as a tale of loyalty, fidelity, and high adventure, but it is also a sacred story to the Hindu people.

One theme that should be familiar to readers of Homer's *Odyssey* is the bow that no one but the hero can draw. In the *Ramayana,* the hero is Rama, while in the *Odyssey,* the hero is Odysseus.

The *Ramayana* was loved and praised by all. It is said, "Men who listen to the *Ramayana* will live a long life. They will be free of sins and will have many sons. Women who listen to the *Ramayana* will be blessed with children like Rama and his brothers. May all who recite it or listen to it regularly find increased love, wisdom, and strength."

In long-past days, the lovely city of Ayodhya, capital of Kosala, stood on the banks of the Sarayu River. The city was filled with wondrous palaces gleaming with gems, and temple spires rose into the sky. Around the city stood a great moat, and within the city, the people of Ayodhya were happy and peaceful.

Only King Dasaratha was not happy. An old man, he had no son to inherit his throne. He told his priest Vasistha, "I long for a son."

The priest knew as well as his king that there must be an heir. "King Dasaratha, you will have sons. I shall perform a sacred rite to please the gods."

Excited by this wonderful news, the king ran to his three wives, Sumitra, Kaikeyi, and Kausalya. "I will have sons!"

Meanwhile, the gods were growing more and more angry with Ravana, king of the *rakshasas,* the demons. Ten-headed, twenty-armed Ravana had great power. But he used that power to keep gods and holy men alike from their sacred rituals. Yet Ravana had been granted a boon by the gods. Thanks to it, he could not be harmed by gods or demons.

The god Vishnu, protector of the universe, thought, "Arrogant Ravana protected himself only from those beings who he thought could hurt him. He failed to protect himself from humans."

So Vishnu made the decision to be born as a human, someone who could kill Ravana. He sent a messenger to King Dasaratha with a special drink.

The messenger told the king, "Give each of your three wives this drink. It will bring sons." Then, the messenger disappeared.

The king gave the drink to each of his wives. Soon the city was filled with great rejoicing when the king announced the birth of four sons. They were named Rama, Lakshmana, Bharata, and Satrughna. Almost from birth, it became clear that Rama and Lakshmana were inseparable friends. People said that it was as if the two were one life in two bodies.

All four sons grew to be wise, kind men. King Dasaratha was finally happy, watching his sons grow. Though he never said it, his favorite son was Rama.

One day, the sage Vishwamitra, whom Dasaratha greatly respected, came to Ayodhya to see the king. "Greetings, oh, wise one," King Dasaratha said. "What brings you to my kingdom?"

"I must ask you for a favor. I have been trying to perform an important sacred rite—yet again and again it has been interrupted by Ravana's demons. My vows prevent me from fighting them."

"How can I help?" the king asked. "Nothing is too great to ask."

"Let me take Rama with me to protect my sacred site."

"But he is only a child, barely sixteen! Let me send you my armies instead. I will lead them into battle myself! Only, do not take my son!" The king began to weep.

Vishwamitra understood the king's pain. But he had no choice. He knew, as the king could not, that Rama was an avatar of Vishnu. Only Vishnu in human form could kill Ravana.

So it was that Rama went with Vishwamitra, and Lakshmana went as well. The two young men followed the sage along the bank of the Sarayu River. Whenever they stopped to rest, the sage taught them how to use their weapons.

They came to a dark and terrible forest, twisted and full of thorns. The sage said, "This was once a beautiful and prosperous land. Now, the terrible she-demon, Tataka, lives here. She attacks and kills anyone who enters."

"We are not afraid," Rama said.

"Excellent. You and your brother must rid the forest of this demon and her underlings. If you can do so, you also will restore the land to peace and beauty."

Rama and Lakshmana followed Vishwamitra into the forest. Each step took them farther into the darkness. They heard eerie howls and weird groans but saw no one.

Then, just as they stepped into a clearing, a huge rock suddenly came hurtling down out of the sky, straight at Rama. He fit an arrow to his bow and fired, splitting the rock in half. The pieces crashed harmlessly into the trees.

But then the huge and hideous demon Tataka sprang into sight. Her eyes were fire and her hands were claws. Before Tataka could attack, Lakshmana loosed an arrow from his bow. He missed a killing shot. But Rama did not. His arrow pierced Tataka's heart, and she fell dead. Lotus blossoms rained down upon Rama, blessings from the gods.

The three men continued through the forest, killing the rest of the forest demons. The land was cleansed.

But the sage knew that it was one thing to kill forest demons, and another to kill the demon king Ravana himself.

He led Rama and Lakshmana to Mithila to visit King Janaka. The king told them the story of his daughter.

"Years back, I found a child in a plowed furrow. I named her Sita, and raised her as my own daughter. Now, she is a beautiful young woman with many royal suitors. But he who wishes to wed Sita must lift and string the ancient bow of Shiva. So far, no man has been able just to lift the bow."

"I will do it," Rama said.

He easily took the bow from its case and started to string it. As he did so, the bow snapped in half. The king exclaimed, "Sita has found her husband! Let a messenger be sent to Ayodhya: Rama is to wed my daughter, Sita."

King Janaka led Sita to Rama. He placed her hand in his and said to Rama, "Sita, my daughter, is from today your partner in life."

Rama and Sita looked at each other and were overjoyed. Following the wedding, they returned to Ayodhya, and everyone in the city cheered their arrival. In the days that followed, Rama and Sita were the perfect husband and wife, utterly devoted to each other.

As the years passed, Rama grew into an excellent young man, learned and kind, following the will of the gods. But his father, King Dasaratha, grew older, and knew that his end was near. "I must be sure that my throne goes to my worthiest son, Rama. I shall step down to have the blessing of seeing him as king before I die."

But the youngest of the king's three wives, Kaikeyi, went to him and said, "Do you remember the day I saved your life? Do you remember how I stopped your runaway chariot?"

"Yes," replied the king.

"And do you remember what you said that day? You promised me two boons. Hear them now, I pray you. First, I wish to have my son, Bharata, placed upon the throne of Ayodhya. Second, I wish to see Rama banished from the kingdom for no less than fourteen years."

The king cried out in horror and fell to his knees. "I beg you not to hold me to these things."

But Kaikeyi showed no mercy. She told Rama that he must go into exile. Rama did not argue, but said to the king, "Father, your word is law. I shall do whatever you bid."

Lakshmana exclaimed, "I shall stop any who oppose your right to the throne!"

"No," Rama said. "You know it is my dharma, my sacred duty, to obey."

"Then I shall follow you!"

Sita, sobbing, added, "And it is my dharma to be at your side, my husband. How could I live without you?"

So the three left together, wearing the clothes not of royalty but of hermits. The people wept as they left, and Dasaratha cried, "Rama! Rama! Do not leave me!"

The king's heart failed within him, and soon after, he died.

Meanwhile, Rama, Lakshmana, and Sita hunted for a land where they could live alone and safe. They built a small hut near a stream.

But then Lakshmana, hunting in the forest, heard hoofbeats and climbed a tree to see who was approaching. To his shock, it was an army from Ayodhya. Bharata had found his brothers. Lakshmana was sure that his brother had come to kill them.

But Bharata embraced his brothers, crying, "My heart is filled with grief and shame. Grief for the loss of our noble father. Shame for being given the throne that should be yours. Come back to Ayodhya and be our king."

"I gave my word," Rama said. "I must stay in exile for fourteen years. Only after that time will I return."

"As long as you are in exile," Bharata stated, "there shall be no king. Give me your sandals and I shall place them on the throne. For the next fourteen years, I will rule in your name. And if you do not return after those fourteen years, I shall die."

Rama, Lakshmana, and Sita traveled on until they finally reached a clearing in a lush forest, sweet with the perfume of flowers and with fruit on every vine. All around them, birds sang joyfully.

"Let us build our home here," Rama said.

The ancient vulture king Jatayu lived nearby. They and he became friends, and Jatayu guarded Sita while the brothers hunted.

Just beyond the clearing lived Shurpanakha the she-demon, Ravana's sister. She had a potbelly, huge ears, clawed fingers and toes, narrow eyes, and long tangles of dirty hair. One day, she saw Rama in the forest. Putting down the bone she was gnawing, she said, "I want him for my husband."

Turning herself into a beautiful maiden, she went to see Rama. "Why does such a strong, handsome man like you live in this forest?"

But when she saw Sita, Shurpanakha frowned. "That woman is not good enough for you. I can make you happy."

When Rama refused her, the demon lost her temper. Returning to demon form, she lunged at Sita. Lakshmana grabbed Shurpanakha and cut off her nose and ears.

Shurpanakha fled, howling in pain, straight to her demon brothers, Khar and Dushan. When they learned that a human had dared to wound her, they cried, "Take us to him. We will kill him!"

"Look!" Lakshmana cried. "The sky is growing dark—with flying demons!"

Rama and Lakshmana fought side by side, firing arrow after arrow skyward. With every arrow, a demon fell dead.

Shurpanakha watched in horror as her brothers and their army were destroyed. She hurried to see Ravana. "Oh, Ravana. Khar, Dushan, and all their warriors have been killed by the two banished princes from Ayodhya!"

Ravana sprang to his feet, staring at his disfigured sister with the eyes of all ten heads. "Those two!"

"Wait, brother. There is one more thing. Rama's wife, Sita, is the most beautiful woman I have ever seen. She would make you a lovely queen."

"So be it!" Ravana cried. "I shall avenge you and our brothers in a way that Rama shall never expect."

The next day, a beautiful deer stepped out of the forest. Sita was enchanted by it.

"Please capture it for me," Sita asked Rama.

Lakshmana said, "No natural deer can be so perfect. Brother, be wary."

"Stay with Sita," Rama said, and set out after the deer. It led him deep into the forest, and then turned into a magician and vanished. "Lakshmana was right," Rama cried, and he ran back toward the hut.

Meanwhile, Sita and Lakshmana heard Rama's voice calling for help. "Lakshmana," Sita gasped, "you must help him!"

Lakshmana drew a magic circle around the hut. "Stay inside, and you will be safe," he said; then he grabbed his bow and quiver and ran after the sound of Rama's voice.

Hidden behind a tree, Ravana stood watching. As soon as Lakshmana was gone, the demon king turned into a *sannyasi,* an old wise man, and approached the hut, clutching a begging bowl. Sita kindly offered the poor man some food. "Please, take this offering," she said.

But Ravana could not cross the magic circle. "As a sannyasi, I cannot enter your house. I cannot accept your offering, I fear."

Sita took a step forward. One foot crossed over the magic circle. Ravana changed back to his demon form and snatched Sita. She screamed, but Ravana's magic chariot soared up into the sky and off to his kingdom.

The old vulture king Jatayu saw this and flew after them. He tore off a railing from the chariot, caught Sita, and set her safely on the ground, then turned to fight Ravana, tearing off arms and heads—but they at once grew back. Jatayu fell back, weary, and Ravana cut off both his wings. Sita had just time enough to bless the dying bird before Ravana dragged her back into his chariot and sped away.

Once he had Sita safely in his palace, Ravana did his best to woo her, begging her to be his queen. But Sita refused to listen, telling the demon king that she loved only Rama.

Ravana set Sita in a palace garden guarded by a hundred demons.

Back at the hut, Rama and Lakshmana were horrified to realize how they had been tricked. Rama cried, "I will slay Ravana and all his kin!"

In their search for Sita, Rama and Lakshmana entered Kiskindha, the kingdom of the monkeys. They met the monkey king Sugriva and told him their story.

Sugriva said, "I, too, am in exile. My brother seized my kingdom. Help me regain my throne, and I will help you find your wife." He added, "One of my people saw Sita being carried off. As she passed overhead, she dropped this."

It was one of Sita's ornaments. Rama took it, and tears filled his eyes.

Rama and Lakshmana defeated Sugriva's brother and won back the monkey king's throne. The monkey warrior Hanuman arrived, together with a great monkey army. Hanuman divided his troops into four divisions, with the plan that each division would go in search of Sita for one month.

At the end of the month, three of the four divisions returned with no word of Sita's whereabouts. Only Hanuman's division had yet to return.

As Hanuman and his men searched for Sita, they came to a mighty ocean. Hanuman prayed for help, and grew miraculously large. Crying "Victory to Rama," he leaped up and flew across the ocean to Ravana's palace.

As he landed, Hanuman returned to his normal size. He searched all through the palace. Then he saw a grove of trees. Beneath one tree, surrounded by she-demon guards, sat the loveliest of women, sobbing, "Rama, Rama."

"I have found Sita!" Hanuman cried.

But before he could speak to her, Hanuman saw Ravana coming, and hid. Ravana pleaded with Sita, "Come with me. Be my queen. You will have everything you wish."

"You have kidnapped me!" Sita replied. "Rama will come to rescue me—and he will kill you!"

Ravana stormed away. Hanuman waited until the she-demon guards fell asleep, then crept to Sita's side and knelt before her. "Do not be afraid. I am Hanuman, Rama's messenger. He has sent me to find you, and weeps for your return." To show that he was not a demon in disguise, Hanuman gave Sita a ring from Rama. "This will prove that Rama sent me."

Sita cried, "Go tell Rama where I am. Give this jewel to my lord as proof of my love."

The demon guards awoke, but Hanuman slew them with ease. More guards rushed in, and at last Hanuman was taken before Ravana. "Set his tail on fire," Ravana ordered. "Let him return home that way."

As the king's men wrapped Hanuman's tail in cloth to set it on fire, he grew it longer and longer. The more they wrapped, the longer Hanuman grew his tail. Finally, Ravana grew impatient. "Set it on fire!"

Hanuman leaped up into the air with his long tail on fire. He flew low over the city, trailing that fiery tail, and set each building, temple, palace, and garden on fire. As he flew over the garden, he made sure that Sita was safe. Then, before he headed home, he dunked his tail in the ocean to put out the fire.

Hanuman and his troops rushed back to tell Rama the good news. By now, Rama had given up all hope of ever seeing Sita alive again. Without saying a word, Hanuman gave Rama Sita's jewel. Rama cried, "You have given me reason to live again."

Meanwhile, back at Ravana's palace, his decent brother, Vibhishana, tried his best to get Ravana to let Sita go, to save both her life and Ravana's kingdom. But Ravana would not listen. At last, Vibhishana flew away to Rama.

"I am Vibhishana, brother to Ravana. No matter what I say to him, he still refuses to release Sita. Now, I wish to join you and fight at your side."

Rama replied, "Welcome, Vibhishana. You have rejected evil for good. For your honesty, you shall become the new king in Ravana's place."

Rama stood on the shoreline of the great ocean. "Hear me!" he called to the ocean god. "I am Rama. My weapons are beyond imagination. In an instant, I can dry your ocean. If you wish to avoid this fate, show me how to reach Lanka."

The ocean said, "Rama, here is Nala, son of the great builder. He will build you a bridge across these waters. I shall support that bridge."

With the help of the monkey army, Nala put up a bridge made of wood, rocks, and stones. Rama, Hanuman, and the monkey army crossed the bridge by nightfall, and surrounded Ravana's city.

Ravana ordered one of his demons, "Make me an exact copy of Rama's head. Soak it in blood. Then bring it to me." He took the head to Sita. "O, Sita, Rama has failed in his attempt to rescue you. His army has been destroyed. Here is the end of your hope."

Sita collapsed in tears. "Alas, O Rama, you have followed your dharma. But I am left alone. You came to save me, but you gave your own life.

"O Rama, you are happy now. You have rejoined your beloved father in heaven. But what shall I do?

"O Rama, I am she who brought all this upon you. Take me too. Take me with you, my love."

Angered by Sita's devotion, Ravana stormed from the garden and ordered all his troops to march toward the city gates.

The great battle began, and soon bodies littered the city and the land outside the walls. Indrajit, Ravana's son, rained poison arrows upon Rama and Lakshmana. So overwhelming was this attack that the two brothers fell to the ground, unconscious.

Meanwhile, Ravana's demons made themselves invisible and attacked the monkey army.

But Hanuman charged forward, smashing the skull of every enemy he could still see. The monkey army rallied behind him and fought more fiercely than before.

Rama and Lakshmana struggled back to consciousness and returned to the battle. Ravana, high over the battle in his magic chariot, shot an arrow that hit Lakshmana. Hanuman rushed to his side and carried him to safety.

By now, things were looking bad for Rama and his forces. Most of the monkeys were dead or wounded. But Hanuman raced off to Kailasa Mountain, where a healing herb grew, and returned in giant form, balancing the mountain in his arms. All the wounded warriors, including Lakshmana, were healed as soon as they inhaled the aroma of the magical herbs.

Rama, Lakshmana, Vibhishana, and Hanuman overpowered Indrajit, Ravana's son, and killed him. But Ravana could not be taken. The battle raged for two days, and at last Rama felt his strength leaving him.

But one of the sages with his army said, "Pray to the Sun, O Rama. It is the heart of the Sun that will bring you victory."

Rama knelt to pray to the Sun, and felt his strength return.

Ravana attacked again, charging forward. Rama stood quietly, and reached for his most powerful weapon, the Brahma-missile, to be used only when all else had failed. As he did so, the earth shook. All the warriors covered their eyes and fell to the ground.

Rama fired. The missile struck Ravana's chest, and Ravana fell dead.

"Victory to Rama!" Rama's men shouted.

Vibhishana knelt at the body of his dead brother and burst into tears. "Why didn't you listen to me? Why were you so overcome with Sita and power?"

Following the funeral rites for Ravana, Rama made Vibhishana the new king.

Vibhishana's wife and maidens took Sita from the garden. She wore a beautiful sari sparkling with jewels. Rama and Sita were reunited and returned to Ayodhya.

But once they were back in Ayodhya, Rama grew troubled. Many people in the city were expressing their doubts about Sita's faithfulness while she had been in Ravana's hands. Even his lowest subjects whispered, "How can Rama forget that Sita was with another man?"

Sorrowing, Rama knew that a king must be above reproach. He ordered that Sita be sent back to the forest.

Sita stood alone on a riverbank. She heard the whisper of the river's goddess saying, "Let life go, Sita. Come home. Dive into me."

But an old man said, "Do not enter the river."

"Who are you?" Sita asked.

"I am Valmiki, a poet and a hermit. I live in this forest. You are welcome to make my home yours."

It was there that Sita gave birth to Rama's twins sons, Kusa and Lava. For the next twelve years, she and her sons lived peacefully with Valmiki. During that time, Valmiki composed a poem he named the *Ramayana,* and taught it to the boys.

In Ayodhya, King Rama held a great public festival. Kusa and Lava came to Ayodhya to perform. Rama heard the boys and asked, "What is this beautiful poem called?"

The boys said, "The *Ramayana.*"

Rama stared at the twins. "These are my sons!" he exclaimed.

He hastily sent a messenger to find Sita and convince her to return to Ayodhya.

The next day, Sita returned. Quietly she said, "I will prove my innocence before you once and for all."

Then Sita took a step back and said, "Mother Earth, if I have been faithful to my husband, take me home."

With a roar, the ground opened and took Sita back, then closed once more.

Rama lived on, ruling Ayodhya alone, for a thousand years. One day, he thought, "I was born of the god Vishnu, and it is time for me to return to him."

He left the palace and the crowded streets. He walked to the banks of the Sarayu River. There, Brahma, the creator of all, appeared to him. "Come, O Vishnu, return to Vishnu. Return to heaven."

Hearing Brahma's words, Rama smiled and stepped into the river and returned to heaven. Rama was home.

Shah-nameh

Iran's Greatest Epic

Known as the greatest epic of Iran, formerly Persia, the *Shah-nameh* was written by the poet Ferdowsi in the eleventh century. It is full of adventure, magic, and heroic deeds, beginning with the world of myth and continuing into folklore, that make it an ideal work for storytellers to read and learn.

Kaiumers was the first king of Persia, and, against him, Ahriman the evil, jealous of his greatness, sent forth a mighty daeva (a devil or evil djinn) to conquer him. By this daeva, Saiamuk, the son of Kaiumers, was slain, and the king himself died of grief at the loss of his son.

Husheng, his grandson, succeeded Kaiumers and was a great and wise king who gave fire to his people, taught them irrigation, instructed them how to till and sow, and gave names to the beasts. Husheng's son and successor, Tahumers, taught his people the arts of spinning, weaving, and writing, and when he died he left his throne to his son, Jemschid.

Jemschid was a mighty monarch who divided men into classes, and the years into periods, and he built mighty walls and cities. But his heart grew proud at the thought of his power, and he was driven away from his land by his people, who called Zohak to the throne of Iran.

Zohak, who came from the deserts of Arabia, was a good and wise young man who had fallen into the power of a daeva. This daeva, in the guise of a skillful servant, asked permission one day to kiss his monarch between the shoulders as a reward for an unusually fine bit of cookery. From the spot he kissed sprang two black serpents, whose only nourishment was the brains of the king's subjects.

The serpent king, as Zohak was now called, was much feared by his subjects, who saw their numbers lessen daily by the demands of the serpents. But when the children of the blacksmith Kawah were demanded as food for the serpents, the blacksmith defied Zohak. He raised his leathern apron as a standard—a banner ever since honored in Persia—and called the people to him to set off in search of Feridoun, an heir of Jemschid. Under the young leader, the oppressed people defeated the tyrant, and they placed Feridoun on the throne.

Feridoun had three sons, Irij, Tur, and Silim. Having tested their bravery, he divided the kingdom among them, giving to Irij the kingdom of Iran. Although the other brothers received equal shares of the kingdom, they were enraged, because Iran was not their portion. When their complaints to their father were not heeded, they slew their brother.

Irij left a son, a babe named Minuchihr, who was reared carefully by Feridoun. In time, Minuchihr avenged his father by defeating the armies of his uncles and slaying them both. Soon after this, Feridoun died, entrusting his grandson to Saum, his favorite *pehliva,* or vassal, who ruled over Seistan.

Saum was a childless monarch. When at last a son was born to him, he was very happy, until he learned that while the child was perfect in every other way, he had the silver hair of an old man. Fearing the talk of his enemies, Saum exposed the child, Zal, on a mountaintop to die. There, the child was found by the simurgh, a remarkable animal, part bird, part human, that was touched by the cries of the helpless infant. She carried him to her great nest of aloe and sandalwood, and reared him with her little ones.

Saum, who had lived to regret his foolish and wicked act, was told in a dream that his son still lived and was being cared for by the simurgh. He accordingly sought the nest, and carried his son away with great thanksgiving. The simurgh parted tenderly with the little Zal, and presented him with a feather from her wing, telling him that whenever he was in danger, he had only to throw it on the fire, and she would instantly come to his aid.

Saum first presented his son at the court of Minuchihr, and then took him home to Zaboulistan, where he was carefully instructed in every art and science.

At one time, while his father was invading a neighboring province, Zal traveled over the kingdom and stopped at the court of Mihrab, a tributary of Saum, who ruled at Kabul. Though a descendant of the serpent king, Mihrab was good, just, and wise, and he received the young warrior with hospitality.

Zal had not been long in Kabul before he heard of the beauty of Rudabeh, the daughter of Mihrab, and she, in turn, of the great exploits of Zal. By an artifice of the princess, they met and vowed to love each other forever, though they knew their love would meet with opposition. Saum and Zal both pleaded Zal's case before Minuchihr, who relented when he heard from the astrologers that a good and mighty warrior would come of the union. Rudabeh's mother won the consent of Mihrab, so that the young people were soon married with great pomp.

To Zal and Rudabeh, a son was born named Rustam, who, when one day old, was as large as a year-old child. When three years old, he could ride a horse, and, at eight years, he was as powerful as any hero of the time.

Nauder succeeded the good Minuchihr. Under him Persia was defeated by the Turanians, and Afrasiyab occupied the Persian throne. But Zal, whose father, Saum, had died, overthrew Afrasiyab and placed Zew upon the throne. Zew's reign was short, and Garshasp, his son, succeeded him.

When Garshasp was threatened by the Turanians, his people went for aid to Zal, who, because he was growing old, referred them to Rustam, yet of tender age. Rustam responded gladly, and his father commanded that all the horses from Zaboulistan to Kabul be brought forth that his son might select a steed therefrom. Every horse bent beneath his grasp until he came to the colt Rakush, which responded to Rustam's voice and suffered Rustam to mount him. From that day to his death, this steed was Rustam's faithful companion and preserver.

Garshasp was too weak to rule over the kingdom, and Zal dispatched Rustam to Mount Alberz, where he had been told in a dream that a youth dwelt called Kai-Kobad, descended from Feridoun. Kai-Kobad welcomed Rustam, and the two, with the noblest of the kingdom, defeated the power of Turan.

After a reign of a hundred years, the wise Kai-Kobad died, and was succeeded by his son, the foolish Kai-Kaus, who, not satisfied with the wealth and extent of his kingdom, determined to conquer the kingdom of Mazinderan, ruled by the daevas. Zal's remonstrances were to no avail: The headstrong Kai-Kaus marched into Mazinderan, and, together with his whole army, was conquered, imprisoned, and blinded by the power of the White Daeva.

When the news of the monarch's misfortune came to Iran, Rustam immediately saddled Rakush, and, choosing the shortest and most peril-beset route, set forth, unaccompanied, for Mazinderan. If he survived the dangers that lurked by the way, he would reach Mazinderan in seven days.

While sleeping in a forest after his first day's journey, Rustam was saved from a fierce lion by Rakush, who stood at Rustam's head. On the second day, just as he believed himself to be perishing of thirst, he was saved by a sheep that he followed to a fountain of water.

On the third night, Rakush, whom he had angrily forbidden to attack any animal without waking him, twice warned him of the approach of a dragon. The first time, the dragon disappeared when Rustam awoke, and he spoke severely to his faithful horse. The second time Rustam slew the dragon. Morning having dawned, Rustam proceeded through a desert where he was offered food and wine by a sorceress. Not recognizing her, and grateful for the food, he offered her a cup of wine in the name of God, and she was immediately converted into a black fiend, whom he slew.

He was next opposed by Aulad, whom he defeated and promised to make ruler of Mazinderan if he would guide him to the caves of the White Daeva. A stony desert and a wide stream lay between him and the demon. But the undaunted Rustam passed over them, and choosing the middle of the day, at which time Aulad told him the daevas slept, he slew the guards, entered the cavern, and after a terrible struggle overcame and slew the great daeva.

He then released Kai-Kaus and his army and restored their sight by touching their eyes with the blood from the daeva's heart.

Kai-Kaus, not satisfied with this adventure, committed many other follies, from which it taxed his warriors sorely to rescue him.

Once, Kai-Kaus was imprisoned by the king of Hamaveran after he had espoused his daughter. Again, he followed the advice of a wicked daeva and tried to search the heavens in a flying machine that descended and left him in a desert wasteland. It was only after this last humiliation that he humbled himself, lay in the dust many days, and at last became worthy of the throne of his fathers.

At one time, Rustam was hunting near the borders of Turan, and fell asleep, leaving Rakush to graze in the forest, where he was espied by the men of Turan, who captured him. When Rustam awoke, he followed his steed by the traces of Rakush's hoofs, until he came to the city of Samengan. The king received Rustam kindly, and promised to restore the horse if he could be found. While his messengers went in search of the horse, the king feasted his guest and led him for the night to a perfumed couch.

In the middle of the night, Rustam awoke to see a beautiful young woman enter the room accompanied by a maid. She proved to be the princess, who had fallen in love with Rustam. She pleaded with him to return her love, promising, if he did so, to restore his cherished horse. Rustam longed for his steed; moreover, the maiden was irresistibly beautiful. He accordingly yielded to her proposals, and the two were wedded the next day, the king having given his consent.

After tarrying some time in Samengan, Rustam was forced to return to Iran. Bidding his bride an affectionate farewell, he presented her with a bracelet.

"If thou art given a daughter, place this amulet in her hair to guard her from harm. If a son, bind it on his arm, that he may possess the valor of Nariman."

In the course of time, the princess bore a boy, christened Sohrab, who was like his father in beauty and boldness. But for fear that she would be deprived of him, she wrote to Rustam that a daughter had been born to her. To her son, she declared the secret of his birth, and urged him to be like his father in all things. But she warned him not to disclose the secret, for she feared that if it came to the ears of Afrasiyab, he would destroy Sohrab because of his hatred of Rustam.

Sohrab, who already cherished dreams of conquest, was elated at the knowledge of his parentage. "Mother," exclaimed he, "I shall gather an army of Turks, conquer Iran, dethrone Kai-Kaus, and place my father on the throne; then both of us will conquer Afrasiyab, and I will mount the throne of Turan."

The mother, pleased with her son's valor, gave him for a horse a foal sprung from Rakush—and fondly watched his preparations for war.

The wicked Afrasiyab well knew that Sohrab was the son of Rustam. He was also aware that it was very dangerous to have two such mighty warriors alive, since if they became known to each other they would form an alliance. He planned, therefore, to aid Sohrab in the war, keeping him in ignorance of his father's identity, and to manage in some way to have the two meet in battle, so that one or both might be slain.

The armies met and the great battle began. Sohrab asked to have Rustam pointed out to him, but the soldiers on his side were all instructed to keep him in ignorance. By some strange mischance, the two men whom his mother had sent to enlighten him were both slain. Rustam was moved at the sight of the brave young warrior, but remembering that Tahmineh's offspring was a daughter, thought nothing more of the thrill he felt at sight of him.

At last, Sohrab and Rustam met in single combat. Sohrab was moved with tenderness for his unknown opponent, and besought him to tell him if he was Rustam, but Rustam declared that he was only a servant of that chief. For three days, they fought bitterly, and on the fourth day, Rustam overthrew his son. When Sohrab felt that the end had come, he threatened his unknown opponent. "Whoever thou art, know that I came out not for empty glory but to find my father, and that though I have found him not, when he hears that thou hast slain his son, he will search thee out and avenge me, no matter where thou hidest thyself. For my father is the great Rustam."

Rustam fell down in agony when he heard his son's words and realized that his guile had prevented him from being made known the day before. He examined the onyx bracelet on Sohrab's arm; it was the same one that he had given Tahmineh. Bethinking himself of a magic ointment possessed by Kai-Kaus, he sent for it that he might heal his dying son, but the foolish king, jealous of his prowess, refused to send it, and Sohrab expired in the arms of his father.

Rustam's heart was broken. He heaped up his armor, his tent, his trappings, and his treasures, and flung them into a great fire. The house of Zal was filled with mourning, and when the news was conveyed to Samengan, he tore his garments, and his daughter grieved herself to death before a year had passed away.

To Kai-Kaus and a wife of the race of Feridoun was born a son called Saiawush, who was beautiful, noble, and virtuous. But his foolish father allowed himself to be prejudiced against the youth by slanderous tongues, so that Saiawush fled from the court and sought shelter with Afrasiyab in Turan. There, he speedily became popular, and took unto himself for a wife the daughter of Afrasiyab. But when he and his wife, Ferandis, built a beautiful city, the hatred and jealousy of Gersiwaz was aroused, so that he lied to Afrasiyab and said that Saiawush was puffed up with pride, and at last induced Afrasiyab to slay his son-in-law.

Saiawush had a son, Kai-Khosrau, who was saved by Piran, a kindhearted nobleman, and given into the care of a goatherd. When Afrasiyab learned of his existence, he summoned him to his presence, but the youth, instructed by Piran, assumed the manners of an imbecile, and was accordingly freed by Afrasiyab, who feared no harm from him.

When the news of the death of Saiawush was conveyed to Iran, there was great mourning, and war was immediately declared against Turan. For seven years, the contest was carried on, always without success, and at the end of that time, Gudarz dreamed that a son of Saiawush was living called Kai-Khosrau, and that until he was sought out and placed at the head of the army, deliverance could not come to Iran. Kai-Khosrau was discovered, and led the armies on to victory. When Kai Kaus found that his grandson not only was a great warrior, skilled in magic, but also possessed wisdom beyond his years, he resigned the throne and made Kai-Khosrau ruler over Iran.

Kai-Khosrau ruled many long years, in which time he brought peace and happiness to his kingdom, avenged the murder of his father, and compassed the death of the wicked Afrasiyab. Then, fearing that he might become puffed up with pride like Jemschid, he longed to depart from this world, and prayed to Ormuzd to take him to his bosom.

The king, after many prayers to Ormuzd, dreamed that his wish would be granted if he set the affairs of his kingdom in order and appointed his successor. Rejoiced, he called his nobles together, divided his treasure among them, and appointed his successor, Lohurasp, whom he commanded to be the woof and warp of justice. Accompanied by a few of his faithful friends, Kai-Khosrau set out on the long journey to the crest of the mountains. At his entreaties, some of his friends turned back; those who stayed overnight in spite of his warnings found upon waking that they were covered by a heavy fall of snow, and were soon frozen. Afterward, their bodies were found and received a royal burial.

Lohurasp had a son, Gushtasp, who greatly desired to rule, and was a just monarch when he succeeded to the throne. Gushtasp, however, was jealous of his son, Isfendiyar, who was a great warrior. When Gushtasp was about to be overcome by the forces of Turan, he promised Isfendiyar the throne if he would destroy the enemy. But when the hosts were scattered, and Isfendiyar reminded his father of his promise, he was cast into a dungeon, there to remain until his services were again needed. When he had again gained a victory, he was told that the throne would be his when he had rescued his sisters from the brazen fortress of Arjasp, where they had been carried and imprisoned.

On his way to this tower, Isfendiyar met with as many terrible foes as Rustam had encountered on his way to the White Daeva, and as successfully overcame them. Wolves, lions, enchantresses, and dragons barred the way to the impregnable fortress, which rose three *farsakhs* high and forty wide, and was constructed entirely of brass and iron. But Isfendiyar, assuming the guise of a merchant and concealing his warriors in chests, won his way into the castle, gained the favor of its inmates, and made them drunk with wine. This done, he freed his sisters, slew the guards, and struck down Arjasp.

Instead of keeping his promise, Gushtasp hastened to set his son another task. Rustam was his pehliva, but it pleased him to send forth Isfendiyar against him, commanding him to bring home the mighty warrior in chains. Isfendiyar pleaded in vain with his father. Then he explained the situation to Rustam, and begged that he would accompany him home in peace to gratify his father. Rustam refused to go in chains, so the two heroes reluctantly began the hardest battle of their lives.

At the end of the first day, Rustam and Rakush were severely wounded, and on his return home, Rustam happened to think of the simurgh. Called by the burning of the feather, the kind bird healed the wounds of the hero and of Rakush, and she instructed Rustam how to slay his foe. "Seek thou the tamarisk tree, and make thereof an arrow. Aim at his eye, and there thou canst blind and slay him."

Rustam followed the directions and laid low the gallant youth. Isfendiyar died exclaiming, "My father has slain me, not thou, Rustam. I die, the victim of my father's hate. Do thou keep for me and rear my son!"

Rustam, who had lived so long and accomplished such great deeds, died at last by the hand of his half brother. This brother, Shugdad, stirred up the king of Kabul, in whose court he was reared, to slay Rustam because he exacted tribute from Kabul.

Rustam was called into Kabul by Shugdad, who claimed that the king mistreated him. When he arrived, the matter was settled amicably, and the brothers set out for a hunt with the king. The hunters were led to a spot where the false king had caused pits to be dug and lined with sharp weapons. Rustam, pleased with his kind reception and suspecting no harm, beat Rakush severely when he paused and would go no farther. Stung by the blows, the gallant horse sprang forward and fell into the pit. As he rose from this, he fell into another, until, clambering from the seventh pit, he and Rustam fell swooning with pain.

"False brother!" cried Rustam. "What hast thou done? Was it for thee to slay thy father's son? Exult now, but thou wilt yet suffer for this crime!" Then, altering his tone, he said gently,

"But give me, I pray thee, my bow and arrows, that I may have them by my side to slay any wild beast that may try to devour me."

Shugdad gave him the bow, and when he saw the gleam in Rustam's eyes, he concealed himself behind a tree. But the angry Rustam, grasping the bow with something of his former strength, sent the arrow through tree and man, transfixing both. Then, thanking his Creator that he had been given the opportunity to slay his murderer, Rustam breathed his last.

Destiny

An American Civil War Tale

During the American Civil War, a variant of the Jewish folktale "Appointment in Samarra" surfaced. The basic tale type features a man, or group of men, fleeing what appears to be imminent death, only to die, ironically, in another place. "Destiny" is a story of a young man establishing his courage, but the irony of his death places it in the category of the "Appointment in Samarra" tale type.

In the summer of 1862, a young man belonging to a Vermont regiment was found sleeping at his post. He was tried and sentenced to be shot. The day was fixed for the execution, and the young soldier calmly prepared to meet his fate.

Friends who knew of the case brought the matter to President Lincoln's attention. It seemed that the boy had been on duty one night, and, on the following night, he had taken the place of a comrade too ill to stand guard. The third night, he had been again called out and, being utterly exhausted, had fallen asleep at his post.

As soon as the president understood the case, he signed a pardon and sent it to the camp. The morning before the execution arrived, but the president had not heard whether the pardon had reached the officers in charge of the matter. He began to feel uneasy. Lincoln ordered a telegram to be sent to the camp, but he received no answer. State

papers could not fix his mind, nor could he banish the condemned soldier boy from his thoughts.

At last, feeling that he must know whether the lad was safe, Lincoln ordered a carriage and rode rapidly for 10 miles over a dusty road beneath a scorching sun. When he reached the camp, he found that the pardon had been received and the execution stayed.

The sentinel was released, and his heart was filled with lasting gratitude. When the campaign opened in the spring, the young man was with his regiment near Yorktown, Virginia. They were ordered to attack a fort, and he fell at the first volley of the enemy.

The young man's comrades caught him up. They carried him bleeding and dying from the field.

"Bear witness," he said, "that I have proved myself not a coward, and I am not afraid to die." Then, making a last effort, with his dying breath he prayed for Abraham Lincoln.

Greatest Liar of Them All

An Apache Folktale

Coyote is an important trickster figure of the American Southwest, specifically the Apache people. Tales about him can be found in almost every tribal group west of the Mississippi River, as far north as Oregon and Idaho, and down into Mexico. Traditionally, tales about him begin, "Coyote was going along..."

Coyote was going along one day when he came to a camp of men just sitting around, waiting for him.

"Coyote," they said, "we hear that you are the greatest liar of them all."

Coyote only shrugged. "How would you know such a thing?"

"Oh, everyone knows it. But how do you tell such great lies? Why does everyone always believe you? Come, show us how to lie."

Coyote shrugged again. "It was no easy thing to learn how to do. I had to pay a great price to learn how to lie so well."

"What price did you pay?"

"One horse, my finest buffalo horse." By that, he meant a horse well trained to run in close among the buffalo so his rider could make many kills.

"What, like this?" asked one man, and led forth a fine horse, his best buffalo horse.

Coyote studied the horse, which sidled nervously at the strange wolfish scent of the trickster. "Yes, this is exactly the sort of horse I mean. It was with one like him that I paid for my power to lie."

"But will you teach us to lie?" the men asked impatiently.

Coyote pretended to think it over. "Let me try to ride this fine buffalo horse. If he doesn't buck, I will explain my power to lie."

That sounded like a good bet to the men. After all, a buffalo horse is trained to be nice and mannerly.

Coyote got up on the horse's back, but he dug in with his claws. Naturally, the horse began to buck, and Coyote leaped off.

"He needs a blanket between him and me," Coyote said. "That is surely the problem."

So the men put a thick saddle blanket on the horse. Coyote mounted again, but his claws were sharp enough to prick right through the blanket. And, of course, the horse began to buck again.

Coyote leaped off. "He still wants something more on his back. A good saddle, I guess."

So the men saddled the horse with their best saddle. They gave Coyote a fine riding crop, too.

"I shall try the horse one more time," Coyote said. "If he still bucks, I won't be able to tell you the secret of my power."

He rode the horse a little distance away, just out of reach of the men, and then stopped.

"This is the secret of my power," Coyote said. "I trick people into giving me things. Like a blanket. Like a good saddle. Like a riding crop and a fine buffalo horse."

And with that, Coyote rode away, and the men could do nothing to stop him.

Why Ananse Owns Every Story

An Ashante Folktale from Ghana

> This retelling of "Why Ananse Owns Every Story," an Ashante folktale from Ghana, features Ananse, who is the primary trickster figure of both West Africa and the Caribbean. He is a spider, though he is sometimes portrayed as a man, or as a cross between a spider and a man, or as a spider with a man's clever eyes.

Kwaku Ananse, the Spider, wanted ownership of all the stories there were. Nyame, the sky god, owned them, so off Ananse went to Nyame.

"I wish to buy all the stories," the Spider said.

"They are, indeed, for sale," Nyame told him. "But the price is very high. Many people have tried to buy the stories, but they were unable to pay the price. Do you really think you can do what they could not?"

"Of course," Ananse said boldly. "What is the price?"

"You must bring me three things. First, bring me fierce Mmoboro."

"The hornets? Done."

"Second, bring me dangerous Onini."

"The python? Done."

"And last, bring me perilous Osebo."

"The leopard?" Ananse laughed. "The stories are as good as mine!"

Ananse scuttled home, cut a gourd from its vine, and drilled a small hole in it. Then he found a nice, large calabash, a bigger gourd, and filled it with water.

Off Ananse went to the tree where the hornets lived. Quickly, the Spider poured water from the calabash all over himself till he was dripping wet. He tossed water from the calabash all over the tree until the hornets were dripping wet as well.

"What are you doing out here in the rain?" Ananse cried. "Foolish people, I am too big to fit in this nice, dry gourd, but you are not. Come inside and stay dry!"

The hornets flew into the hole in the gourd. Ananse hastily plugged up the hole with a wad of grass. "You really *are* fools," he laughed, and scuttled to Nyame.

"I have brought you Mmoboro."

The sky god nodded. "That is one-third of the price. But now you must bring me dangerous Onini the python."

Ananse went home, cut himself a sturdy bamboo pole and a strong vine, and went looking for Onini the python.

As he went, Ananse pretended to be talking to himself. "My wife is foolish," he muttered. "I say he's longer. She says he's shorter. I say he's stronger. She says he's weaker. I am right. I know I am right."

Onini was overcome by curiosity. "Who is stronger? Who is longer?"

Ananse pretended to be startled. "Oh, it's nothing, mighty Onini."

"Tell me."

"Why, I have argued with my wife. She says you, mighty Onini, are shorter and weaker than this bamboo pole. Isn't that a foolish thing?"

"Foolish, indeed. Come, put the pole down, and I'll show you how much longer I am."

Ananse put the pole down and Onini stretched out beside it. "No," the Spider said, "not quite. That's better . . . no. You keep slipping, Onini. I can't really tell if you are longer or shorter than the pole. Let me tie you at one

542

end so you can stretch out all the way without slipping."

Ananse used the vine to tie Onini's head firmly to the pole. He scuttled to the other end of the pole and tied Onini's tail to the pole, then wrapped the vine about every bit of the snake.

"Look at this," the Spider said. "My wife was right after all. You *are* shorter and weaker than the pole. I was foolish. But you are the bigger fool, since you are now my prisoner!"

Off Ananse staggered with Onini and the pole. "Here is the python."

Was Nyame surprised? The sky god only nodded. "That is two-thirds of the price. Now, though, you must bring me the perilous Osebo the leopard."

Ananse went into the forest where Osebo lived and dug a deep pit, covering it over with branches and dust until it was invisible.

"Hey, Osebo!" he called. "Here is someone for you to eat!"

Osebo came running. With a snarl and a crash, he fell right into the pit. Ananse waited a bit, then strolled up to the edge of the pit.

"Why, what is this?" he asked as though surprised. "Is that you, great Osebo? What are you doing in that hole?"

"I fell," Osebo snarled. "Help me out of here."

"Oh, no; oh, no. I would love to help you; I would. But if I pull you out, you will surely eat me."

"I will not."

"Then you will eat my wife."

"I will not."

"I don't know. . . ."

"I swear," shouted the leopard, "that I will not eat you or your wife or any spider anywhere! Now, help me out of here."

"Well . . . since you did make a promise . . . ," Ananse said. "Very well."

He pulled the top of a springy sapling down over the pit and tied it there with a vine. Then Ananse tied one end of a second vine to the top of that young tree and dropped the other end of the vine into the pit.

"Tie the vine to your tail," Ananse called. "Be sure to tie it tightly!"

Osebo tied the vine tightly to his tail. Ananse laughed and cut the first vine, the one that tied down the top of the springy sapling. It shot upright, snatching Osebo out of the pit. But now, the leopard hung upside down by his tail! Ananse quickly killed Osebo, then carried the leopard to Nyame.

"Here is Osebo," he said. "The third part of the price has been paid."

This time, the sky god was truly surprised. "From now on, all stories belong to you. From now on, whenever a story is told, the teller must say that it belongs to Ananse."

And so, from that day to this, all stories told by the Ashante are called Anansesem, the stories of Ananse the Spider.

Brewery of Eggshells

A Changeling Folktale from Wales

Until the twentieth century, the fear of losing a baby to death or disease was a very real one in many countries, including Great Britain. In areas such as Wales, people held a strong belief in fairy folk. This led to an equally strong folk belief that a human baby might be exchanged by the fairies for one of their own, a changeling. There were even some tragic nineteenth-century accounts of parents so sure that their sickly baby was a changeling that they tried to kill it, sure the fairies would come to save the changeling and return their true child. Ways of revealing a changeling were said to be trickery to make it speak out or cruelty, such as holding it over a fire.

In Treneglwys (Wales), there was a certain shepherd's cot, or cottage, known by the name of Twt y Cymrws because of the strange strife that occurred there. A man and his wife lived there and had twins, whom the woman nursed tenderly. One day, while her husband was away in the fields, she was called away to the house of a neighbor who lived some distance away. She did not much like going and leaving her little ones all alone in a solitary house, especially as she had heard tell of the good folk (the fairy folk) haunting the neighborhood.

Well, she went and came back as soon as she could, but on her way back she was frightened to see some old elves of the blue petticoat crossing her path, even though it was midday. She rushed home, but she found her two little ones in the cradle, and everything seemed as it had been before.

After a time, the good people began to suspect that something was wrong, for the twins did not grow at all.

The man said, "They're not ours."

The woman said, "Whose else should they be?"

And so arose the great strife that the neighbors named the cottage after. It made the woman very sad, so one evening she made up her mind to go and see the Wise Man of Llanidloes, for he knew everything and would tell her what to do.

So she went to Llanidloes and told the case to the wise man. Now, there was soon to be a harvest of rye and oats, so the wise man said to her, "When you are getting dinner for the reapers, clear out the shell of a hen's egg and boil some potage in it, and then take it to the door as if you meant it as a dinner for the reapers. Then listen if the twins say anything. If you hear them speaking of things beyond the understanding of children, go back and take them up and throw them into the waters of Lake Elvyn. But if you don't hear anything remarkable, do them no injury."

So when the day of the reaping came, the woman did all that the wise man had ordered. She put the eggshell on the fire and took it off and carried it to the door, and there she stood and listened. Then she heard one of the children say to the other:

Acorn before oak I knew,
An egg before a hen,
But I never heard of an
*   eggshell brew*
A dinner for harvest men.

So she went back into the house, seized the children, and threw them into the lake. The goblins in their blue trousers came and saved their little ones, and the mother had her own children back. And so the great strife ended.

Tam Lin

A British Folktale

The romantic fantasy ballad "Tam Lin" from Great Britain has been the subject of various novels and makes a good story for storytellers with fantasy-loving teenage or adult audiences. Although its original age is unknown, it was first collected by Sir Francis J. Child and is listed by him as Ballad 39 in his *English and Scottish Popular Ballads* (1882-1898). Sir Walter Scott also included it in his *Minstrelsy of the Scottish Border* (1802). It also can be found in prose form in *A Collection of Ballads* (1910) by Andrew Lang.

Briefly summarized, it is the story of Janet, a young noblewoman, who saves her lover, Tam Lin, from the Queen of Faerie.

O I forbid you, maidens a',
That wear gowd on your hair,
To come or gae by Carterhaugh,
For young Tam Lin is there.

There's nane that gaes by Carterhaugh
But they leave him a wad,
Either their rings, or green mantles,
Or else their maidenhead.
Janet has kilted her green kirtle
A little aboon her knee,
And she has broded her yellow hair
A little aboon her bree,
And she's away to Carterhaugh
As fast as she can hie.

When she came to Carterhaugh
Tam Lin was at the well,
And there she fand his steed standing,
But away was himsel.

She had na pu'd a double rose,
A rose but only twa,
Till upon then started young Tam Lin,
Says, Lady, thou's pu nae mae.

Why pu's thou the rose, Janet,
And why breaks thou the wand?

Or why comes thou to Carterhaugh
Withoutten my command?
"Carterhaugh, it is my own,
My daddy gave it me,
I'll come and gang by Carterhaugh,
And ask nae leave at thee."

Janet has kilted her green kirtle
A little aboon her knee,
And she has broded her yellow hair
A little aboon her bree,
And she is to her father's ha,
As fast as she can hie.

Four and twenty ladies fair
Were playing at the ba,
And out then came the fair Janet,
The flower among them a'.

Four and twenty ladies fair
Were playing at the chess,
And out then came the fair Janet,
As green as onie glass.

Out then spake an auld gray knight,
Lay oer the castle wa,
And says, Alas, fair Janet, for thee,
But we'll be blamed a'.

"Haud your tongue, ye auld fac'd
    knight,
Some ill death may ye die!
Father my bairn on whom I will,
I'll father none on thee."

Out then spak her father dear,
And he spak meek and mild,
"And ever alas, sweet Janet," he says,
"I think thou gaest wi child."

"If that I gae wi child, father,
Mysel maun bear the blame,
There's neer a laird about your ha,
Shall get the bairn's name.

"If my love were an earthly knight,
As he's an elfin gray,
I wad na gie my ain true-love
For nae lord that ye hae.
"The steed that my true love rides on
Is lighter than the wind,
Wi siller he is shod before,
Wi burning gowd behind."

Janet has kilted her green kirtle
A little aboon her knee,
And she has broded her yellow hair
A little aboon her bree,
And she's away to Carterhaugh
As fast as she can hie.

When she came to Carterhaugh,
Tam Lin was at the well,
And there she fand his steed standing,
But away was himsel.

She had na pu'd a double rose,
A rose but only twa,
Till up then started young Tam Lin,
Says, Lady, thou pu's nae mae.
"Why pu's thou the rose, Janet,
Amang the groves sae green,
And a' to kill the bonny babe
That we gat us between?"

"O tell me, tell me, Tam Lin," she says,
"For's sake that died on tree,

If eer ye was in holy chapel,
Or christendom did see?"

"Roxbrugh he was my grandfather,
Took me with him to bide
And ance it fell upon a day
That wae did me betide.

"And ance it fell upon a day
A cauld day and a snell,
When we were frae the hunting
    come,
That frae my horse I fell,
The Queen o' Fairies she caught me,
In yon green hill do dwell.

"And pleasant is the fairy land,
But, an eerie tale to tell,
Ay at the end of seven years,
We pay a tiend to hell,
I am sae fair and fu o flesh,
I'm feard it be mysel.

"But the night is Halloween, lady,
The morn is Hallowday,
Then win me, win me, an ye will,
For weel I wat ye may.

"Just at the mirk and midnight hour
The fairy folk will ride,
And they that wad their true-love
    win,
At Miles Cross they maun bide."

"But how shall I thee ken, Tam Lin,
Or how my true-love know,
Amang sa mony unco knights,
The like I never saw?"

"O first let pass the black, lady,
And syne let pass the brown,
But quickly run to the milk-white steed,
Pu ye his rider down.

"For I'll ride on the milk-white steed,
And ay nearest the town,
Because I was an earthly knight
They gie me that renown.

"My right hand will be gloved, lady,
My left hand will be bare,
Cockt up shall my bonnet be,
And kaimed down shall my hair,
And thae's the takens I gie thee,
Nae doubt I will be there.

"They'll turn me in your arms, lady,
Into an esk and adder,
But hold me fast, and fear me not,
I am your bairn's father.

"They'll turn me to a bear sae grim,
And then a lion bold,
But hold me fast, and fear me not,
And ye shall love your child.

"Again they'll turn me in your arms
To a red het gand of airn,
But hold me fast, and fear me not,
I'll do you nae harm.

"And last they'll turn me in your
    arms
Into the burning gleed,
Then throw me into well water,
O throw me in with speed.

"And then I'll be your ain true-love,
I'll turn a naked knight,
Then cover me wi your green mantle,
And hide me out o sight."

Gloomy, gloomy was the night,
And eerie was the way,

As fair Jenny in her green mantle
To Miles Cross she did gae.

At the mirk and midnight hour
She heard the bridles sing,
She was as glad at that
As any earthly thing.

First she let the black pass by,
And syne she let the brown,
But quickly she ran to the milk-white
    steed,
And pu'd the rider down.

Sae weel she minded what he did say,
And young Tam Lin did win,
Syne covered him wi her green mantle,
As blythe's a bird in spring

Out then spak the Queen o Fairies,
Out of a bush o broom,
"Them that has gotten young Tam Lin
Has gotten a stately-groom."

Out then spak the Queen o Fairies,
And an angry woman was she,
"Shame betide her ill-far'd face,
And an ill death may she die,
For she's taen away the bonniest knight
In a' my companie.

"But had I kend, Tam Lin," said she,
"What now this night I see,
I wad hae taen out thy twa grey een,
And put in twa een o tree."

The Smart Man and the Fool

A Fjort (Congolese) Folktale

In the late nineteenth century, English folklorist Richard Edward Dennett collected folktales from the Fjort people of what is now the Republic of the Congo. Dennett recorded both the style of the storytelling and the stories. The style, which incorporates audience participation, is practiced today. The following is an adaptation of Dennett's telling. Note that although the storyteller here is male, Dennett stated that both Fjort men and women told stories.

Imagine, then, a village in a grove of graceful palm trees. The full moon is shining brightly upon a small crowd . . . seated round a fire in an open space in the center of the village. One of them has just told a story, and his delighted audience demands another.

Thus he begins: "Let us tell another story; let us be off!"

All then shout: "Pull away!"

"Let us be off!" he repeats.

And they answer again: "Pull away!"

Then the storyteller commences:

There were two brothers, the Smart Man and the Fool. And it was their habit to go out shooting to keep their parents supplied with food. Thus, one day, they went together into the mangrove swamp, just as the tide was going down, to watch for the fish as they nibbled at the roots of the trees. Fool saw a fish, fired at it, and killed it. Smart Man fired also, but at nothing, and then ran up to Fool and said, "Fool, have you killed anything?"

"Yes, Smart Man, I am a fool, but I killed a fish."

"Indeed, you are a fool," answered Smart Man, "for when I fired I hit the fish that went your way, so that the fish you think you killed is mine. Here, give it to me."

The fool gave Smart Man the fish. Then, they went to their town, and Smart Man, addressing his father, said, "Father, here is a fish that your son shot, but Fool got nothing."

Here the crowd joins in and sings over the last sentence two or three times. Then the narrator continues:

The mother prepared and cooked the fish, and the father and Smart Man ate it, giving none to Fool.

Then they went again. And Fool fired, and with his first shot killed a big fish.

"Did you hear me fire?" said Smart Man.

"No," answered Fool.

"No?" returned Smart Man. "See, then, the fish I killed."

"All right," said Fool, "take the fish."

When they reached home, they gave the fish to their mother, and after she had cooked it, Smart Man and his father ate it, but gave none to Fool. As they were enjoying the fish, a bone stuck in the father's throat. Then Smart Man called to Fool and bade him go for a doctor.

"No," said Fool, "I cannot. I felt that something would happen." And he sang:
"Every day you eat my fish,
You call me Fool,
And would let me starve."

The crowd here joins in, and sings Fool's song over and over again.

"How can you sing?" said Smart Man,
"when you see that our father is
    suffering?"
But Fool went on singing:
"You eat and eat unto repletion;
A bone sticks in your throat;
And now your life is near completion,
The bone is still within your throat.

So you, smart brother, killed the fish,
And gave the fool to eat?
Nay! But now he's dead perhaps you
    wish
You'd given the fool to eat."

The crowd goes on singing this until they are tired; and the storyteller continues:

While Fool was still singing, the father died. Then, the neighbors came and joined the family circle, and asked Fool how it was that he could go on singing now that his father was dead. And Fool answered them, saying: "Our father made us both, one a smart man, the other a fool. The Fool killed the food, and they ate it, giving none to the Fool. They must not blame him, therefore, if he sings while they suffer. He suffered hunger while they had plenty."

And when the people had considered the matter, they gave judgment in favor of the Fool, and departed.

The father died, and so had been justly punished for not having given food to the Fool.

He who eats fish with much oil must suffer from indigestion.

And now I have finished my story.

All answer, "Just so!"
"To-morrow may you chop palm kernels," says the narrator as he gets up and walks away.

The Cauld Lad of Hilton

An English Folktale

In English folklore, a brownie generally is a helpful little spirit, usually male, that will straighten up the house in which he lives with "his" humans—as long as they never thank him or offer him clothes. The brownie in the following tale clearly is fed up with his job and is trying to find a way to convince the humans to get rid of him.

At Hilton Hall, long years ago, there lived a brownie that was the contrariest brownie you ever knew. At night, after the servants had gone to bed, it would turn everything topsy-turvy, put sugar in the salt cellars and pepper into the beer, and was up to all kinds of pranks. It would throw the chairs down, put tables on their backs, rake out fires, and do as much mischief as could be. But sometimes, it would be in a good temper, and then!

"What's a brownie?" you say. Oh, it's a kind of a sort of a bogle, but it isn't so cruel as a redcap! What! You don't know what's a bogle or a redcap! Ah, me! What's the world a-coming to? Of course, a brownie is a funny little thing, half man, half goblin, with pointed ears and a hairy hide. When you bury a treasure, you scatter over it blood drops of a newly slain kid or lamb, or, better still, bury the animal with the treasure, and a brownie will watch over it for you and frighten everybody else away.

Where was I? Well, as I was a-saying, the brownie at Hilton Hall would play at mischief, but if the servants laid out for it a bowl of cream, or a knuckle cake spread with honey, it would clear away things for them, and make everything tidy in the kitchen. One night, however, when the servants had stopped up late, they heard a noise in the kitchen, and, peeping in, they saw the brownie swinging to and fro on the jack chain, and saying:

> *Woe's me! woe's me!*
> *The acorn's not yet*
> *Fallen from the tree,*
> *That's to grow the wood,*
> *That's to make the cradle,*
> *That's to rock the bairn,*
> *That's to grow to the man,*
> *That's to lay me.*
> *Woe's me! Woe's me!*

So they took pity on the poor brownie, and asked the nearest henwife what they should do to send it away. "That's easy enough," said the henwife, and told them that a brownie that's paid for its service, in aught that's not perishable, goes away at once. So they made a cloak of Lincoln green, with a hood to it, and put it by the hearth and watched. They saw the brownie come up, and seeing the hood and cloak, put them on, and frisk about, dancing on one leg and saying:

> *I've taken your cloak, I've taken your hood;*
> *The Cauld Lad of Hilton will do no*
> *   more good.*

And with that, the brownie vanished, and it was never seen or heard of afterward.

551

The Cuckoo

A "Fool" Folktale of Gotham, England

A "fool" folktale is about a foolish but generally endearing person or a town of such people. One such town is Chelm, Poland. Another is Gotham, England, a real town, and one of the mysteries of the folk process is how it became known as a place of foolish people.

Once, in the long-ago days, spring came to the pretty little town of Gotham, England. All the people strolled about the streets, smelling the sweet flowers, feeling the warm air, and listening to the happy songs of the birds.

"Listen to the cuckoo," they said. "How sweetly she sings."

"What a pity she doesn't sing like this all the year round!" they added. "How nice it would be if we could always hear her. It would be like having spring with us all the year round."

Then one of the good folks had an idea. "What if we kept the cuckoo with us always? If we kept the cuckoo with us always, then spring would stay with us all the time, too!"

Spring all the time! How wonderful that sounded to everyone!

But how were they to keep the cuckoo with them? This was a problem, a true problem. The people of Gotham sat and thought about it a long, long time. Then all at once, the wisest of the wise men sprang to his feet.

"I know what we'll do," he cried. "We'll build a wall around the cuckoo. That way she will have to stay with us forever!"

This seemed like a wonderful idea to everyone, a splendid idea indeed! They grabbed bricks and pieces of wood and set about building a wall all around the tree in which the cuckoo sat.

All the while that they worked, the cuckoo kept singing, now and then cocking her head to look down in curiosity at what the humans did. Higher and higher grew the wall, while the cuckoo watched and sang, sang and watched. Higher and higher—

But all at once, the cuckoo grew bored with sitting still. She spread her wings, and of course, she flew lightly right over the top of the wall.

"Oh no!" the people cried. "Alas, alack! We almost had her. It was the wall that was at fault."

"Of course it was the wall," everyone agreed. "It wasn't tall enough! If only we'd built the wall just a little bit higher, the cuckoo would never have been able to fly over it!"

Being the good people of Gotham, not once did one of them ever realize that without a roof, not even the highest wall could hold in a bird!

"If only we had built the wall just a little bit higher," they said again, and sighed. But it was springtime, and the day was so bright and sunny that before long all the good folk of Gotham were smiling again.

Dick Whittington and His Cat

A Medieval Folktale from England

The historic Richard Whittington (c. 1350–1423) was a merchant and the mayor of London during the reign of King Edward III. Although the tale of Whittington and his cat is pure fiction, the story is better known in Great Britain and the United States than is the actual man.

In the reign of the famous King Edward III, there was a little boy called Dick Whittington, whose father and mother died when he was very young. The boy remembered nothing at all about his parents and was left a ragged little fellow running about a country village.

For all this, Dick Whittington was a very sharp boy and was always listening to what everybody talked about. In this manner, Dick heard a great many very strange things about the great city called London, and he finally set out for it.

There, he nearly starved, but he finally found work in the house of a merchant, where he did whatever dirty work he was able for the cook. His bed stood in a garret, where there were so many holes in the floor and the walls that every night he was tormented by rats and mice. A gentleman gave Dick a penny for cleaning his shoes, so the boy bought a cat and, in a short time, had no more trouble with the rats and mice.

Soon after this, the master had a ship ready to sail, and as he thought it right that all his servants should have some chance for good fortune as well as for himself, he asked them all what they would send out. Poor Dick had nothing but his cat, which he sent on to find its fortune.

Now, Dick was more miserable than before. He decided to run away. So he packed up his few things and started very early in the morning, on All Hallow's Day, which is the first of November. The boy walked as far as Holloway, and there sat down on a stone, which to this day is called Whittington's stone, and began to think to himself which road he should take as he proceeded onward.

While he was thinking what he should do, the bells of Bow Church in London began to ring, and he fancied their sound seemed to say to him:

Turn again, Whittington
Lord Mayor of London.

He listened, and returned to London.

Meanwhile, the ship, with the cat on board, was a long time at sea. It was at last driven by the winds on a part of the coast of Barbary. The people treated the sailors very civilly and were very eager to buy the fine things that the ship had on board.

The captain was invited to the royal palace. But there he saw rats and mice everywhere, and the king and queen were quite unhappy about it. This land had no cats! So the captain hastily told the king he had a creature on board the ship that would dispatch all these vermin immediately. The king promised to load the ship with gold and jewels in exchange for the wonder.

Sure enough, the cat took care of the rats and mice, and the captain sailed with a fair wind for England. The ship arrived safely in

London with the load of gold and jewels. The honest merchant promptly sent for Dick, who was overwhelmed by his sudden good fortune.

In time, history tells, Dick Whittington did, indeed, become mayor of London and was knighted by King Henry V. The carved figure of Sir Richard Whittington with his cat in his arms was to be seen until the year 1780 over the archway of the old prison of Newgate.

Fire! Fire! Burn Stick!

A Cumulative Folktale from England

"Fire! Fire! Burn Stick!" is a classic example of a cumulative tale from England. Elements are added as the story progresses. Then, the elements are removed until nothing but the happy ending is left.

An old woman was sweeping her house, and she found a little crooked sixpence. "What," said she, "shall I do with this little sixpence? I will go to market and buy a little pig." As she was coming home, she came to a stile; the piggy would not go over the stile.

She went a little farther, and she met a dog. So she said to the dog, "Dog! Dog! Bite pig; piggy won't get over the stile, and I shan't get home tonight." But the dog would not.

She went a little farther, and she met a stick. So she said, "Stick! Stick! Beat dog; dog won't bite pig, piggy won't get over the stile, and I shan't get home tonight." But the stick would not.

She went a little farther, and she met a fire. So she said, "Fire! Fire! Burn stick; stick won't beat dog, dog won't bite pig, piggy won't get over the stile, and I shan't get home tonight." But the fire would not.

She went a little farther, and she met some water. So she said, "Water! Water! Quench fire; fire won't burn stick, stick won't beat dog, dog won't bite pig, piggy won't get over the stile, and I shan't get home tonight." But the water would not.

She went a little farther, and she met an ox. So she said, "Ox! Ox! Drink water; water won't quench fire, fire won't burn stick, stick won't beat dog, dog won't bite pig, piggy won't get over the stile, and I shan't get home tonight." But the ox would not.

She went a little farther, and she met a butcher. So she said, "Butcher! Butcher! Kill ox; ox won't drink water, water won't quench fire, fire won't burn stick, stick won't beat dog, dog won't bite pig, piggy won't get over the stile, and I shan't get home tonight." But the butcher would not.

She went a little farther, and she met a rope. So she said, "Rope! Rope! Hang butcher; butcher won't kill ox, ox won't drink water, water won't quench fire, fire won't burn stick, stick won't beat dog, dog won't bite pig, piggy won't get over the stile, and I shan't get home tonight." But the rope would not.

So she went a little farther, and she met a rat. So she said, "Rat! Rat! Gnaw rope; rope won't hang butcher, butcher won't kill ox, ox won't drink water, water won't quench fire, fire won't burn stick, stick won't beat dog, dog won't bite pig, piggy won't get over the stile, and I shan't get home tonight." But the rat would not.

So she went a little farther, and she met a cat. So she said, "Cat! Cat! Kill rat; rat won't gnaw rope, rope won't hang butcher, butcher won't kill ox, ox won't drink water, water won't quench fire, fire won't burn stick, stick won't beat dog, dog won't bite pig, piggy won't get over the stile, and I shan't get home tonight." But the cat said to her, "If you will go to yonder cow and fetch me a saucer of milk, I will kill the rat."

So away went the old woman to the cow. But the cow said to her, "If you will go to yonder haystack and fetch me a handful of hay, I'll give you the milk."

So away went the old woman to the haystack, and she brought the hay to the cow.

As soon as the cow had eaten the hay, she gave the old woman the milk, and away the old woman went with it in a saucer to the cat.

As soon as the cat had lapped up the milk, the cat began to kill the rat, the rat began to gnaw the rope, the rope began to hang the butcher, the butcher began to kill the ox, the ox began to drink the water, the water began to quench the fire, the fire began to burn the stick, the stick began to beat the dog, the dog began to bite the pig, the little pig in a fright jumped over the stile, and so the old woman got home that night.

The Gingerbread Boy

An English Folktale

While this particular version of "The Gingerbread Boy" is from England, the story of the runaway gingerbread boy—or man, or animated pancake—also can be found in other countries, including India. In all versions, the tale ends badly for the animated food, which gets eaten.

There was once a little old man and a little old woman who lived in a little old house at the edge of a wood. They would have been a very happy old couple but for one thing— they had no little child, and they wished for one very much. One day, when the little old woman was baking gingerbread, she cut a cake in the shape of a little boy and put it into the oven.

Presently, she went to the oven to see if the cake was baked. As soon as the oven door was opened, the little gingerbread boy jumped out and began to run away as fast as he could go.

The little old woman called her husband, and they both ran after him. But they could not catch him. And soon, the gingerbread boy came to a barn full of threshers. He called out to them as he went by, saying:

I've run away from a little old woman,
A little old man,
And I can run away from you, I can!

Then, the barn full of threshers set out to run after him. But though they ran fast, they could not catch him. And he ran on, till he came to a field full of mowers. He called out to them:

I've run away from a little old woman,
A little old man,
A barn full of threshers,
And I can run away from you, I can!

Then, the mowers began to run after him, but they couldn't catch him. And he ran on, till he came to a cow. He called out to her:

I've run away from a little old
    woman,
A little old man,
A barn full of threshers,
A field full of mowers,
And I can run away from you, I can!

But though the cow started at once, she couldn't catch him. And soon, he came to a pig. He called out to the pig:

I've run away from a little old
    woman,
A little old man,
A barn full of threshers,
A field full of mowers,
A cow,
And I can run away from you, I can!

But the pig ran and couldn't catch him. And he ran on, till he came across a fox, and to him he called out:

I've run away from a little old woman,
A little old man,
A barn full of threshers,
A field full of mowers,
A cow and a pig,
And I can run away from you, I can!

Then, the fox set out to run. Now, foxes can run very fast, and so the fox soon caught the gingerbread boy and began to eat him up.

Presently, the gingerbread boy said, "Oh dear! I'm quarter gone!" And then, "Oh, I'm half gone!" And soon, "I'm three-quarters gone!"

And, at the very last, with the fox's final bite, the gingerbread boy said, "I'm all gone!" and he never spoke again.

A Grain of Corn

A Cumulative Folktale from England

"A Grain of Corn" is a cumulative tale and rhyme from the English countryside. Like many of these types of tales and rhymes, it shows the standard threats of violence but manages at the end to skirt any actual killings.

Once upon a time, a farmer's wife was winnowing corn, when a crow, flying past, swooped off with a grain from the winnowing basket and perched on a tree close by to eat it. The farmer's wife, greatly enraged, flung a clod of dirt at the bird with such good aim that the crow fell to the ground and dropped the grain of corn, which rolled into a crack in the tree.

The farmer's wife, seeing the crow fall, ran up to it and seized it by the tail, crying, "Give me back my grain of corn, or I will kill you!"

The wretched bird, in fear of death, promised to do so, but when he searched for the grain, it had rolled so far into the crack that by neither beak nor claw could he reach it.

So he flew off to a woodman, and said:

> Man! Man! Cut tree;
> I can't get the grain of corn
> To save my life from the farmer's wife!

But the woodman refused to cut the tree; so the crow flew on to the king's palace, and said:

> King! King! Kill man;
> Man won't cut tree;
> I can't get the grain of corn
> To save my life from the farmer's wife!

But the king refused to kill the man; so the crow flew on to the queen, and said:

> Queen! Queen! Coax king;
> King won't kill man;
> Man won't cut tree.

> I can't get the grain of corn
> To save my life from the farmer's wife!

But the queen refused to coax the king; so the crow flew on till he met a snake, and said:

> Snake! Snake! Bite queen;
> Queen won't coax king;
> King won't kill man;
> Man won't cut tree;
> I can't get the grain of corn
> To save my life from the farmer's wife!

But the snake refused to bite the queen; so the crow flew on till he met a stick, and said:

> Stick! Stick! Beat snake;
> Snake won't bite queen;
> Queen won't coax king;
> King won't kill man:
> Man won't cut tree;
> I can't get the grain of corn
> To save my life from the farmer's wife!

But the stick refused to beat the snake; so the crow flew on till he saw a fire, and said:

> Fire! Fire! Burn stick;
> Stick won't beat snake;
> Snake won't bite queen;
> Queen won't coax king;
> King won't kill man;
> Man won't cut tree;
> I can't get the grain of corn
> To save my life from the farmer's wife!

But the fire refused to burn the stick; so the crow flew on till he met some water, and said:

> Water! Water! Quench fire;
> Fire won't burn stick;
> Stick won't beat snake;
> Snake won't bite queen;
> Queen won't coax king;
> King won't kill man;
> Man won't cut tree;
> I can't get the grain of corn
> To save my life from the farmer's wife!

But the water refused to quench the fire; so the crow flew on till he met an ox, and said:

> Ox! Ox! Drink water;
> Water won't quench fire;
> Fire won't burn stick;
> Stick won't beat snake;
> Snake won't bite queen;
> Queen won't coax king;
> King won't kill man;
> Man won't cut tree;
> I can't get the grain of corn
> To save my life from the farmer's wife!

But the ox refused to drink the water; so the crow flew on till he met a rope, and said:

> Rope! Rope! Bind ox;
> Ox won't drink water;
> Water won't quench fire;
> Fire won't burn stick;
> Stick won't beat snake;
> Snake won't bite queen;
> Queen won't coax king;
> King won't kill man;
> Man won't cut tree;
> I can't get the grain of corn
> To save my life from the farmer's wife!

But the rope wouldn't bind the ox; so the crow flew on till he met a mouse, and said:

> Mouse! Mouse! Gnaw rope;
> Rope won't bind ox;

> Ox won't drink water;
> Water won't quench fire;
> Fire won't burn stick;
> Stick won't beat snake;
> Snake won't bite queen;
> Queen won't coax king;
> King won't kill man;
> Man won't cut tree;
> I can't get the grain of corn
> To save my life from the farmer's wife!

But the mouse wouldn't gnaw the rope; so the crow flew on until he met a cat, and said:

> Cat! Cat! Catch mouse;
> Mouse won't gnaw rope;
> Rope won't bind ox;
> Ox won't drink water;
> Water won't quench fire;
> Fire won't burn stick;
> Stick won't beat snake;
> Snake won't bite queen;
> Queen won't coax king;
> King won't kill man;
> Man won't cut tree;
> And I can't get the grain of corn
> To save my life from the farmer's wife!

The moment the cat heard the name of mouse, she was after it; for the world will come to an end, before a cat will leave a mouse alone.

> So the cat began to catch the mouse,
> The mouse began to gnaw the rope,
> The rope began to bind the ox,
> The ox began to drink the water,
> The water began to quench the fire,
> The fire began to burn the stick,
> The stick began to beat the snake,
> The snake began to bite the queen,
> The queen began to coax the king,
> The king began to kill the man,
> The man began to cut the tree;
> So the crow got the grain of corn,
> And saved his life from the farmer's
>   wife!

The Sorcerer's Apprentice

An English Version of a World Folktale

"The Sorcerer's Apprentice," a world folktale, may be most familiar to modern story-tellers from Walt Disney's *Fantasia* (1940). However, the tale turns up in various versions from Egypt, most of Europe, and much of Asia. Sometimes, the conjuration is of an inanimate object, such as a broom; other times, the apprentice conjures a more dangerous being, such as a devil.

The following is an English version, as collected at the turn of the twentieth century by English folklorist Joseph Jacobs. It shows that a little learning can, indeed, be a dangerous thing.

There was once a very learned man in the north country who knew all the languages under the Sun, and who was acquainted with all the mysteries of creation. He had one big book bound in black calfskin and clasped with iron, and with iron corners, and chained to a table that was made fast to the floor. When he read out of this book, he unlocked it with an iron key, and none but he read from it, for it contained all the secrets of the spiritual world.

The book told how many angels there were in heaven, and how they marched in their ranks, and sang in their choirs, and what were their several functions, and what was the name of each great angel of might. And it told of the demons, how many of them there were, and what were their several powers, and their labors, and their names, and how they might be summoned, and how tasks might be imposed on them, and how they might be chained to be as slaves to man.

Now, the master had a pupil who was but a foolish lad. He acted as servant to the great master, but never was he suffered to look into the black book, hardly to enter the private room.

One day, the master was out. Then, the lad, as curious as could be, hurried to the chamber where his master kept his wondrous apparatus for changing copper into gold, and lead into silver, and where he kept his mirror in which he could see all that was passing in the world, and where he stored the shell which when held to the ear whispered all the words that were being spoken by anyone the master desired to know about.

The lad tried in vain with the crucibles to turn copper and lead into gold and silver. He looked long and vainly into the mirror; smoke and clouds passed over it, but he saw nothing plain. And the shell to his ear produced only indistinct murmurings, like the breaking of distant seas on an unknown shore. "I can do nothing," he said, "as I don't know the right words to utter, and they are locked up in yon book."

He looked round, and, see! The book was unfastened; the master had forgotten to lock it before he went out. The boy rushed to it and opened the volume. It was written with red and black ink, and much of it he could not understand; but he put his finger on a line and spelled it out.

At once, the room was darkened, and the house trembled; a clap of thunder rolled through the passage and the old room, and there stood before him a horrible, horrible form, breathing fire, and with eyes like burning lamps. It was the demon Beelzebub, whom he had called up to serve him.

"Set me a task!" said he, with a voice like the roaring of an iron furnace.

The boy only trembled, and his hair stood up.

"Set me a task, or I shall strangle thee!"

But the lad could not speak. Then the evil spirit stepped toward him, and putting forth his hands touched his throat. The fingers burned his flesh. "Set me a task!"

"Water yon flower," cried the boy in despair, pointing to a geranium that stood in a pot on the floor. Instantly, the spirit left the room, but in another instant, he returned with a barrel on his back, and poured its contents over the flower. Again and again, he went and came, and poured more and more water, till the water on the floor of the room was ankle deep.

"Enough; enough!" gasped the lad, but the demon heeded him not; the lad didn't know the words by which to send him away, and still the demon fetched water.

It rose to the boy's knees, and still more water was poured. It mounted to his waist, and Beelzebub still kept on bringing barrels full. It rose to his armpits, and he scrambled to the tabletop. And now, the water in the room stood up to the window and washed against the glass, and swirled around his feet on the table. It still rose; it reached his breast.

In vain, the boy cried; the evil spirit would not be dismissed, and, to this day, he would have been pouring water, and would have drowned all Yorkshire. But the master remembered on his journey that he had not locked his book, and therefore returned. At the moment when the water was bubbling about the pupil's chin, the master rushed into the room and spoke the words that cast Beelzebub back into his fiery home.

Tom Thumb's Adventures

A Medieval English Folktale

The folktale of Tom Thumb first appeared in print in the seventeenth century in both England and in a French version by the writer Charles Perrault. But the original story goes back in less complete form to at least the sixteenth century.

It is said that in the days of the famed Prince Arthur, who was king of Britain in the year 516, there lived a great magician, called Merlin, the most learned and skillful enchanter in the world at that time.

This great magician, who could assume any form he pleased, was traveling in the disguise of a poor beggar. Being very much fatigued, he stopped at the cottage of an honest plowman to rest himself, and asked for some refreshment.

The countryman gave the magician a hearty welcome. His wife, who was a very good-hearted, hospitable woman, soon brought him some milk in a wooden bowl and some coarse brown bread on a platter.

Merlin was much pleased with this homely repast and the kindness of the plowman and his wife, but he could not help seeing that though everything was neat and comfortable in the cottage, they seemed to be sad and much cast down. He therefore questioned them on the cause of their sadness and learned they were miserable because they had no children.

The poor woman declared, with tears in her eyes, that she should be the happiest creature in the world if she had a son. Even if he was no bigger than her husband's thumb, she would be satisfied.

Merlin was so much amused with the idea of a boy no bigger than a man's thumb that he made up his mind to pay a visit to the queen of the fairies and ask her to grant the poor woman's wish. The droll fancy of such a little person among the human race pleased the fairy queen, too, and she promised Merlin that the wish would be granted. A short time afterward, the plowman's wife had a son, who, wonderful to relate, was no bigger than his father's thumb.

The fairy queen, wishing to see the little fellow thus born into the world, came in at the window while the mother was sitting up in bed admiring him. The queen kissed the child, and, giving him the name of Tom Thumb, sent for some of the fairies, who dressed her little favorite as she bade them.

An oak-leaf hat he had for his crown;
His shirt of web by spiders spun;
With jacket wove of thistle's down;
His trousers were of feathers done.
His stockings, of apple-rind they tie
With eyelash from his mother's eye:
His shoes were made of mouse's skin
Tann'd with the downy hair within.

It is remarkable that Tom never grew any larger than his father's thumb, which was only of an ordinary size; but as he got older, he became very cunning and full of tricks. When he was old enough to play with the boys, and had lost all his own cherrystones, he used to creep into the bags of his playfellows, fill his pockets, and, getting out unseen, again join in the game.

One day, however, as he was coming out of a bag of cherrystones, where he had been pilfering as usual, the boy to whom it belonged chanced to see him. "Aha, my little Tommy," said the boy. "So I have caught you stealing my cherrystones at last, and you shall be rewarded for your thievish tricks." On saying this, he drew the string tight around Tom's neck and gave the bag such a hearty shake that poor little Tom's legs, thighs, and body were sadly bruised. Tom roared out in pain and begged to be let out, promising never to be guilty of such bad practices again.

A short time afterward, his mother was making a batter pudding, and Tom, being very anxious to see how it was made, climbed up to the edge of the bowl. Unfortunately, his foot slipped, and he plumped over, unseen by his mother, head and ears into the batter. His mother stirred him into the pudding bag and put him in the pot to boil.

The batter had filled Tom's mouth and prevented him from crying out; but, on feeling the hot water, he kicked and struggled so much in the pot that his mother thought that the pudding was bewitched. Instantly, she pulled it out of the pot and threw it to the door. A poor tinker was passing by, spied the pudding, lifted it up, put it into his budget (bag), and walked off. As Tom had now got his mouth cleared of the batter, he began to cry aloud, which so frightened the tinker that he flung down the pudding and ran away.

The pudding having broken to pieces by the fall, Tom crept out covered over with the batter, and with difficulty he walked home. His mother, who was very sorry to see her darling in such a woeful state, put him into a teacup, and soon washed off the batter, after which, she kissed him and laid him in bed.

Soon after the adventure of the pudding, Tom's mother went to milk her cow in the meadow, and she took Tom along with her. As the wind was very high, fearing lest he should be blown away, she tied him to a thistle with a piece of fine thread. The cow soon saw the oak-leaf hat, and, liking the look of it, took poor Tom and the thistle at one mouthful. While the cow was chewing the thistle, Tom was afraid of her great teeth, which threatened to crush him to pieces, and he roared out as loud as he could, "Mother! Mother!"

"Where are you, Tommy, my dear Tommy?" cried his mother.

"Here, mother," replied he, "in the red cow's mouth."

His mother began to cry and wring her hands; but the cow, surprised at the odd noise in her throat, opened her mouth and let Tom drop out. Fortunately, Tom's mother caught him in her apron as he was falling to the ground, or he would have been dreadfully hurt. She then put Tom in her bosom and ran home with him.

Tom's father made him a whip of barley straw to drive the cattle with. One day, Tom went into the fields, but his foot slipped, and he rolled into a furrow. A raven that was flying overhead picked him up, flew with him to the top of a giant's castle that was near the seaside, and left him there.

Tom was in a dreadful state and did not know what to do; but he was soon even more dreadfully frightened, for old Grumbo, the giant, came up to walk on the terrace, and seeing Tom, he took him up and swallowed him like a pill. The giant had no sooner swallowed Tom, than he began to repent what he had done, for Tom began to kick and jump about so much that Grumbo felt very uncomfortable, and at last threw him up into the sea.

A large fish swallowed Tom the moment he fell into the sea, but the fish was caught soon after and was bought for the table of King Arthur. When the fish was opened to be cooked, everyone was astonished to find such a little boy, and Tom was quite delighted to be out again. They carried him to the king, who made Tom his dwarf.

Tom soon became a great favorite at court, for by his tricks and gambols he amused not only the king and queen, but also all the Knights of the Round Table. It is said that when the king rode out on horseback, he often took Tom along with him, and if a shower came on, Tom used to creep into His Majesty's waistcoat pocket, where he slept till the rain shower was over.

One day, King Arthur asked Tom about his parents, wishing to know if they were as small as he was, and whether they were rich or poor. Tom told the king that his father and mother were as tall as any of the persons about the court, but rather poor. On hearing this, the king carried Tom to the treasure, the place where he kept all his money, and told him to take as much money as he could carry home to his parents, which made the poor little fellow caper with joy. Tom went immediately to fetch a purse, which was made of a water bubble, and then returned to the treasury, where he got a silver threepenny piece to put into it.

Our little hero had some trouble in lifting the burden upon his back, but he at last succeeded in getting it placed to his satisfaction, and set forward on his journey. Without meeting with any accidents, and after resting himself more than a hundred times by the way, in two days and two nights, he reached his father's house in safety. Tom had traveled forty-eight hours with a huge silver piece on his back, and was almost tired to death when his mother ran out to meet him and carried him into the house.

Tom's parents were both happy to see him, and the more so as he had brought such an amazing sum of money with him, but the poor little fellow was excessively wearied, having traveled a half mile in forty-eight hours, with a huge silver threepenny piece on his back. His mother, in order to revive him, placed him in a walnut shell by the fireside, and feasted him for three days on a hazelnut, which made him very sick, for a whole nut used to serve him for a month.

Tom was soon well again, but as there had been a fall of rain, and the ground was very wet, he could not travel back to King Arthur's court; therefore, his mother, one day when the wind was blowing in that direction, made a little parasol of cambric paper and tied Tom to it. She gave him a puff into the air with her mouth, and he was soon carried on the wind to the king's palace.

Just at the time when Tom came flying across the courtyard, the cook happened to be passing with the king's great bowl of furmenty, which was a dish His Majesty was very fond of. Unfortunately, the poor little fellow fell plump into the middle of it, and splashed the hot furmenty about the cook's face.

The cook, who was an ill-natured fellow, being in a terrible rage at Tom for frightening and scalding him with the furmenty, went straight to the king and said that Tom had jumped into the royal furmenty and thrown it down out of mere mischief. The king was so enraged when he heard this that he ordered Tom to be seized and tried for high treason. There being no person who dared to plead for Tom, he was condemned to be beheaded immediately.

On hearing this dreadful sentence pronounced, poor Tom fell a-trembling with fear, but, seeing no means of escape, and observing a miller close to him gaping with his great mouth, as country boobies do at a fair, he took a leap, and fairly jumped down the miller's throat. This exploit was done with such agility that not one person present saw it, and even the miller did not know the trick that Tom had played upon him. Now, as Tom had disappeared, the court broke up, and the miller went home to his mill.

When Tom heard the mill at work, he knew he was clear of the court, and therefore he began to tumble and roll about, so that the poor miller could get no rest, thinking he was bewitched, so he sent for a doctor. When the doctor came, Tom began to dance and sing, and the doctor, being as much frightened as the miller, sent in haste for five other doctors and twenty learned men.

While they were debating this extraordinary case, the miller happened to yawn. Tom, seizing the chance, made another jump and alighted safely upon his feet in the middle of the table.

The miller, who was very much provoked at being tormented by such a little pygmy creature, fell into a terrible rage, and, laying hold of Tom, ran to the king with him; but His Majesty, being engaged with state affairs, ordered him to be taken away and kept in custody till he sent for him.

The cook was determined that Tom should not slip out of his hands this time, so he put him into a mousetrap and left him to peep through the wires. Tom had remained in the trap a whole week when he was sent for by King Arthur, who pardoned him for throwing down the furmenty, and took him again into favor.

On account of his wonderful feats of activity, Tom was knighted by the king, and went under the name of the renowned Sir Thomas Thumb. As Tom's clothes had suffered much in the batter pudding, the furmenty, and the insides of the giant, fish, and miller, his majesty ordered him a new suit of clothes, and decreed that he be made a knight.

Of Butterfly's wings his shirt was made,
His boots of chicken's hide;
And by a nimble fairy blade,
Well learned in the tailoring trade,
His clothing was supplied.
A needle dangled by his side;
A dapper mouse he used to ride,
Thus strutted Tom in stately pride!

It was certainly very diverting to see Tom in this dress, and mounted on the mouse, as he rode out a-hunting with the king and nobility, who were all ready to expire with laughter at Tom and his fine prancing charger.

One day, as they were riding by a farmhouse, a large cat, which was lurking about the door, made a spring, and seized both Tom and his mouse. She then ran up a tree with them and was beginning to devour the mouse. Tom boldly drew his sword and attacked the cat so fiercely that she let them both fall. One of the nobles caught him in his hat and laid him on a bed of down in a little ivory cabinet.

The queen of fairies came soon after to pay Tom a visit, and carried him back to Fairyland, where he lived for several years. During his residence there, King Arthur and all the persons who knew Tom had died, and as he was desirous of being again at court, the fairy queen, after dressing him in a suit of clothes, sent him flying through the air to the palace, in the days of King Thunstone, Arthur's successor. Everyone flocked around to see him, and being carried to the king, he was asked who he was, whence he came, and where he lived. Tom answered:

My name is Tom Thumb,
From the fairies I've come.
When King Arthur shone,
His court was my home.
In me he delighted,
By him I was knighted;
Did you never hear of Sir Thomas
    Thumb?

The king was so charmed with this address that he ordered a little chair to be made, in order that Tom might sit upon his table, and also a palace of gold that was to be a span high with a door an inch wide for Sir Tom to live in. He also gave him a coach, drawn by six small mice.

The queen was so enraged at the honor paid to Sir Thomas that she resolved to ruin him, so she told the king that the little knight had been saucy to her.

The king sent for Tom in great haste. Tom was fully aware of the danger of royal anger, so he crept into an empty snail shell and lay for a long time, until he was almost starved with hunger. When at last he ventured to peep out, he saw a fine large butterfly on the ground, near his hiding place. Tom approached very cautiously and climbed astride it, and he was immediately carried up into the air. The butterfly flew with him from tree to tree and from field to field, and at last returned to the court, where the king and nobility all strove to catch him. At last, poor Tom fell from his seat into a watering pot, in which he was almost drowned.

When the queen saw him, she was in a rage and said he should be beheaded; and he was again put into a mousetrap until the time of his execution.

However, a cat, observing something alive in the trap, patted it about till the wires broke, which set Tom free.

The king again received Tom into favor, but Tom did not live to enjoy it. For a large spider one day attacked him, and although Tom drew his sword and fought well, the spider's poisonous breath at last overcame him: "He fell dead on the ground where he stood, and the spider suck'd every drop of his blood."

King Thunstone and his whole court were so sorry at the loss of their little favorite that they went into mourning and raised a fine white marble monument over his grave with the following epitaph:

Here lies Tom Thumb, King Arthur's
knight,
Who died by a spider's cruel bite.
He was well-known in Arthur's court,
Where he afforded gallant sport;
He rode at tilt and tournament,
And on a mouse a-hunting went.
Alive he filled the court with mirth;
His death to sorrow soon gave birth.
Wipe, wipe your eyes, and shake your
head,
And cry,—Alas! Tom Thumb is dead!

Virgil the Magician

A Medieval English Folktale

Virgil the magician is actually the first-century C.E. Roman poet Virgil, author of the epic *Aeneid*. Why folk belief gradually turned a poet into a master magician is not known, but by the time of the Middle Ages, a series of folktales had evolved that feature him.

Some say that Virgil was the son of a nobleman; others say nothing about his rank at all. But all the tales agree that Virgil started his life as an ordinary boy, without a trace of magic but with a quick, inquiring mind.

One day, bored with his schoolwork since he had already outpaced all his teachers, he went walking in the wild hills, where he discovered a dark, mysterious cave and plunged inside to explore.

Virgil had gone quite a way into the cave, and was beginning to wonder if he shouldn't turn around while he could still find his way out, when he heard a cold voice whispering his name.

"Virgil . . . Virgil . . ."

"Who is it? Who calls?"

"Look, Virgil," the voice whispered. "Do you see the round stone set in the floor?"

By now, the boy's eyes had grown accustomed to the dim light filtering in from outside through cracks in the rock. "I see it," he said warily, "and the bolt holding it in place."

"I am trapped beneath that stone. Free me, Virgil."

"Not so quickly. First, who and what are you?"

"I am a mighty spirit," the cold voice whispered, "trapped under here till doomsday. Free me, Virgil, and I will give you books to make you the mightiest of all magicians."

That sounded intriguing to Virgil. But the boy wasn't about to act so trustingly, not when what was almost certainly an evil spirit was involved. "Not so quickly," he said. "First give me the books. Then I will free you."

The spirit ranted for a bit, but what choice was there? "The books are hidden behind rocks to your left and right," the cold voice whispered.

Sure enough, they were. A glance through them sent excitement racing through Virgil, for they were full of marvels.

But now he must free the spirit. Virgil pulled the bolt and stone aside, revealing a small opening. A great dark shape swirled up out of it, filling the cave in a moment, and the boy fell back against a rock. No doubt about what he had just released! He could feel evil whirling around that shape like a cold, cold mist.

But Virgil was ready. "You lied!" he said in seeming contempt. "You are no mighty spirit at all!"

"What's this? What's this? I *am* mighty, boy! I will show you just how great my powers are!"

Virgil only yawned. "Nonsense. No mighty spirit could ever have fit through such a tiny opening."

"I did! I did!"

"Bah. I don't believe you. You are nothing but a fraud."

"Why, you foolish little worm of a boy! Watch this!"

The evil spirit swirled back down into the opening. Virgil quickly replaced the stone, bolting it back in place. "You are the fool, spirit, not me. Stay there, you evil thing, as it was meant to be. Stay there till doomsday!"

He took the magic books and left. Alone in the hills, Virgil hungrily began his magical studies. The days turned to months, and the months to years—ten years in all. At the end of those years, even though he was still a young man, Virgil had become a true magician.

But then he received a desperate message from his widowed mother. While he had been lost in the study of wonders, she had been slowly cheated by the rich relatives of her deceased husband. Now, she was at the edge of poverty.

Virgil hurried home, abashed that with all his magic, he had never realized his mother's peril. "But now I shall set things to rights," he assured her.

At first, he decided against using magic. Surely, such arts were not needed here! But the rich relatives merely shook their heads at his protests, claiming that they had taken no more than their just due. And when Virgil appealed to the emperor of Rome, he received not a word of satisfaction.

"We shall," the emperor's message read, "take the matter under advisement. It shall take years to check every record."

"The emperor," Virgil translated drily, "has been getting a percentage of the stolen profits from our relatives. Well, now, I can play games, too."

When the emperor's tax collectors came to claim the royal share of profits due from the corn harvest, Virgil shrugged. "Do you see any corn?"

He had, of course, hidden it all by magic. "Then we shall tax the profits from your wine harvest," the tax collectors decided.

Virgil shrugged. "Do you see any grapes?"

He'd hidden all the grapes away by magic, too. No matter what the tax collectors tried to tax, Virgil had hidden it away. At last, muttering angrily, they returned to court.

"You shouldn't have made an enemy of the emperor," Virgil's mother warned.

"He shouldn't have made an enemy of me!" the magician replied.

Sure enough, the emperor declared Virgil a rebel, and sent soldiers to besiege his castle. But Virgil cast a mighty spell that froze the soldiers in their tracks like so many statues. He left them there all day in warning. When he let them go again, the soldiers fled without a word.

"You cowards!" the emperor raged at them. "Are you afraid of one man?"

Yes, after spending that time as statues, they certainly were! But one didn't admit such things to the emperor.

The emperor sent a whole army after Virgil. But Virgil cast a mighty spell that created the illusion of an icy, raging river before them and a river behind them, trapping the army on a narrow strip of land. There, they stayed all day and night with no food or drink, smelling the delicious scents of roasting meat coming from the castle and hearing the sound of happy laughter.

One soldier, however, had been lagging behind and hadn't been caught by either river. He rode at full tilt for Rome and cried out to the emperor, "Your army is trapped and starving because of Virgil's magic!"

The emperor set out with every court magician he could find. Together, they all cast a sleep spell—and it caught Virgil off guard. His servants fell instantly asleep, and he managed to stay awake only by fighting the spell with all his will. Mind foggy and hands feeling heavier than stone, Virgil struggled to open his magic books, slowly turning page after page to find the spell he wanted.

Yes! Here it was, "Battling the Sleep Spell." Virgil shouted out a fierce word of power. Instantly, the sleep spell recoiled on the court magicians, and they fell fast asleep, while all of Virgil's men awoke.

The illusion of the two rivers was broken and vanished—but the emperor's soldiers and even the emperor himself were turned into living statues. There they were and there they stayed for a full two days.

On the morning of the third day, Virgil canceled his spell. The emperor and his soldiers became living folk once more. The emperor wisely sued for peace. He repaid Virgil's mother all the money owed to her and punished the rich relatives who had cheated her.

"Will you be my court magician?" he asked Virgil.

Virgil knew that the emperor feared him. Fearful men never trust those who frighten them. But at least as court magician, he would know more easily if another attack on him or his people was planned. "I will," he agreed. "But I will not live in your palace. That would be too dangerous for your people when I work my magical experiments."

This was perfectly true. The emperor gave Virgil permission to build a fine castle for himself. Virgil's Castle of Eggs was, of course, magical. It was called this because its foundation rested on eggs, and nothing more solid than that. Virgil also built a tower for the emperor from which he could overhear any words of treason. And if there wasn't exactly peace between Virgil and the emperor, neither was there war.

There was another matter in which Virgil was not so successful. Magician or no, he was still human, young, and romantic. Alas, his magic frightened away the young women at court, and some of them mocked him. His anger at that mockery only made matters worse. Lonely because of all his powers, Virgil thought he would never find true love.

But then, traveling the world by magic, he landed in a beautiful garden by moonlight and came face-to-face with a young woman wandering alone. Virgil fell in love with her on the spot. And, more wonderful than any magic, so did she fall instantly in love with him.

"But you must not stay here!" she cried. "My father is the sultan of Babylon, and if he finds you here, he will slay you!"

"I'm not afraid, Princess. I am Virgil the magician. Let me show you the wonders of my castle."

To his delight, she had no fear of his magic. She gladly flew with him and wandered with him through his castle's halls and gardens, and they were joyous in each other's company. But at sunrise, Virgil returned her to her father's palace.

"Will you come to me tomorrow?" the princess asked.

"I will," Virgil promised, "though all your father's guards should block my path."

Alas, a servant heard and raced off to the sultan. "Your daughter has allowed a—a sorcerer to visit her!"

The sultan slipped a powerful sleeping potion into some wine and left it where his daughter was sure to find it and give it to her mysterious guest. So she did, and Virgil fell into a deep, drugged sleep.

He woke to find himself in prison, and the princess chained in there as well. "You have betrayed me!" the sultan shouted at them. "You have both brought dishonor to my name!"

"I have done nothing dishonorable," Virgil protested, "and neither has your daughter. This I swear on my magic."

"The oath of a sorcerer is worthless! And the fate of a sorcerer is the stake and the flame! You shall die this very day at sunrise."

"Then I shall die as well!" the princess cried.

"So you shall," the sultan said coldly. "He has corrupted you with his darkness."

The dawn came. Virgil and the princess were led to the stake, which was piled high with dry wood. But Virgil showed not the slightest sign of fear. He was waiting for the moment when the guards would release his chains so that they could bind him to the stake. For that instant, he would be free!

When the moment arrived, Virgil flung up his arms and shouted out a word of power. Suddenly, everyone there, all save Virgil and the princess, thought that a great flood had roared down upon them. They all began frantically trying to swim.

"Hurry," Virgil whispered to the princess, "before they realize this is only illusion. Will you come with me? Will you wed me?"

"Yes and yes," the princess told him.

The two of them flew magically away from Babylon to Virgil's castle. There, they were wed, and there, they lived in joy and magic for the rest of their lives.

The Laplander Wizard

An Estonian Folktale of a Magician

Laplanders—or more properly, Saami, as they prefer to be called—are fair-haired, fair-skinned people, an ancient race of nomadic reindeer-herders who live in the northern reaches of Scandinavia, Finland, and Russia. There was a long-standing belief in Teutonic and Slavic countries that the Saami, particularly those who lived among the darker Finns (who have no genetic or cultural links with the Saami but with whom they are often confused in folklore), were, like the Finns, skilled in magic, possibly because both peoples had a tradition of shamanism. Laplander or Finnish wizards often make appearances in Scandinavian tales, usually as evil sorcerers.

While this may seem to be a very localized tale, it has its parallels in both Finnish and Swiss stories, while the motif of the wizard, sorcerer, or witch traveling in a whirlwind and being wounded or even slain by knife or sword is even more widespread, appearing in Finnish, Swiss, Bohemian, Italian, and even Appalachian American tales. As for the element of the black ox, it turns up in over a hundred variants collected in Finland, as well as in some from Switzerland and northern Italy.

Now, here is another wizard, a shaman, really, whose name we know not; perhaps it was lost in too many tellings of the tale, or perhaps he wished to keep such a powerful thing as a name secret.

At any rate, there he was in the land of the Laplanders, among whom, it was believed, were many powerful magicians. But magicians grow restless. And so one day, the Laplander wizard went traveling in the form of a whirlwind. Such traveling covers much ground but takes much strength. It was hard work even for a wizard, and he snatched up food as he went to keep the whirlwind from collapsing and himself with it.

Unfortunately, some of that food was wheat from a farm in Estonia, a farm owned by a good man but a rash one. The farmer was too furious at seeing his wheat disappearing to think about what he was doing. He snatched

out his good, sturdy knife and threw it at the whirlwind with all his might—and sure enough, he heard a cry of pain. The whirlwind sped out of sight, and the farmer nodded in satisfaction. He'd chased away that whatever-it-had-been, that uncanny thief!

The next day, the farmer fell ill. No one could quite puzzle out what ailed him: He suffered no fever, no chill, nothing but a strange lack of strength.

"It is a spell," a doctor whispered at last, embarrassed at having to admit such a strange thing. "Go to Lapland. There are many powerful magicians there and surely you'll find one to heal you."

It was a long, weary journey for the farmer, but at last he reached the land of the Laplanders. Now where should he go? Where could he find the magician he needed? The farmer felt drawn to one house, and to that house he went.

The first thing he saw as he entered was his own knife, stabbed into the wall. "My knife!" he gasped.

"So it was you who threw it," a voice said from the shadows. A stern-faced man in the brightly embroidered woolen robe of a Laplander stepped forward, limping slightly. "Yes," he told the farmer, who was wide-eyed with fright, "I was that whirlwind. It was me you wounded, and wounded quite badly."

"Y-you shouldn't have been stealing my wheat."

"Did that give you any right to try to kill me? You hit my leg; you might have pierced my heart."

The farmer winced. True, he realized only now, he *could* have shouted a warning instead of blindly throwing the knife. He would have done just that if the thief had been an ordinary man.

"I'm sorry," he murmured. "I was afraid and angry both; I wasn't thinking. What can I do to repay you?"

"You must serve me for seven years."

"B-but I'm ill."

"You are not ill," the Laplander wizard said.

And just as suddenly as that, it was true.

So, for seven years, the farmer served the Laplander wizard, doing the ordinary jobs little different from those he'd done on his own farm. He learned almost nothing about magic in those years, but if the Laplander wizard wasn't overly kind to him, he wasn't cruel either. The wizard's son, his father's apprentice, was a little more friendly, enough to keep the farmer from truly despairing.

But seven years is a long time to live away from home. One Christmas Eve, the loneliness grew too great, and the farmer wept. "My poor wife! Will I ever see her again?"

The Laplander wizard overheard him and sighed ever so softly. "You truly long for her."

"Wizard, nothing could give me greater joy than to be at home at her side for Christmas."

"You have served me honestly, without a word of complaint. But we agreed on seven years of servitude. Seven is no ordinary number, and if I let you go now, the loss of its magic can only be balanced by a gift."

"I—I'll give you an ox, a fine, fat ox. The black ox, if he's still living."

"He is," the Laplander wizard said, his eyes strange and vague for a moment; he was using, the farmer knew, far-sight. "So be it. You shall be home before morning."

"But how—"

"My son will see you there. Go."

Hardly daring to hope, the farmer went outside. There sat the wizard's son in what looked very much like a great feed trough. "Come, get in!" the boy cried.

No sooner had the farmer seated himself, than the trough soared up in the sky, riding the winds as lightly as a bird. The farmer gasped at the speed and height. "My cap!" he cried as the wind tore it from his head.

"Too late!" the wizard-boy laughed. "We are already far from there. Look, here is your farm. Hold fast!"

They spiraled down to a landing, soft as a fallen leaf. The farmer scrambled out and raced into his house. Oh, what a wonderful, wonderful reunion he had with his wife!

"The boy!" he remembered suddenly, "The wizard's son! I promised the wizard our black ox, if the ox still lives."

"It does," his wife assured him.

The farmer went outside, looking for the wizard's son, but he failed to find him. "Has he already gone home? And left my debt with his father unpaid?"

He hurried into the barn. Sure enough, the black ox was gone. The wizard's son had taken the payment and left without a word.

The Laplander wizard never came to the farmer's lands again. And as for the farmer, well, he never acted rashly again. In fact, in the years that followed, he gained a fine name for himself as a happy, prudent man.

The Brave Little Tailor

A German Folktale

"The Brave Little Tailor" is a classic tale, most familiar in the West as the version printed by the Brothers Grimm in their *Household Tales*. The basic theme is of the "little" man overcoming all obstacles—including his original boast—by his basic cleverness, or downright trickery. All cultures enjoy seeing the ordinary person triumphing over the mighty, which may explain the story's popularity.

The earliest written evidence of this German version dates to 1557, but there are also oral versions from Armenia, Cambodia, Italy, Russia, and many more places. While the hero's tests vary, the basic story remains the same.

A little tailor sat sewing by the window. He was in good spirits, finishing off a jacket before taking a bite of his bread and jam, enjoying the sweet aroma rising from the jam. But when he was ready to eat, he found a flock of flies attacking his food. The little tailor grabbed a piece of cloth and smote seven of them. He was so satisfied that he made a belt embroidered with the words "Seven at one blow!"

Inspired by his own bravado, the little tailor set out into the world, in his pocket a cheese from his pantry and a bird he had caught.

At the top of a mountain, he found a giant. The giant was not at all impressed with this small human until he saw that "Seven at one blow!" and was sure it meant that the tailor had killed seven men with one blow.

Now, the giant decided to test the tailor. Taking up a stone, he squeezed it till water dropped from it. The tailor took out the cheese and squeezed it till the liquid dropped from it. The giant picked up a stone and threw it so high, it couldn't be seen. The tailor said that he could throw something that would never come back to Earth and launched the bird, which of course flew off. Now the giant challenged the tailor to help carry a mighty tree out of the forest. The tailor perched on a branch, and the giant never saw that he was carrying the whole tree by himself.

The trickery continued, until the giant and his colleagues tried to murder the tailor while he slept. The tailor hid and watched the giants smash the bed on which they thought he was lying. In the morning, the tailor cheerfully walked up to them, and they fled in terror.

The tailor went on to the royal court, and the king, sure this was a mighty warrior, took him into the royal service. The soldiers were angry that this nobody was with them, one who might slay seven of them at a blow if he was angered. But the king did not know how to get rid of the tailor. So he set him on a task to kill two murderous giants. If he did this, the king said he would give him the hand of his daughter and half the kingdom.

Refusing to let any of the guards go with him, the little tailor entered the forest and found the two giants asleep under a tree. He took up two pocketfuls of stones, climbed a tree, and started a fight between the giants by dropping stones first on one, then on the other, until they were so angry about having rocks thrown at them—they thought by each other—that they killed each other.

The little tailor wanted the promised reward. The king, however, had second thoughts. He ordered the tailor to catch a dangerous unicorn. The tailor took a rope and an axe with him into the forest, and when the unicorn charged him, he dodged. The unicorn's horn went into the trunk of a tree, the tailor roped the animal, cut the horn free, and brought the unicorn back to the king.

Now, the king demanded that the tailor catch a fierce wild boar. The tailor lured the boar into chasing him, ran into a chapel with the boar following, then leaped out the one small window—too small for the boar—and locked the door.

Now, the king had no choice. He gave the tailor the hand of his daughter and half the kingdom. The princess, though, soon realized that her warrior husband was actually a tailor and wanted her father to get rid of this mere nobody. The king told her to leave the door open that night so his servants could enter, carry off the tailor as he slept, and toss him on board a ship, which would carry him into the wide world.

But the tailor, who had made friends with many at the court by this time, was warned in time. And so, when the servants came for him, he shouted out while pretending to be asleep, "I smote seven at one blow. I killed two giants. I brought away one unicorn and caught a wild boar. Am I to fear those who are standing outside the room?"

The servants were terrified and ran away. After that, no one raised a hand to the tailor, and he became a king and stayed king to the end of his life.

Rumpelstiltskin

A German Folktale

"Rumpelstiltskin" is a popular world folktale that centers on the power of the name as magic, a common folk belief. Versions of this tale have been collected in France, Great Britain, Iceland, Italy, and Scandinavia. The best-known version of this story is surely that from the Brothers Grimm.

A poor miller with a beautiful daughter told the king that she could spin straw into gold. The king took him up on the promise and had the girl brought to a room full of straw. Giving her a spinning wheel and spindle, he told her that she had one night to spin all the straw into gold—or die.

The poor girl, all alone, burst into tears. Suddenly, there appeared a tiny man who asked why she wept. She told him that she had to spin the straw into gold and had no idea how to do it. The little man asked what she would give if he did the job, and she gave him her necklace. Sure enough, he spun the straw into gold.

That morning, the king saw the gold but wanted even more straw spun into gold. Again, the poor girl was left alone in a room filled with straw. And again, the tiny man appeared. This time, he demanded the ring from her finger. Getting that, he spun all the straw into gold.

Now, the king said that he would marry the miller's daughter—but only if she could spin straw into gold a third time.

This time, when the tiny man appeared, he made her promise to give him her first child when she became queen. The girl, thinking that would never happen, agreed, and he spun the straw into gold.

When the king came in the morning and saw the gold, he made the miller's daughter his queen. A year later, she had a beautiful son. That day, the tiny man appeared and demanded the child. The queen frantically bargained with him and wept. At last, he agreed: She had three days to guess his name—or lose her child.

For two days and nights, the queen tried to guess his name—and failed. But on the third day, a messenger said that he'd come to an odd house in front of which danced an odd little man, who cried:

Tomorrow I brew, today I bake,
And then the child away I'll take;
For little deems my royal dame
That Rumpelstiltskin is my name!

When the tiny man appeared before the queen, she twice pretended not to know his name, but on the third try, she asked him, "Is your name, perhaps, Rumpelstiltskin?"

The tiny man was so furious that in his rage he drove his right foot so far into the ground that it sank in up to his waist. Then, in a passion, he seized his left foot with both hands and tore himself in two.

The Six Swans

A Shape-Shifting Folktale from Germany

The widely told folktale "The Six Swans," probably best known in the version collected by the Brothers Grimm, features shape-shifting and the courage of a sister determined to save her brothers. Versions of this tale have been found in the Arab Near East, England, France, Greece, Italy, Russia, and Scandinavia. Perhaps the reason the folktale has remained so popular is that it is both magical and a firm story of familiar love.

Once upon a time, a king went hunting and got so lost that he agreed to marry a strange old woman's beautiful daughter in exchange for a rescue. After he had taken the beautiful but inexplicably frightening maiden up on his horse, the old woman showed him the way, and the king reached his royal palace again, where the wedding was celebrated.

The king had already been married once, and he had by his first wife seven children, six boys and a girl, whom he loved better than anything else in the world. But the new queen hated them, so for the boys she made little shirts of white silk with charms sewn inside them. She threw one of the little shirts over each of the boys, and, as soon as the shirts touched their bodies, they were changed into swans and flew away over the forest.

But the girl escaped. She told her father what had happened, and even gave him some shed feathers as proof. But he refused to believe that his wife was responsible. The girl knew she wasn't safe at home and went to seek her brothers.

Eventually, she caught up with the six swans just as they transformed back into her brothers. They told her that they could shed their swan skins and be human for only one-quarter of an hour every night. The only way they could be rescued was if their sister agreed to neither speak nor laugh for six years, and during that time to sew six shirts of starwort (or, in some translations, stinging nettles). If she said so much as a word, all would be lost.

The brothers flew away. Their sister was determined to rescue them, even if it meant her life. She began to work right away on the starwort shirts.

Time passed, and the king of that country came to hunt in the forest. His men found the girl and wondered who she was. But she said nothing. They brought her before the king, who instantly fell in love with her, even though she said nothing, not even when he took her back to his castle and declared his love to her and his court. Even though she still said nothing, they soon were wed.

The king's mother, though, hated the idea of her son being married to a woman who never spoke and continued to sew those odd shirts. After a year, the young queen had a son, but the evil mother stole it away and made it seem like the young queen had murdered it. Since she would not speak, she could not defend herself. The king, however, would not believe she was guilty. But when this happened three times over the years, the king at last had to sentence her to death by fire.

When the day came for the sentence to be executed, it was the last day of the six years during which she was not to speak or laugh. The six shirts were ready, with only the left sleeve of the sixth still missing. Even as she was led to the stake, she frantically tried to finish it, and clung to all six shirts.

Just as the fire was about to be lit, six swans came flying through the air toward her and sank down so that she could throw the shirts over them. As each was touched by a shirt, the swan's skin fell away, and he became human once again. The youngest lacked only his left arm, and had in the place of it a swan's wing on his shoulder.

Now, the young queen could defend herself. She told the king all that had happened, and how his mother had hidden away their three children.

Then, to the great joy of the king, the missing children were found. The king's evil mother was executed, and the king and queen, their children, and her six brothers lived many years in happiness and peace.

The Twelve Dancing Princesses

A German Folktale

"The Twelve Dancing Princesses," a rather odd folktale, is a familiar one in Europe and the United States. While it is known in various forms throughout Europe, it is perhaps best known in the version published by the Brothers Grimm. Versions of this story have been collected in the Cape Verde Islands, as well as in France, Portugal, and Russia.

That the princesses seem so heartless may offend some modern storytellers and listeners. Indeed, Victorian tellers and writers often left out the detail about the young men who failed to discover the princesses' secret being put to death. There is also no clear explanation of who the mysterious princesses might be, or whether the underground world is or is not Faerie. It is up to each storyteller to decide whether or not to alter details, since there is no such thing as a right or wrong version of a world tale.

There was a king who had twelve beautiful daughters. They slept in twelve beds all in one room, and when they went to bed, the doors were shut and locked up. However, every morning, their shoes were found to be quite worn through, as if they had been danced in all night. Nobody could find out how it happened, or where the princesses had been.

So the king made it known to all the land that if any man could discover the secret and find out where it was that the princesses danced in the night, he could take the one he liked best as his wife, and would be king after the death of the princesses' father. But those who tried and did not succeed, after three days and nights, would be put to death.

Everyone who tried to discover the secret failed, falling asleep and seeing nothing.

Then an old soldier, back from the wars, happened to meet an old woman in the woods. She asked him where he was going, and he answered that he was going to find out where the princesses went each night. The old woman warned him not to drink anything the princesses gave him at night, and to only pretend to sleep. She also gave him a cloak of invisibility.

That night, the soldier was welcomed at court and was shown to an outer chamber where the princesses slept. The eldest of the princesses brought him a cup of wine, but he only pretended to drink and to fall asleep. He watched the princesses dress in fine clothes and seem delighted about going dancing. Only the youngest was uneasy, sure something bad was going to happen.

Then, the eldest princess clapped her hands, and a trapdoor flew open where her bed had been. The twelve princesses started down into the opening, and the soldier wrapped his cloak of invisibility about himself and followed. On the way down the stairway, he accidentally stepped on the hem of the youngest princess's gown, and she cried out, but the others told her it had been nothing but a nail snagging the cloth.

At the bottom of the stairway was a grove of glittering silver-leaved trees. The soldier broke off a twig as evidence. They came to another grove, this one of golden trees, then a third made all of diamonds, and in these groves, too, the soldier broke off a twig. Each time he did this, the youngest princess jumped at the noise, but the others only scoffed at her nervousness.

They came to a great lake on which lay twelve little boats with twelve handsome princes in them. One princess went into each boat; the soldier slipped into the same boat as the youngest.

On the other side of the lake stood a castle from which came merry music. There, each prince danced with his princess. They danced on till all their shoes were worn out.

Then, the princes rowed the princesses back again over the lake. On the opposite shore, they took leave of each other, the princesses promising to come again the next night.

The soldier was brought before the king, who asked him where his daughters danced at night. The soldier told the king all that had happened, and showed him the evidence that he had brought with him.

The twelve princesses confessed everything. The king asked the soldier which princess he would take as his wife.

Since he was no longer young, the soldier chose the eldest princess. They were wed, and the soldier became the heir to the throne.

Cuchulain and the Green Man

An Ancient Irish Folktale

Cuchulain is a hero out of Irish myth and folklore, a culture hero whose mother is a mortal princess but whose father is said to be the god Lugh. Cuchulain's most famous exploits appear in the *Tain*, or *Táin Bó Cúailnge* (*Cattle Raid of Cooley*), the epic of Ulster, Ireland, from the eleventh or twelfth century C.E. The tale "Cuchulain and the Green Man" was later absorbed into the Arthurian cycle as an exploit not of Cuchulain but of the knightly hero Gawain.

Now, no one ever denied that Cuchulain was the nephew of King Conor of Ulster, since he was the son of the king's sister Dechtire. But it was said, and for all anyone knew said truly, since Dechtire was dead and had never spoken of the boy's sire, that his father was no mortal man, but the great god Lugh of the Sun's splendor.

Whether or not he was half divine, Cuchulain was raised by his uncle, and, even as a young boy, he showed signs that he would grow into a true hero. Indeed, by the time Cuchulain was seventeen, he had no equal among the warriors of Ulster. And since he was a handsome youngster, Conor's men were glad that he was a modest sort who never looked for trouble with other men's wives. Still, they were also glad when he won the hand of Emer, daughter of Forgall the Wily.

But not everyone appreciates peace and tranquility. One of King Conor's men was known as Bricriu of the Bitter Tongue, since he forever liked making barbed remarks and delighted in making mischief. Inviting the members of King Conor's court to dinner, Bricriu arranged that a contest should arise over who should have the "champion's portion," knowing that there were three hot-blooded young men who could claim that honor. They were Laegire, Conall Cearnach, and Cuchulain.

So successful was Bricriu in playing to their pride and to the secret insecurity of young men, that there was nearly a fight there and then. King Conor, furious at this breaking of the laws of hospitality, ordered the three hotbloods to take their argument elsewhere. So to avoid a bloody fight, the three heroes went off to submit their claims to the championship of Ireland to King Ailill of Connaught.

Ailill put the heroes to a strange test. Their dinner was served them in a separate room. Suddenly, three monstrous cats, as black as night and blazing red of eyes, burst into the room. The startled Laegire and Conall leaped up among the rafters, but Cuchulain stood his ground. He waited until a cat attacked, then struck it a sharp blow with his sword. With that, the three monstrous cats disappeared.

Cuchulain claimed that he had won the championship. But Laegire and Conall protested fiercely that they had been too startled to have a chance to properly react, and that this test had been an unfair one.

King Ailill must have sighed with frustration, or perhaps shaken his head wryly, remembering his own youth. But without any argument, he sent the three rivals off to Curoi of Kerry, who was a just and wise man—and one who was wise in the ways of magic. Curoi ordered that the three, in turn, stand watch outside his castle that night.

First it was Laegire's turn. He was confronted by a huge giant, a great boulder of a being who hurled spears that were the trunks of trees at Laegaire. The young man dodged and tried to attack, but the giant reached down, caught him up like an unwanted kitten, and hurled him over the castle wall. Laegire landed with a thump, too winded and bruised to go back outside.

"You are no champion!" Conall sneered, and went to take his turn on guard. But he, too, was confronted by the huge giant, who hurled those terrible spears at him. Conall, too, dodged and tried to attack. But he met with the same fate as Laegire, being caught up and hurled over the castle wall. He, too, landed too winded and bruised to go back outside.

Cuchulain did not sneer or boast. He simply went outside to stand watch. The giant loomed out of the darkness and began hurling his terrible tree-trunk spears. Cuchulain dodged, but waited to attack, biding his time. Only when the giant moved in to seize him did Cuchulain cast his own spear. He pierced the giant to the heart—and the giant vanished.

But that was not the end of Cuchulain's trials. The young man was beset by monsters on every side, and he fought fiercely with sword and spear to survive. Then a great winged creature came lunging down at him. Cuchulain sprang up with a great hero-leap, thrust his hand down the thing's throat, and tore out its heart. As the monsters disappeared as the giant had done, Cuchulain made another great hero-leap over the castle wall in triumph.

"Not fair!" was the cry of his rivals. "He used magic to win, where we had none."

"So be it," Curoi said. "Return to King Conor's court at Armagh and await my judgment."

Off the three went, and soon they joined all the Ulster heroes in King Conor's great hall. Suddenly, a stranger entered, hideous and gigantic, with eyes of blazing yellow. In one mighty hand, he clasped a great, gleaming axe.

"What business have you here?" King Conor asked as calmly as though this were just an ordinary man.

The stranger replied in a voice that boomed like thunder, "Behold my axe! Whoever grasps it today may behead me—if I may, in the same way, cut off his head tomorrow. Come, who will take up the challenge? If there is none who dare face me, I will state that Ulster has lost her courage and her honor!"

Laegire sprang to his feet, shouting, "Ulster has not lost her courage! I accept your challenge."

With a shrug, the giant laid his head on a block. Laegire swung the axe with all his force and, with one blow, severed the giant's head from his body. But to the horror of everyone in the hall, the giant got to his feet, took his axe in one and his head in the other, and strode from the hall.

The following night, the giant returned, head on his shoulders and as sound as ever. But Laegire's courage failed him, and he snuck off into the night.

"So *this* is the courage of Ulster!" the giant sneered.

Conall Cearnach sprang to his feet. "I will not fail you!" he shouted.

Once again, the giant knelt, and once again, he was beheaded. Once again, he stalked off, head in hand—but when he returned, there was no Conall Cearnach to be found.

"Is there no true warrior in all Ulster?" the giant jeered.

"There is," Cuchulain said quietly.

As the other two had done, he cut off the giant's head at one stroke. As before, the giant strode away with head in hand.

The next night, Conor and his men waited to see what Cuchulain would do. He did nothing, save sit quietly. To Conor, he murmured, "This night will surely see my death. But I would rather die than break my sworn word."

The giant strode into the hall, swinging his axe. "Where is Cuchulain?" he cried.

Cuchulain got to his feet. "Here I am."

"Ah, poor boy!" the giant said. "The fear of death lies heavy on you. At least, you have kept your word and have not failed me."

As the giant stood with the great axe ready, Cuchulain knelt to receive the blow and laid his head on the block.

But the giant wasn't satisfied. "Don't cringe. Stretch out your neck."

"Slay me quickly," Cuchulain retorted. "I did not keep you waiting last night."

The giant raised his axe till it crashed upward through the rafters of the hall, then swept it down with a crash like thunder. The men of Ulster closed their eyes in horror. But when they looked for Cuchulain, they cried out in surprise. The axe hadn't so much as scratched him. It had struck the ground instead, and the young man knelt where he was, unharmed.

The giant was no longer the giant. Smiling and leaning on his axe was none other than Curoi of Kerry.

"Rise," he told Cuchulain. "I proclaim that the Championship of the Heroes of Ireland is yours from this day forth, and the Champion's Portion at all feasts; and to your wife I adjudge the first place among all the women of Ulster. Woe to any who dares dispute this decision!"

With that, Curoi vanished. The warriors with one voice proclaimed Cuchulain as the Champion of the Heroes of all Ireland. And, as promised by Curoi of Kerry, Cuchulain kept that title for all his days.

A Leprechaun's Gold

An Irish Folktale

Leprechauns usually stand well under 2 feet tall. While the other fairy folk find them less than handsome, leprechauns often dress in what they consider good fashion: perhaps a green jacket with silver buttons, bright blue hose, a three-cornered hat, and nicely buckled shoes. They often wear a leather apron over the lot, since leprechauns are the shoemakers for all the fairy folk of Ireland. They owe no one allegiance, though, save their own king, and prefer to live by themselves. Leprechauns are also often keepers of fairy treasure, but any human who thinks such small beings make poor guardians will soon learn otherwise.

One day a young farmer, Thomas—or Tom, as his neighbors most often called him—was walking through the fields when he heard an odd tapping sound coming from behind a hedge. Warily, Tom tiptoed forward, and his eyes grew wide with astonishment. For there, tapping away on a tiny shoe (and stopping now and then to take a drink from the jug at his side), was a small being who could be nothing else but a leprechaun. Now, Tom, being a local lad, knew all the stories about these creatures—particularly the one that said they guarded wondrous treasures.

But a leprechaun is almost impossible for a big, clumsy human to surprise. As Tom tried his best to be as stealthy as a cat, the little being looked up at him. "God bless your work," Tom said politely, trying to pretend he hadn't been about to grab the leprechaun.

"Thank you, and good day to you," the little man replied, going back to his cobbling.

Tom, trying to keep the conversation going so he might work the subject of treasure into it, asked, "May I know what's in that jug at your side?"

"Beer," the leprechaun answered. "And good beer it is. Made it myself out of the heather."

"Out of heather!" Tom said with a laugh. "There's no such thing possible!"

"Is there not? I tell you, the way of brewing such fine beer's been a family secret for longer than you could ever guess."

Could it be that maybe there was such a thing as heather beer after all? "Might I be having a taste?" Tom asked.

"I tell you, young man," the leprechaun said sternly, "you'd be better off watching your cows than begging after drink. Look, now, they're out. And they've gotten into the oats!"

Tom started to turn almost before he'd realized it—but then he remembered more about the old tales and the way leprechauns tricked unwary humans: The moment they looked away, the leprechaun would be off and away. Instead, Tom whirled, pounced like a cat on a mouse, and caught the small shoemaker in his hand.

The leprechaun squirmed something fierce, but he couldn't get free. "Hey, man, let me go!"

"Not till you show me where your treasure's hidden."

"What would you want with treasure? It's more trouble than it's worth to your kind."

"It will be trouble to you if you don't show me, and *now*!"

"Ah, well," the leprechaun said, pathetic as a child, "there's no softening your heart of stone, is there?"

"There'll be no softening of my heart till you show me that treasure."

"So be it. Come along, young man. We have some walking to do."

Held firm in Tom's hand, the leprechaun directed him to this field and that, and finally told him, "Stop here."

"Here? But this is just a field of thistles!"

"Nevertheless, a nice fat pot of gold is buried right here. Start digging under this thistle, and you'll have your pockets full of treasure. Well, man, why are you waiting?"

How could Tom dig without a shovel? And how could he dig and not lose hold of the leprechaun? Suddenly, an idea came to him. He removed his scarf, and a nice, bright red one it was, too, and he tied it about the thick stem of the thistle.

"Now," he said, "swear to me you'll not so much as touch that thistle or that scarf."

"How could I not agree to swear it when so clever a lad holds me hostage? There; I have sworn. Now, will you not release me? I have shoes that need mending and—"

"Not yet. Swear to me you won't remove the gold this day or night."

"Och, and is he not the cleverest of men? I swear I shall not remove the gold this day or night. I shall not touch the scarf or the thistle. Now, may I kindly have my freedom?"

"You may. And good luck to you."

"Good luck to you, too, man. And much good may the gold do you when you get it."

The leprechaun vanished into the fields. Tom ran home as though devils were after him. He hunted wildly through his farming tools till he'd found a shovel and raced just as swiftly back to the field of thistles.

There Tom stopped dead, staring. Och, yes, the leprechaun had kept his word. He'd kept the very letter of his word. The thistle with the red scarf about it had not been touched at all. But each and every thistle in that entire field bore a red scarf as well. There was no telling which scarf belonged to Tom. There was no telling which was the thistle under which the gold lay!

What could Tom do? The only thing he could. He stood and laughed at the fool he'd been to think that he could ever out-trick a leprechaun.

The Storyteller at Fault

An Irish Folktale

"The Storyteller at Fault" is an old Irish folktale, dating to at least the fourteenth century and possibly much earlier, that all storytellers can take to heart. It is about a storyteller and the problem he had in finding stories to tell.

In the ancient days of Ireland, there reigned in Leinster a king who was remarkably fond of hearing stories. Like the other princes and chieftains of the island, he had a favorite storyteller, who held a large estate from the king—which he kept only on the condition of telling the king a new story every night of his life.

Many indeed were the stories this teller knew, so that he had already reached a good old age without failing even for a single night in his task. And such was the skill he displayed that whatever cares of state or other annoyances might prey upon the monarch's mind, his storyteller was sure to send him to sleep.

One morning, the storyteller strolled out into his garden, turning over in his mind incidents that he might weave into a story for the king at night. But this morning, he found himself quite at fault; after pacing his whole estate, he returned to his house without being able to think of anything new or strange. He found no difficulty in "there was once a king who had three sons" or "one day, the king of all Ireland," but further than that he could not get.

At length, he went in to breakfast, and told his wife, "I have no mind to eat anything. For as long as I have been in the service of the king of Leinster, I never sat down to breakfast without having a new story ready for the evening, but this morning, my mind is quite shut up, and I don't know what to do. I might as well lie down and die at once. I'll be disgraced forever this evening, when the king calls for his storyteller."

Just at this moment, the lady looked out the window. There was a strange object lying in the fields. When the storyteller and his wife went to investigate, they found a miserable-looking old man lying on the ground with a wooden leg placed beside him.

"Who are you?" asked the storyteller.

"I'm but a poor, old, lame, decrepit, miserable creature, sitting down here to rest awhile and wait for someone to play a game of dice with me. I have one hundred pieces of gold in this leathern purse."

"You may as well play with him," said the storyteller's wife, "and perhaps you'll have something to tell the king in the evening."

A smooth stone was placed between them, and, upon it, they cast their throws. Soon, though, the storyteller had lost every penny.

"Will you play again?" asked the old man.

"Don't be talking, man; you have all my money."

"Haven't you chariot and horses and hounds? I'll stake all the money I have against them."

"Nonsense, man! Do you think for all the money in Ireland, I'd run the risk of seeing my lady tramp home on foot?"

"Maybe you'd win."

"Maybe I wouldn't," said the storyteller.

"Play with him, husband," said his wife. "I don't mind walking if you don't, love."

"I never refused you before," said the storyteller, "and I won't do so now." Down he sat again, and, in one throw, lost horses, hounds, and chariot.

"Will you play again?" asked the beggar.

"Are you making game of me, man? What else have I to stake?"

"I'll stake all my winnings against your wife," said the old man.

The storyteller turned away in silence, but his wife stopped him.

"Accept his offer," said she. "This is the third time, and who knows what luck you may have? You'll surely win now."

They played again, and the storyteller lost. No sooner had he done so than to his sorrow and surprise, his wife went and sat down near the beggar.

"I'll stake the whole now, wife and all, against your own self," said the beggar.

Again they played, and again the storyteller lost. The beggar took from his pocket a long cord and a wand. "What kind of animal would you rather be, a deer, a fox, or a hare?"

The storyteller chose a hare. The beggar threw the cord round him, struck him with the wand, and, suddenly, a long-eared, frisking hare was skipping and jumping on the green. But it wasn't for long, because his wife set the hounds on him.

The hare fled; the dogs followed. Round the field ran a high wall, so that run as he might, the hare couldn't get out, and mightily diverted were beggar and lady to see him twist and double. In vain, did he take refuge with his wife; she kicked him back again to the hounds, until, at last, the beggar stopped the hounds, and with a stroke of the wand, the storyteller, panting and breathless, stood before them again.

"And how did you like the sport?" asked the beggar.

"It might be sport to others," replied the storyteller, looking at his wife. "For my part, I could well put up without. Would it be asking too much," he went on to the beggar, "to know who you are, or where you come from, or why you take pleasure in plaguing me?"

"Oh!" replied the stranger. "I'm an odd kind of good-for-little fellow, one day poor, another day rich, but if you wish to know more about me or my habits, come with me."

With that, he drew out of his wallet a well-looking middle-aged man, to whom he said, "By all you heard and saw since I put you into my wallet, take charge of this lady and of the carriage and horses, and have them ready for me whenever I want them."

Suddenly, the storyteller found himself at the Foxes' Ford, near the castle of Red Hugh O'Donnell. He could see all, but none could see him.

O'Donnell was in his hall, weariness of spirit upon him. "Save you, O'Donnell," said the beggar. "For five pieces of silver you shall see a trick of mine."

"You shall have them," said O'Donnell.

The beggar placed three small straws in his hand. "The middle one," said he, "I'll blow away; the other two, I'll leave."

"You cannot do it," said one and all.

But the beggar put a finger on either outside straw and blew away the middle one.

"A good trick," said O'Donnell, and paid him his five pieces of silver.

"Six more pieces, O'Donnell, and I'll do another trick," said the beggar.

"Six you shall have."

"Do you see my two ears? One, I'll move but not the other."

"You can never move one ear and not the two together."

The beggar put his hand to one ear and gave it a pull. O'Donnell laughed and paid him the six pieces.

"Well, O'Donnell," said the beggar, "strange are the tricks I've shown you, but I'll show you a stranger one yet for the same money."

"My word on it," said O'Donnell.

With that, the beggar took a bag from under his armpit, and from out of the bag a ball of silk. He unwound the ball and flung it up into the clear blue heavens, and it became a ladder. Then, he took a hare and placed it upon the thread, and up it ran. He took out a red-eared hound, and it swiftly ran up after the hare.

"Now," said the beggar, "has anyone a mind to run after the dog?"

"I will," said a lad of O'Donnell's.

"Up with you, then," said the juggler. "But I warn you, if you let my hare be killed, I'll cut off your head when you come down."

The lad ran up the thread, and all three soon disappeared. After looking up for a long time, the beggar said, "I'm afraid the hound is eating the hare, and that our friend has fallen asleep."

Saying this, he began to wind the thread, and down came the lad fast asleep, and down came the red-eared hound, and in his mouth was the last morsel of the hare. The beggar struck off the heads of lad and hound.

O'Donnell was sorely angered at the death of lad and hound.

"Five pieces of silver twice over for each of them," said the beggar, "and their heads shall be on them as before."

Five pieces, and again five were paid him, and, suddenly, the lad had his head and the hound his. In that instant, the gray beggar vanished.

Now, all this while, the king of Leinster's spirit was heavy. It was the time when he was used to hearing a story, but there was not a word about his storyteller.

The beggar entered, and in his hand was a three-stringed harp.

"I already have the best harpers in the five-fifths of Ireland," the king said, and he signed them to play.

"Did you ever hear the like?" he asked the beggar.

"Did you ever, O King, hear a cat purring over a bowl of broth, or the buzzing of beetles in the twilight, or a shrill-tongued old woman scolding your head off? More melodious to me were the worst of these sounds than the sweetest harping of thy harpers."

When the harpers heard this, they drew their swords and rushed at him, but instead of striking him, their blows fell on one another. When the king saw this, he thought the harpers weren't content with murdering their music, but must needs murder one another.

"Hang the fellow who began it all," he ordered, "and if I can't have a story, let me have peace."

Up came the guards, who seized the beggar, marched him to the gallows, and hanged him high. Back they marched to the hall, and who should they see but the beggar seated on a bench with a flagon of ale. Three times, they tried to hang him, and, three times, they found him sitting there in the hall.

"Are you wishing to hang me again?" he asked.

"Go where you will," said the captain, "and as fast as you please, if you'll only go far enough. It's trouble enough you've given us already."

As he said these words, the captain vanished, and the storyteller found himself on the spot where he had first met the beggar, and where his wife still was with the carriage and horses.

"Now," said the beggar, "I'll torment you no longer. There's your carriage and your horses, and your money and your wife. And as for your wife, don't think ill of her for what she did, for she couldn't help it."

"Not help it! Not help kicking me into the mouth of my own hounds! Not help casting me off for the sake of a beggarly old—"

"I'm not as beggarly or as old as ye think. I am Angus of the Bruff. Many a good turn you've done me with the king of Leinster. This morning, my magic told me the difficulty you were in, and I made up my mind to get you out of it. As for your wife there, the power that changed your body changed her mind. Forget and forgive as man and wife should do, and now you have a story for the king of Leinster when he calls for one."

With that, the beggar disappeared.

It's true enough that the storyteller now had a story fit for a king. After he'd finished telling it, the king who heard it laughed so long and hard that he couldn't go to sleep at all. And from that day on, the storyteller never had to trouble to find new stories, since every night from then on, the king listened to and laughed anew at the tale of the gray beggar.

The Crystal Casket

An Italian Snow White Folktale

"The Crystal Casket" is a tale from Italy, first recorded in English in 1885. There is a rather disturbing necrophilic touch to it, as the king is willing to marry a corpse, but we know what the king does not—that the heroine is still alive.

There was once a widower who had a daughter between ten and twelve years old. Her father sent her to school and, as she was all alone in the world, commended her always to her teacher.

Now, the teacher, seeing that the child had no mother, fell in love with the father and kept saying to the girl, "Ask your father if he would like me for a wife."

This the teacher said to the girl every day, and at last the girl said, "Papa, the schoolmistress is always asking me if you will marry her."

The father said, "Eh! My daughter, if I take another wife, you will have great troubles."

But the girl persisted, and finally the father was persuaded to go one evening to the schoolmistress's house. When she saw him, she was well pleased, and they settled the marriage in a few days.

Poor child! How bitterly she had to repent having found a stepmother so ungrateful and cruel to her! Every day, the schoolmistress sent her stepdaughter out on a terrace to water a pot of basil, and it was so dangerous that if she fell, she would plunge into a deep river.

One day, there came a large eagle, who said to her, "What are you doing here?" The girl was weeping because she saw how great the danger was of falling into the river. The eagle said to her, "Get on my back, and I will carry you away, and you will be happier than with your new mama."

After a long journey, they reached a great plain, where they found a beautiful palace all of crystal. The eagle knocked at the door and said, "Open, my ladies, open! For I have brought you a pretty girl." When the people in the palace opened the door and saw that lovely girl, they were amazed, and they kissed and caressed her.

One day, the eagle flew away to the terrace where the stepmother was watering the basil. "Where is your daughter?" asked the eagle.

"Eh!" she replied. "Perhaps she fell from this terrace and went into the river; I have not heard from her in ten days."

The eagle answered, "What a fool you are! I carried her away; seeing that you treated her so harshly, I carried her away to my fairies, and she is very well." Then, the eagle flew away.

The stepmother, filled with rage and jealousy, called a witch from the city and said to her, "You see my daughter is alive, and she is in the house of some fairies of an eagle which often comes upon my terrace. Now, you must do me the favor to find some way to kill this stepdaughter of mine, for I am afraid that some day or other she will return, and my husband, discovering this matter, will certainly kill me."

The witch answered, "Oh, you need not be afraid of that; leave it to me."

What did the witch do? She made a little basketful of sweetmeats, in which she put poison; then she wrote a letter to the girl, pretending that it was her father who had learned where she was and wished to make her this

588

present. The letter said that her father was glad to hear that she was with the fairies.

Let us leave the witch who is arranging all this deception, and return to Ermellina, for so the young girl was named. The fairies said to her, "See, Ermellina, we are going away, and shall be absent four days. Now, in this time take good care not to open the door to anyone, for some treachery is being prepared for you by your stepmother."

She promised to open the door to no one. "Do not be anxious," she said. "I am well off, and my stepmother has nothing to do with me."

But it was not so. The fairies went away, and, the next day when Ermellina was alone, she heard a knocking at the door. She said to herself, "Knock away! I don't open to anyone."

But meanwhile, the blows redoubled, and curiosity forced her to look out the window. What did she see? She saw one of the servant girls of her own home (for the witch had disguised herself as one of her father's servants).

"O my dear Ermellina," the servant said, "your father is shedding tears of sorrow for you, because he really believed you were dead, but the eagle that carried you off came and told him the good news that you were here with the fairies. Meanwhile, your father, not knowing what civility to show you, for he understands very well that you are in need of nothing, has thought to send you this little basket of sweetmeats."

At first, Ermellina did not open the door; the servant begged her to come down and take the basket and the letter, but she said, "No, I wish nothing!" Finally, though, since women, and especially young girls, are fond of sweetmeats, Ermellina descended and opened the door.

When the witch, disguised as the servant, had given Ermellina the basket, she said, "Eat this," and broke off for her a piece of the sweetmeats, which she had poisoned. When Ermellina took the first mouthful, the old woman, in the form of the servant girl, disappeared. Ermellina had scarcely time to close the door before she fell down on the stairs.

When the fairies returned, they knocked at the door, but no one opened it for them; then, they perceived that there had been some treachery and began to weep. The chief of the fairies said, "We must break open the door," and so they did, and saw Ermellina dead on the stairs.

Her other friends who loved her so dearly begged the chief of the fairies to bring her to life, but she would not, "for," she said, "she has disobeyed me." But one and the other asked her until she consented. She opened Ermellina's mouth, took out a piece of the sweetmeat that the girl had not yet swallowed, and raised her up, and Ermellina came to life again.

We can imagine what a pleasure it was for her friends; but the chief of the fairies reproved her for her disobedience. Ermellina promised not to disobey the fairies again.

Once more, the fairies were obliged to depart. Their chief said, "Remember, Ermellina: The first time I cured you, but the second I will have nothing to do with you."

Ermellina said they need not worry, that she would not open the door to anyone. But it was not so; for the eagle, thinking to increase her stepmother's anger, told her again that Ermellina was alive. The stepmother denied it all to the eagle, but she summoned anew the witch and told her that her stepdaughter was still alive, saying, "Either you will really kill her, or I will be avenged on you."

The old witch, finding herself caught, told her to buy a very handsome dress, one of the handsomest she could find. The witch transformed herself into a tailor belonging to the family, took the dress, departed, and went to poor Ermellina. The witch knocked at the door and said, "Open, open, for I am your tailor. Come down; I must fit a dress on you."

Ermellina replied, "No, no, for I have been deceived once."

"But I am not the old woman," replied the tailor. "You know me, for I have always made your dresses."

Poor Ermellina was persuaded and descended the stairs; the tailor took to flight and disappeared while Ermellina was yet buttoning up the dress. Ermellina closed the door and was mounting the stairs, but she was not permitted to go up, for she fell down dead.

Let us return to the fairies, who came home and knocked at the door. But what good did it do to knock? There was no longer anyone there. They began to weep. The chief of the fairies said, "I told you that she would betray me again; but now, I will have nothing more to do with her."

So they broke open the door and saw the poor girl with the beautiful dress on, but she was dead. They all wept, because they really loved her. But there was nothing to do.

The chief of the fairies struck her enchanted wand and commanded a beautiful rich casket all covered with diamonds and other precious stones to appear; then the others made a beautiful garland of flowers and gold, put it on the young girl, and then laid her in the casket, which was so rich and beautiful that it was marvelous to behold. Then the old fairy struck her wand as usual and commanded a handsome horse, the likes of which not even the king possessed. Then they took the casket, put it on the horse's back, and led him into the public square of the city, and the chief of the fairies said, "Go, and do not stop until you find someone who says to you, 'Stop, for pity's sake, for I have lost my horse for you.'"

Now let us leave the afflicted fairies and turn our attention to the horse, which ran away at full speed. Who happened to pass at that moment? None other than a king saw this horse with that wonder on its back. Then, the king began to spur his horse, and he rode him so hard that he killed him and had to leave him dead in the road; but the king kept running after the other horse. The poor king could endure it no longer; he saw himself lost, and exclaimed, "Stop, for pity's sake, for I have lost my horse for you!"

Then the horse stopped (for those were the words). When the king saw that beautiful girl dead in the casket, he thought no more about his own horse, but took the other to the city. The king's mother knew that her son had gone hunting; when she saw him returning with this loaded horse, she did not know what to think. The son had no father, wherefore he was all-powerful.

The king reached the palace and had the horse unloaded and the casket carried to his chamber; then, he called his mother and said, "Mother, I went hunting, but I have found a wife."

"But what is it? A doll? A dead woman?"

"Mother," replied her son, "don't trouble yourself about what it is; it is my wife."

His mother began to laugh, and withdrew to her own room. (What could she do, poor mother?)

Now, this poor king no longer went hunting, took no diversion, did not even go to the table, but ate in his own room. By a fatality, it happened that war was declared against him, and he was obliged to depart.

He called his mother, and said, "Mother, I wish two careful chambermaids, whose business it shall be to guard this casket, for if on my return I find that anything has happened to my casket, I shall have the chambermaids killed."

His mother, who loved him, said, "Go, my son; fear nothing, for I myself will watch over your casket."

He wept several days at being obliged to abandon this treasure of his, but there was no help for it; he had to go. After his departure, he did nothing but commend his wife (so he called her) to his mother in his letters.

Let us return to the mother, who no longer thought about the matter, not even to have the casket dusted. But all at once, there came a letter that informed her that the king had been victorious and would return to his palace in a few days. The mother called the chambermaids and said to them, "Girls, we are ruined."

They replied, "Why, Highness?"

"Because my son will be back in a few days, and how have we taken care of the doll?"

They answered, "True, true; now let us go and wash the doll's face."

They went to the king's room and saw that the doll's face and hands were covered with dust and fly specks, so they took a sponge and washed her face, but some drops of water fell on her dress and spotted it. The poor chambermaids began to weep, and went to the queen for advice.

The queen said, "Do you know what to do? Call a tailor, and have a dress precisely like this brought, and take off this one before my son comes."

They did so, and the chambermaids went to the room and began to unbutton the dress. The moment that they took off the first sleeve, Ermellina opened her eyes. The poor chambermaids sprang up in terror, but one of the most courageous said, "I am a woman, and so is this one; she will not eat me."

To cut the matter short, the chambermaid took off the dress; when it was removed, Ermellina began to get out of the casket to walk about and see where she was. The chambermaids fell on their knees before her and begged her to tell them who she was. She, poor girl, told them the whole story. Then she said, "I wish to know where I am."

Then, the chambermaids called the king's mother to explain it to her. The mother did not fail to tell her everything, and she, poor girl, did nothing but weep penitently, thinking of what the fairies had done for her.

The king was on the point of arriving, and his mother said to the girl-doll, "Come here; put on one of my best dresses." In short, she arrayed her like a queen.

Then came her son. They shut the doll up in a small room so that she could not be seen. The king came with great joy, with trumpets blowing and banners flying for the victory. But he took no interest in all this, and ran at once to his room to see the doll; the chambermaids fell on their knees before him, saying that the doll smelled so badly that they could not stay in the palace, and they were obliged to bury her.

The king would not listen to this excuse, but at once called two of the palace servants to erect the gallows. His mother comforted him in vain: "My son, it was a dead woman."

"No, no; I will not listen to any reasons. Dead or alive, you should have left it for me."

Finally, when his mother saw that he was in earnest about the gallows, she rang a little bell, and there came forth no longer the doll, but a very beautiful girl, whose like was never seen. The king was amazed, and said, "What is this?"

Then his mother, the chambermaids, and Ermellina were obliged to tell him all that had happened.

He said, "Mother, since I adored her when dead and called her my wife, now I mean her to be my wife in truth."

"Yes, my son," replied his mother. "Do so, for I am willing."

They arranged the wedding, and, in a few days, the two were man and wife.

Appointment in Samarra

A Folktale from the Talmud, the Jewish Book of Religious Wisdom

> "Appointment in Samarra" refers to a type of Jewish folktale in which a man or group of men flee death only to die in the new location. This, it turns out, is the place in which they were destined to die.

There were two Cushites, called Elichoreph and Achiyah, who attended King Solomon. They were sons of Shisha, the scribes of Solomon.

One day, Solomon noticed that the Angel of Death looked sad. Solomon asked him, "Why are you sad?"

The angel replied. "Because they have demanded from me the two Cushites that dwell here."

Solomon had demons take Elichoreph and Achiyah to the city of Luz, which was a legendary city where no one ever died. However, as soon as they reached the gates of Luz, they died.

The next day, Solomon noticed that the Angel of Death was happy. He asked him, "Why are you so happy?"

The angel replied, "Because you sent them to the very place where they were supposed to die."

The Golem of Prague

A Jewish Folktale

Although Jewish folk stories of artificial life date back as far as the Talmud, about 600 C.E., the tales of golems began to be told in Jewish communities during the time of Christian persecution of Jews in the Middle Ages. This was particularly so in Prague, when anti-Semitic sentiment grew so powerful that Jews finally fled the city.

Once, long ago in the city of Prague, there were people who hated the Jews who lived in that city. Why? Jews and Christians both worship the same God, but they worship in different ways. Those wicked people hated the Jews just because they weren't Christians. And so they began to spread terrible rumors that the Jews of Prague were murdering Christian children. Of course, this wasn't true, but when people are afraid, they believe even the strangest rumors.

The chief rabbi of Prague, a wise and wonderworking man known as the Maharal, was worried for his congregation. Surely, it was just a matter of time before fear turned to violence. Surely, the Jews needed a guardian!

So the holy Maharal went down to the river with two apprentices. Out of the clay of the river's bank, they formed the figure of a gigantic man. The Maharal spoke words from the Holy Scriptures over it, and the clay figure, the golem, opened his eyes.

"Stand," the Maharal told him.

The golem stood. The three men dressed him and took him back with them to Prague.

"But—but we can't tell anyone what he really is!" one apprentice said. "People would think he was a monster."

"No one shall know," the Maharal agreed. He told the golem, "You are Joseph. And you will serve me, even if I tell you to jump into fire."

The golem, being only a thing of clay, could not speak, but he nodded obediently.

The Maharal added firmly, "Your purpose in being is to protect the Jews of Prague from harm."

Again, the golem nodded obediently.

The Maharal brought the golem to his home, where everyone took Joseph to be no more than a poor, weak-witted servant. Even the Maharal's own wife, Perele, believed it.

One day, Perele asked Joseph to fill the water barrels—but she forgot to tell him to stop! The golem kept on bringing bucket after bucket of water, till the Maharal's house was nearly flooded.

"Why do you keep such a foolish servant?" Perele angrily asked her husband.

"He will prove his worth," the Maharal assured her.

And, of course, the Maharal was right. When evil men threatened the Jews, Joseph patrolled the streets like a huge, silent soldier. Again and again, he saved the Jews from anyone who tried to hurt them.

The people who hated the Jews were furious. They would not let any huge, silent soldier stop them! So they decided on a terribly cruel plot. They went to the Christian cemetery and dug up the body of a boy.

"We'll hide it in the home of the Maharal himself," they decided. "Then, we will call in the guards. Everyone will believe the Jews

593

have been murdering Christian children, and that will be the end of the Jews of Prague!"

But even as they plotted, not one of those hate-filled people realized that Joseph was following them like a giant silent shadow. Just before they were about to throw the boy's body into the Maharal's house, the golem caught them. He scooped them all up in his mighty arms, carried them to the house of the city's watchman, and dropped them all right in the courtyard.

The noise woke the watchman and his neighbors. They came running and found the grave robbers and the boy's body. Once the watchman learned of the plot, he hurried to the palace to tell Prague's ruler, King Rudolf.

"What a horrible thing!" the king exclaimed. "But how fortunate we all are that these cruel people were stopped in time!"

And he issued a royal decree on the spot: On pain of banishment, none of his people should ever again spread rumors about the Jews.

Life grew peaceful for the Jews of Prague after that. When a whole year had passed without trouble, the Maharal knew the golem was no longer needed. He led Joseph to the attic, where the Maharal and his apprentice spoke holy and magical words over him.

When they were finished, the golem was no more than lifeless clay. The Maharal hid the clay under a pile of papers and books.

"Sleep well, Joseph," he murmured.

And who knows? For all anyone can tell, the golem is sleeping there still, waiting for the time when he will be needed once more.

King Solomon and the Demon

A Jewish Folktale

The historical King Solomon lived in and ruled the biblical land of Israel around 900 B.C.E. He was known for his wisdom, and this trait became part of folk belief. Later folktales claimed that Solomon could control all manner of magic beings, including demons.

King Solomon, ruler of the land of Israel, was, as is well known, the wisest of men, ruler of humankind, and master of spirits and demons. He was also a pious man and had determined to build a temple to the glory of God.

But the king remembered the holy words that said that no altar may be built of hewn stone. For stone is hewn by iron, symbolic of the sword, and the touch of a metal of war on a building of peace would be sure desecration.

Then how could a temple be built? Solomon the Wise pondered this problem, and, at last, he found a solution: the shamir. This creature, the diamond insect, was tiny but incredibly strong, and it could surely hew stones and split mighty trees for the temple's walls and roof beams.

Ah, but where was the shamir to be found? That was an even greater problem, and one that even Solomon the Wise could not solve. So the king, alone in his chambers, held out his hand that bore a signet ring engraved with the holy name. No sooner had he proclaimed that name than a demon appeared, kneeling before the king and trembling.

"What is your will, oh wisest of kings?"

King Solomon gestured to the demon to stand. "I command you to tell me where the shamir may be found."

But the demon only trembled the more. "Mighty king, don't be angry. I am your servant; I do not wish to disobey. But I don't have an answer for you. Only our own king, Ashmodai, has the knowledge you seek."

"And where," the king asked sternly, "is Ashmodai, king of demons, to be found?"

"Far from here, mighty king; far from the homes of men. His palace stands on the very top of a towering mountain. In that mountain is a wonderful well, guarded jealously by Ashmodai. When he is not at home, he keeps the opening to that well carefully closed with a great rock sealed with the touch of his signet ring. Whenever Ashmodai returns, he first examines the seal on the rock to be sure no one has tampered with it, then he drinks deeply of the pure water and seals the well anew."

Not a word of this did Solomon the Wise forget. He dismissed the demon, then summoned Benaiah, son of Jebodiah, the captain of the royal guard. "I wish you to capture Ashmodai, king of demons, and bring him to me."

The king gave Benaiah a golden chain inscribed with the holy name and a sack of the strongest wine, and he lent him his royal signet ring as well. Off the brave warrior went, traveling through the desert waste, climbing the harsh, terrifying height of Ashmodai's mountain, fearing nothing, since he bore King Solomon's signet ring with the holy name upon it.

Benaiah grinned with relief. Ashmodai was not at home. Now, he had a chance to perform the king's plan. There was the well, blocked with the rock and sealed with Ashmodai's seal. Benaiah didn't try to move the massive rock, but he bore a small hole through it. And through that hole, Benaiah poured the whole sackful of that strongest wine.

Sure enough, when Ashmodai returned, tall and terrible, with great, blazing eyes, he went straight for the well. Never noticing the tiny hole in the rock, he opened the well and drank deeply. Demons are unfamiliar with wine—and this was, after all, the strongest wine—and very soon Ashmodai was sound asleep. Benaiah crept forward and bound the demon in the golden chain, then waited.

At last, Ashmodai yawned and woke. Finding himself bound, he fought to free himself, but no demon could break a chain marked with the holy name.

"Come," Benaiah said, "we are going to King Solomon, he who is your master."

Ashmodai gave no argument. But strange incidents happened along the way. Once, he saw a happy bridal party and began to weep.

"Monster!" Benaiah cried. "Why do you weep at the happiness of others?"

"I weep because I see the future; the groom will be dead within three days."

They went on, and they overheard a man insisting that the boot maker make him shoes to last at least seven years. Ashmodai burst into laughter.

"Why do you laugh?" Benaiah asked.

"That foolish man will not live seven days longer, yet he wishes shoes that will outlive him by seven years!"

Benaiah, sharply reminded that his companion was, after all, a demon who could not see things as did humans, said nothing.

Many other strange events befell them, but, at last, Ashmodai stood before King Solomon. The demon shivered at the sight of the ruler of all spirits and demons, then threw down a long staff before the king.

Solomon never flinched. "What does this mean?"

"With all your majesty, mighty king, after your death you will own no more space in the earth than is measured by that staff. Yet you would rule not just your own kind but spirits and demons as well!"

"Control your anger," Solomon said mildly. "I seek only the smallest of services from you. I wish to build a temple to the glory of God—ah, yes, demon; tremble at that—and I need to find the shamir."

"I have it not!"

"Gently, Ashmodai. Who does?"

"Mighty king, it was the shamir that was used to carve the two tablets borne by Moses. But since that day, the shamir has been in the care of the prince of the sea, who has placed it under the guardianship of the woodcock. The woodcock lives in its nest on a mountain peak and keeps the shamir ever with it, tucked under one wing."

"So be it," the king said. "You shall bide here, Ashmodai, till the temple is built."

He summoned Benaiah. "I have a second task for you, brave captain. You must find the shamir in the nest of the woodcock of the mountain peak and bring it back with you. Take this with you."

He gave Benaiah a sturdy lead-lined box and a thick pane of glass and told him how to use them. Off Benaiah went to the mountain, hunting till he found the woodcock's nest. The woodcock was away, but there in the nest, as Solomon had known there would be, were several of the bird's fledglings. Benaiah quickly covered the nest with the thick pane of glass, then hid and waited for the woodcock to return.

Here the bird came. It saw the glass and its fledglings trapped underneath and began to shriek, flapping its wings, clawing at the glass, and beating at it with its beak. But the glass would not break. The fledglings remained trapped. At last, the woodcock took the shamir, the diamond insect, from under its wing. The moment that the shamir touched the glass, the glass fell apart into two pieces.

"Oh, wonderful!" cried Benaiah, and he leaped out of hiding. He quickly slipped the shamir into the lead-lined box and returned all that long way to King Solomon.

And so it was that with the help of the magical shamir, the diamond insect, the holy temple was built. And Solomon the Wise released Ashmodai as he had promised.

As for the shamir—the moment that Solomon's temple to the glory of God was finished, the shamir vanished. And, to this day, no one has seen the shamir again.

No Escape from Fate

A Persian Folktale

"No Escape from Fate" is a familiar folktale about the inevitability of destiny, a variant on the "Appointment in Samarra" theme, possibly dating from ninth-century Persia. It still has quite an ironic impact, particularly since the city of Samarra was the scene of some fighting during the Iraq War, begun in 2003, and so many foreign soldiers traveled to Iraq to fight and met their deaths there.

Many years ago, there was a man in Bathsheba who asked his servant to go to the market. The servant went to the market, and among the throng he saw Death. Death made a gesture, and the servant grew frightened and ran home to his master.

The servant said, "Master, today I saw Death in the market amid the throng. And he made a threatening gesture to me. Master, I shall make haste, and I shall ride like the wind to Samarra, for Samarra is many miles from here, and Death will not find me there."

So the servant rode away to Samarra, and his master was sorely troubled. He went to the market, and he sought out Death. And the master said to Death, "Why did you make a threatening gesture at my servant? He has done me good service and is old in years."

And Death replied, "I made no threatening gesture at your servant. That was a start of surprise. For I saw him this morning in Bathsheba, but this night I was to meet him many miles away in Samarra."

Koschei the Deathless

A Russian Folktale

Koschei is a powerful figure in Russian folklore, immortal because he has hidden his life force outside of his body. There is scant evidence about his origins, whether or not he was originally a dark deity, but he always is portrayed in stories or paintings as a sinister figure, either as an old, gaunt man or as a skeletal figure.

Once there was a king with but one child, a son named Ivan. As Ivan grew, his nurse sang magical songs to him. Among them was one that she sang over and over till he knew it would be his destiny:

"Prince Ivan, when you are grown, you shall seek a bride. Beyond three times nine kingdoms she lives, and Princess Vasilisa is she called."

So it was that Prince Ivan, when he had grown into a fine young man, rode off to find his promised bride. But as he traveled beyond three times nine kingdoms, he came to a city where a man was being flogged. This was a poor man who could not repay a small loan. But when Prince Ivan tried to repay it for him, the prince was warned, "He who settles this loan will have his wife stolen by Koschei the Deathless."

"I have no wife," Prince Ivan said truthfully, and he settled the loan.

Then the prince went on his way. And, at last, weary but full of hope, he reached the last of the kingdoms. There was Princess Vasilisa in her castle tower. She, too, had heard songs, but hers had been about her promised groom. He looked at her, she looked at him, and they swore their vows there and then.

But as soon as they had, Koschei the Deathless came swooping down like a great black cloud. Before Prince Ivan could even draw his sword, Koschei had carried the princess away.

Prince Ivan rode in search of Koschei's lands. He rode high, he rode low, and, at last, he came to Koschei's castle, there at the end of

Nowhere. Koschei the Deathless was away at the hunt, and Ivan stole inside. Princess Vasilisa was there, but there was no way to steal her away again.

"And Koschei cannot be slain like mortal men!" she warned Ivan. "You must hide, and I will try to trick the truth from him."

So Ivan hid. Koschei came swooping in, now seeming to be a skeleton, now an ancient man, and now like nothing but darkness. "A mortal man has been here!" he shouted. "I smell him!"

"You were hunting mortal men," Princess Vasilisa answered. "Their smell is still in your nostrils."

Koschei threw himself down to rest. Vasilisa petted his head and stroked it, as though she were pleased he had returned. "I was so worried," she said. "I feared you would never return. I feared a wild beast had slain you."

Koschei laughed. "Foolish woman! Do you think mere beasts could devour me? My life and death lie in that broom by the door."

When he left, Ivan raced to the broom. Bah, no, it was nothing but a broom, with no magic about it.

When Koschei returned, he found that Vasilisa had gilded the broom and placed it on the table. "What is this?"

"Oh, I could not leave your life and death to lie on the floor!"

Koschei laughed. "Foolish woman! Do you think my death is here? My life and death lie in that goat at the window."

As soon as he left, Ivan raced to the goat. Bah, no, it was nothing but an animal, with no magic about it.

When Koschei returned, he found that Vasilisa had combed the goat's hair and woven golden ribbons in its horns. "What is this?"

"Oh, I could not let your life and death sit in a plain old goat!"

Koschei laughed. "Foolish woman! My death is far away. In the sea, there sits an island, and, on that island, there stands an oak. Under the oak is a chest. In the chest is a hare. In the hare is a duck. In the duck is an egg. And in the egg lies my heart."

Prince Ivan rode off to find Koschei's heart. On the way, he saved a dog from drowning. "Thank you!" the dog said. "I will come when you need aid."

Prince Ivan rode on. He saved an eagle from a net. "Thank you!" the eagle said. "I will come when you need aid."

Prince Ivan rode on. He saved a lobster that was stranded on the shore. "Thank you!" the lobster said. "I will come when you need aid."

At last, Prince Ivan reached the island. There stood the oak. Prince Ivan dug and dug at its roots. Here was the buried chest! He opened it carefully—but the hare sprang out and raced away.

"Dog I saved!" Prince Ivan cried. "Catch that hare!"

The dog appeared and caught the hare.

Ivan carefully cut open the hare—but the duck leaped out and flapped away.

"Eagle I saved!" Prince Ivan cried. "Catch that duck!"

The eagle appeared and caught the duck.

Ivan carefully cut open the duck—but the egg rolled out and fell into the sea.

"Lobster I saved!" Prince Ivan cried. "Catch that egg!"

The lobster caught the egg in a claw and brought it to Ivan.

"Thank you, my friends," Ivan cried, and he rode back to Koschei's castle.

Koschei the Deathless stormed outside, dragging Vasilisa with him. "I smell a mortal man!" he roared. "You shall die!"

"Not today!" Prince Ivan cried.

He sprang at Koschei and struck him on the head with the egg. The egg shattered, and with it, Koschei's heart shattered as well. Without a word, the monster fell down dead.

And Prince Ivan and Princess Vasilisa rode off together to their wedding. We were there, we ate, we drank, and we were joyous.

Gold-Tree and Silver-Tree

A Scottish Snow White Folktale

Storytellers and others may be surprised to learn that Snow White has a good many "sisters," the central characters in folk stories from around the world that tell the same basic tale. "Gold-Tree and Silver-Tree," a version from Scotland, was published by Joseph Jacobs in his *Celtic Tales* (1892).

Notice that this version depicts a clear mother-daughter rivalry, rather than a conflict between stepmother and stepdaughter. Also note the odd addition of the two wives. Folklorists have debated whether that element dates back to a time of polygamy, or whether the nameless storyteller who added that detail simply forgot that there already was a wife in the story and could not figure out how to eliminate the second one.

Once upon a time there was a king who had a wife, called Silver-Tree, and a daughter, whose name was Gold-Tree. On a certain day of the days, Gold-Tree and Silver-Tree went to a glen where there was a well, and in it there was a trout.

Said Silver-Tree, "Troutie, bonny little fellow, am not I the most beautiful queen in the world?"

"Oh! Indeed you are not."

"Who, then?"

"Why, Gold-Tree, your daughter."

Silver-Tree went home blind with rage. She lay down on the bed and vowed she would never be well until she could get the heart and the liver of her daughter to eat.

At nightfall, the king came home, and he was told that Silver-Tree was very ill. He went where she was and asked her what was wrong with her.

"Oh! Only a thing which you may heal if you like."

"Oh! Indeed there is nothing at all that I could do for you that I would not do."

"If I get the heart and the liver of Gold-Tree, my daughter, to eat, I shall be well."

Now, it happened that about this time the son of a great king had come from abroad to ask Gold-Tree for marrying. The king now agreed to this, and the couple went abroad.

The king then went and sent his lads to the hunting hill for a he-goat; he gave its heart and its liver to his wife to eat, and she rose well and healthy.

A year after this, Silver-Tree went to the glen where there was the well in which there was the trout.

"Troutie, bonny little fellow," said she, "am not I the most beautiful queen in the world?"

"Oh! Indeed you are not."

"Who, then?"

"Why, Gold-Tree, your daughter."

"Oh! Well, it is long since she was living. It is a year since I ate her heart and liver."

"Oh! Indeed she is not dead. She is married to a great prince abroad."

Silver-Tree went home and begged the king to put the long ship in order. She said, "I am going to see my dear Gold-Tree, for it is so long since I have seen her." The long ship was put in order, and they went away.

601

Silver-Tree herself was at the helm, and she steered the ship so well that they were not long at all before they arrived.

The prince was out hunting on the hills. Gold-Tree recognized the long ship of her father approaching.

"Oh!" said she to the servants, "my mother is coming, and she will kill me."

"She shall not kill you at all; we will lock you in a room where she cannot get near you."

This is how it was done, and when Silver-Tree came ashore, she began to cry out, "Come to meet your own mother when she comes to see you."

Gold-Tree said that she could not, that she was locked in the room, and that she could not get out of it.

"Will you not put out your little finger through the keyhole, so that your own mother may give a kiss to it?" asked Silver-Tree.

Gold-Tree put out her little finger, Silver-Tree stuck it with a poisoned stab, and Gold-Tree fell dead.

When the prince came home and found Gold-Tree dead, he was in great sorrow, and when he saw how beautiful she was, he did not bury her at all, but he locked her in a room where nobody would get near her.

In the course of time he married again, and the whole house was under the hand of his wife but one room, and he himself always kept the key to that room. On a certain day of the days, he forgot to take the key with him, and the second wife got into the room. What did she see there but the most beautiful woman that she had ever seen. She began to turn and try to wake her, and she noticed the poisoned stab in her finger. She took the stab out, and Gold-Tree rose alive, as beautiful as she had ever been.

At the fall of night, the prince came home from the hunting hill looking very downcast.

"What gift," said his wife, "would you give me if I could make you laugh?"

"Oh! Indeed, nothing could make me laugh, except were Gold-Tree to come alive again."

"Well, you'll find her alive down there in the room."

When the prince saw Gold-Tree alive, he made great rejoicings, and he began to kiss her, and kiss her, and kiss her.

Said the second wife, "Since she is the first one you had, it is better for you to stick to her, and I will go away."

"Oh! Indeed you shall not go away, but I shall have both of you."

At the end of the year, Silver-Tree went to the glen where there was the well in which there was the trout.

"Troutie, bonny little fellow," said she, "am not I the most beautiful queen in the world?"

"Oh! Indeed you are not."

"Who, then?"

"Why, Gold-Tree, your daughter."

"Oh! Well, she is not alive. It is a year since I put the poisoned stab into her finger."

"Oh! Indeed, she is not dead at all, at all."

Silver-Tree went home and begged the king to put the long ship in order, because she was going to see her dear Gold-Tree, as it was so long since she had seen her. The long ship was put in order, and they went away.

Again, it was Silver-Tree herself who was at the helm, and she steered the ship so well that they were not long at all before they arrived.

The prince was out hunting on the hills. Gold-Tree recognized her father's ship approaching.

"Oh!" said she, "my mother is coming, and she will kill me."

"Not at all," said the second wife; "we will go down to meet her."

Silver-Tree came ashore. "Come down, Gold-Tree, love," said she, "for your own mother has come to you with a precious drink."

"It is a custom in this country," said the second wife, "that the person who offers a drink takes a draught out of it first."

Silver-Tree put her mouth to it, and the second wife went and struck it so that some of it went down her throat, and she fell dead. They had only to carry her home a dead corpse and bury her.

The prince and his two wives were long alive after this, pleased and peaceful.

I left them there.

Geser

A Folktale of the Culture Hero of Tibet

Geser is the culture hero of Tibet, with so many tales in his collective epic that they would fill several volumes. Even in modern times, the tales of Geser remain popular, as much in defiance of Chinese occupation as a way to keep Tibet's culture alive.

In the very earliest times, in the upper world there were the fifty-five *tenger,* the divine spirits of the western direction, and the forty-four tenger of the eastern direction.

The leader of the western tenger was Han Hormasta, and the leader of the eastern tenger was Atai Ulaan. There was such anger between them that at last they fought. Han Hormasta won, tearing Atai Ulaan to bits. But when the pieces drifted down to Earth, they turned into evil spirits and disease.

Soon, the people were in despair. There was a powerful female shaman, Sharnaihan Shara, who threw her drumstick to the sky with such magical force that it landed on the table of Manzan Gurme Toodei, mother of all the sky spirits. Manzan Gurme Toodei took out her shaman mirror and saw the perils from evil and disease that faced humanity. She called a meeting of the tenger to decide how to save the people.

Han Hormasta had three sons. He decided to send the middle one, Bukhe Beligte, down to Earth. Reborn as a human, he would become the protector of the people.

Meanwhile, on Earth, there lived a poor husband and wife named Sengelen Noyon and Naran Goohon. They had no dog, no livestock, and practically no possessions, and they survived by gathering wild onions and garlic, netting small fish, and catching rabbits with snares. But despite their poverty, they were overjoyed when Naran Goohon found that she would have a child.

Soon after the baby was born, he lifted his right hand as though about to strike someone, bent his left leg, then looked at his parents with his right eye wide open and his left eye squinted. To his parents' amazement, the baby spoke.

"I hold up my right hand to show that I will always strike my enemies. I bend my left leg to show that I will always kick my enemies. My open right eye shows that I will always see the right path. My squinted left eye shows that I will always see through deceit."

Thus was Bukhe Beligte reborn as a human being.

Meanwhile, the evil spirits had discovered this fact. Meeting in their barren, sunless home, they plotted to kill the newborn child. They sent a giant rat with a bronze muzzle to kill him. But the baby struck the rat so hard that it shattered into ninety mice.

Then, the evil spirits sent a raven with an iron beak and claws to kill the baby. The baby smashed the raven into bits and threw the bits all the way back to where the evil spirits were meeting.

Last, the evil spirits sent a mosquito as large as a horse to kill the baby. The baby cried, "Be forever hungry and fly among the grass!" and struck it so hard that the giant mosquito shattered into a cloud of gnats.

The evil spirits were stunned. Their enemy had destroyed three monsters—and he was still just a baby!

So they went to their foul leader and cried, "Oh most powerful evil one, a magical boy has been born. We need to kill him, smash him, crush him!"

"I shall do this," their leader snapped.

He took on the guise of a human shaman and appeared before Sengelen Noyon and his wife. "I am a shaman who has come to help and protect your new son."

But as soon as the baby saw who had entered, he started screaming.

The shaman said, "Why is the boy making so much noise? Is he ill?"

He approached the cradle, ready to snatch up the baby. But as soon as he grew near, his disguise vanished. The hideous creature gnashed his iron fangs and roared, "I shall cut off your life and eat your soul!"

The baby simply grabbed the iron muzzle of the monster and kicked out so hard that the evil thing's head flew off.

The evil spirits left the baby alone after that.

The young hero grew rapidly—as much in a day as ordinary children grew in a year. He was never ill and never tired, and he played happily every day.

One day, Sengelen Noyon's older brother came to visit. When he saw that they had a child, he was very happy. "But the boy needs playmates," he said. "Let me take this child with me so that he can grow up and play with my own two sons."

The boy's parents agreed.

When Sargal Noyon got home, he held a feast to celebrate the boy's arrival. He told his guests, "Up to this time this boy has had no name. To whomever gives him a name, I will give meat and fat in exchange."

An old man leaning on a walking stick said, "The boy is sweaty and muddy. Why not call him Nuhata Nurgai, Slimy Face?"

Everybody laughed. It was a silly name, a perfect name for a boy who had not yet earned an adult name. And so it was that the newly named Nuhata Nurgai watched Sargal Noyon's animals and played with Sargal Noyon's own sons, Altan Shagai and Mungun Shagai. They were older than the boy, and were forever trying his strength and the quickness of his mind. But Nuhata Nurgai never failed. He grew and thrived.

Now, the ruler of the northwestern lands, Temeen Ulaan, had a beautiful daughter, Tumen Jargalan. He announced that he would give his daughter in marriage to any man who was able to win three contests of strength. Warriors came from far and wide for the contest. Nuhata Nurgai also was there, wearing old clothes and riding a mouse brown colt.

Then the contests began. For the first, Nuhata Nurgai picked up a boulder and threw it so hard that it shattered into flints. For the second, he uprooted a pine tree and threw it so hard that it shattered into splinters. For the third, he pulled up an ephedra bush and threw it so far that no one could see it land.

No one else could match him, and so Nuhata Nurgai took Tumen Jargalan home as his wife. But he left behind a jealous rival, his uncle Hara Zutan, who hated him from that moment on.

Soon after returning home, Nuhata Nurgai set out again, riding his mouse brown colt. He reached a country where the ruler, Shaazgai Bayan, was promising to give his daughter in marriage to any man who could defeat a giant warrior.

The giant had a powerful body, with a chest as wide as the sea. His armor was of black forged iron, his bow was the trunk of a tree, and his quiver was made of planks. But Nuhata Nurgai dodged his arrows, caught him up, and threw him out of sight. He took Shaazgai Bayan's daughter, Urmai Goohon, back to his home, and as the custom was for their people, she became his second wife.

Tumen Jargalan and Urmai Goohon got along well together. But they could not understand why Nuhata Nurgai seemed to want the three of them to have a very dull life together. They didn't know that their husband was only waiting for the right time.

And then, one night Nuhata Nurgai climbed to the summit of Mount Sumber and performed a ritual to honor the tengers. Then and there, he changed into his true form as Bukhe Beligte, with a warrior's strong face and body, blazing eyes, and long black hair.

Looking down from the upper world, Han Hormasta saw his son and nodded. He was ready. So Han Hormasta sent down a warrior's horse and equipment. The horse was a bay, with hooves like iron and legs that would never tire. Lightning glittered in its eyes, and its name was Beligen, which means "gift."

The warrior, who was now known as Geser, grabbed the red reins of the horse, put his feet into the silver stirrups, sat upon the silver saddle, and rode down into the world.

Sengelen Noyon and Naran Goohon rejoiced to know they had borne such a heroic son, and Tumen Jargalan and Urmai Goohon rejoiced to realize they were married to such a handsome warrior.

One day, Geser went hunting in the Altai Mountains. After three days of hunting, he had not found a single deer. On the fourth day, he saw a spotted deer running in the forest and followed it. Just as he was about to shoot, a young man on a chestnut horse dashed out of the forest, shot the deer, swung it up on his horse, and galloped away.

Geser rode after him, angry at losing the deer. They came to the shores of Lake Baikal, but the young man never stopped. He rode his horse right into the water and disappeared.

Geser left his horse and warily followed, down into the land of Uha Loson, chief of the water spirits. The rider of the chestnut horse was none other than the chief's daughter, Alma Mergen, who had disguised herself as a young man while hunting. Uha Loson was delighted to see Geser, because he had known Geser's father, Han Hormasta, quite well. The two men had once agreed that their children would be married. According to this custom, Alma Mergen became Geser's third wife.

Geser and Alma Mergen rode to his home, where he built three houses for his three wives. All was happiness for a time. Geser would say to his family, "Is the Sun in the sky beautiful, or is Tumen Jargalan beautiful? Is the Sun in the heavens beautiful, or is Urmai Goohon beautiful? Is the golden Sun beautiful, or is Alma Mergen beautiful?"

But life could not stay so peaceful for long. The head of Atai Ulaan, the tenger who had been slain and dismembered by Han Hormasta, had turned into the monster Arhan Chotgor. Now, the monster was near Geser's home, lying in wait.

Arhan Chotgor grabbed the first man who came by—but it wasn't Geser. It was Geser's uncle Hara Zutan, who still hated Geser. Terrified, Hara Zutan told the monster, "I will help you hurt him. I will break Geser's bow and arrows. I will steal his wife Urmai Goohon, and you can have Tumen Jargalan."

The monster agreed. Late that night, Hara Zutan stole into Geser's house, broke the antler arrowheads off Geser's arrows, cut his bowstring, broke his sword, and smashed the tip of his spear.

When Geser came home and found that he was weaponless, he dared not wait, not with the lives of his wives at stake. He caught up with Arhan Chotgor and, without weapons, fought with all his skill. At last, he managed to break the monster's neck and slay him.

Then, he went after Hara Zutan, who fell to his knees before Geser, promising, "I won't do anything like this again!"

Since this was Geser's uncle, the hero reluctantly forgave Hara Zutan and sent him home.

But his trouble with Atai Ulaan had not ended just yet. Another demonic creature, Gal Nurman Khan, had sprung from the first vertebra of Atai Ulaan's severed neck. This monster sprang up from the dry, desolate home of the evil spirits and attacked the human world, setting things on fire wherever he went.

Geser tracked Gal Nurman Khan to his wilderness home, and they fought. The fiery demon was stronger than Geser, and, this time, things looked bleak for the hero. But the force of their fight sent a large chunk of rock crashing down from a cliff onto the evil being, crushing him.

Geser knew that Gal Nurman Khan did not live alone. He went on to fight and slay the evil demon-wife and demon-child as well.

As time passed, Geser's fame grew. He tracked down the monster deer Orgoli, which had swallowed forty people whole. Orgoli tried to swallow Geser as well, but as Orgoli tried to suck him in, Geser wedged his spear crosswise in the deer's mouth and held on. Drawing his sword, he chopped off Orgoli's head. Out from the deer's vast body, saved by Geser, crawled the forty people Orgoli had swallowed.

Many other adventures followed in the ensuing years. Geser was not too proud to seek help when it was needed. Once, when he knew he could not defeat a monster, the powerful Sherem Minaata Khan, Geser listened to the advice of his wives and went to the upper world. There, he asked his immortal grandmother for aid. She gave him a stick that she used to beat fleece for felt making. Sure enough, that simple little stick was the one thing that could slay Sherem Minaata Khan. One blow over the monster's head, and he lay dead.

Returning home, Geser said to his wives, "Now that it is a good time, I will fill my quiver with arrows; now that it is a peaceful time I will collect my arrows."

But there can never be rest for a hero. Geser's life was forever full of adventures, far too many to be recounted here. He defeated monsters, demons, and enemies of the realm, and, with his efforts, continually kept peace and happiness for the people.

Geser and his wives lived happily for three days and three years—which was to be the only respite from the hero's never-ending adventures.

A Bagful of Tricks

A Uighur Folktale from China

The Uighurs, powerful in Mongolia between the eighth and twelfth centuries, are Turkic-speaking people who live in northwestern China. The Uighur folktale "A Bagful of Tricks" tells of the trickster figure Effendi Nasreddin. The written record of this character's exploits first started appearing in about the thirteenth century C.E., and there may have been earlier oral tales.

The many tales of Effendi Nasreddin, a fellow who tends to get the better of the high and mighty, are popular from China to Turkey, where he is called Nasreddin Hodja, and the Middle East, where he may be called Mullah Nasreddin. All the honorifics—*effendi* means "master" in Turkish, a *hodja* is a scholar, and a mullah is a religious teacher or leader—attached to his name do not change the fact that Nasreddin is a gadfly, a satiric wise man who never hesitates to play the fool to make his point.

Once there was and once there was not a *padishah*, a great ruler, who heard of the tricks played on the high and mighty by the Effendi Nasreddin.

"I have heard this fellow is able even to trick a padishah. Can such a thing be?" he asked.

"It is true, your majesty," his ministers warily assured him. "This Nasreddin may be of common blood, but he is truly clever enough to trick anyone, even a padishah."

"That's impossible!" raged the padishah. "What, a—a nobody more clever than a ruler? It cannot be so!"

To prove his point, the padishah disguised himself as a common man and rode off to the village of the effendi. There, he greeted Nasreddin, who was sitting peacefully in front of his house. The padishah said to him, "It is said that here there lives a most clever man, the Effendi Nasreddin."

"So it is said."

"I have heard amazing tales of his cleverness, so amazing that I doubt they can be true. Can his fame for trickery possibly be justified?"

"I believe that it can," said the effendi, getting to his feet, "for Nasreddin I am. What can I do for you?"

"I have heard much about you," said the padishah. "I have heard that you can trick anyone and everyone. But I am here to warn you that today you shall not win your little game. For no one born has ever been able to fool me."

"So, now!" the effendi exclaimed as he scratched his head. "You are a difficult opponent; I can see that. For you no common trick will do. No, I must first go home and get my special bag full of tricks. Unless, of course, you are afraid of that bag!"

"Nonsense! Get whatever bag you wish—but be quick about it!"

"Well, now, my home is a good distance from here. If you would lend me your horse, I could be there and back again in almost no time. Otherwise, I would have to walk and walk and—"

607

"Never mind! Here is my horse. Now, go get your bag of tricks. And hurry back here as quickly as you can ride. I am eager to test your cleverness!"

Effendi Nasreddin bowed low, then leaped into the saddle and rode off as swiftly as an arrow from a bow. The padishah stood impatiently waiting.

And waiting.

And waiting.

Night fell. At last, the truth struck the padishah: Nasreddin was not coming back.

"He tricked me!" the padishah admitted. "He did just what he set out to do. The Effendi Nasreddin has tricked the padishah!"

The Story of Gelert

A Welsh Local Folktale

The story of the faithful dog Gelert is an example of a local legend—the Welsh town of Beddgelert (also called Beth-Gelert), or "Gelert's Grave," was named for it—and of a world tale, since similar stories of similarly faithful dogs and mistrustful masters can be found around the world. This particular version dates from the nineteenth century.

Somewhere around the year 1200, Prince Llewellyn had a castle at Aber. Indeed, parts of the towers remain to this day. His consort was Princess Joan, the daughter of King John. Llewellyn was a great hunter of wolves and foxes, for the hills of Carnarvonshire were infested with wolves in those days, after the young lambs.

Now, the prince had several hunting houses, and one of them was at the place now called Beth-Gelert, where the wolves were very thick at this time. The prince used to travel from farmhouse to farmhouse with his family and friends when going on these hunting parties.

One season, they went hunting from Aber, and they stopped at the house where Beth-Gelert is now—which was about 14 miles away. The prince had all his hounds with him, but his favorite was Gelert, a hound who had never let off a wolf for six years.

The prince loved the dog like a child, and, at the sound of his horn, Gelert was always the first to come bounding up. There was company at the house, and, one day, they went hunting, leaving Llewellyn's wife behind at the farmhouse with their child in a big wooden cradle.

The hunting party killed three or four wolves. About two hours before the word passed for returning home, Llewellyn missed Gelert, and he asked his huntsmen:

"Where's Gelert? I don't see him."

"Well, indeed, master, I've missed him this half hour."

And Llewellyn blew his horn, but no Gelert came at the sound.

Indeed, Gelert had gotten on to a wolves' track that led to the house.

The prince sounded the return, and they went home, the prince lamenting Gelert. "He's sure to have been slain—he's sure to have been slain since he did not answer the horn. Oh, my Gelert!"

And they approached the house, and the prince went into the house, and saw Gelert lying by the overturned cradle, and blood all about the room.

"What! Hast thou slain my child?" asked the prince, and ran his sword through the dog.

After that, he lifted up the cradle to look for his child and found underneath it the body of a big wolf that Gelert had slain. His child was safe. Gelert had capsized the cradle in the scuffle.

"Oh, Gelert! Oh, Gelert!" said the prince. "My favorite hound! My favorite hound! Thou hast been slain by thy master's hand, and in death thou hast licked thy master's hand!" He patted the dog, but it was too late, and poor Gelert died licking his master's hand.

The next day, they made a coffin and had a regular funeral, the same as if Gelert were a human being, all the servants and everybody else in deep mourning.

They made Gelert a grave, and the village was called after the dog, Beth-Gelert (Gelert's Grave). The prince planted a tree and laid a gravestone of slate, though it was before the days of quarries. And they are to be seen there to this day.

Vainamoinen

A Finnish Hero Tale

Vainamoinen is one of the heroes of the Finnish epic the *Kalevala*, which was compiled from epic ballads by Elias Lönnrot in the late nineteenth century. Although Vainamoinen looks like an old man, he has the magical strength of a true wizard and the spirit of a warrior.

Vainamoinen was the son not of a mortal woman but of an air spirit, Ilmatar. Ilmatar, impregnated by the wind, came to rest on the earth ocean for long years while the world formed around her, and her son grew in her womb. For sixty years, Vainamoinen lived and grew in that warm, safe prison, but, at last, he could stand this strange captivity no longer and burst free into the world.

His long time in the womb had marked him. Vainamoinen was no babe, no young boy. He was a gray-bearded man, old yet not old, wise with more than human knowledge, a skilled singer of magic songs.

But the world into which he'd arrived was still barren and bleak. Vainamoinen set about sowing the world for humankind, fruit and field and forest, and he sang the world's first magic sowing song as he did, ensuring fertile crops forever after. Now, the world was done, and humans flourished like the forest trees.

Word of Vainamoinen's primal deeds and magic songs spread. And whenever there is one well known for a skill, along will come a younger one to challenge him.

Joukahaimen was a young magician, a spell singer who fancied himself quite a master of the craft. He was full of pride and the arrogance of the untried, and he meant to pick fights with other wizards, singing them into defeat.

His father forbade it, and his mother pleaded, "They will bewitch you; they will destroy you, sing you into helpless snow!"

"I will sing the best singer into the worst!" Joukahaimen replied, and he set out, heedless of his parents' pain.

It was Vainamoinen whom Joukahaimen truly wished to meet and defeat. It was Vainamoinen he did meet, quite by accident. The winter snow was heavy, leaving only a narrow road down which he drove his sleigh, just as Vainamoinen was driving the other way. Vainamoinen had the right of way, but Joukahaimen refused to give it. Shaft tangled with shaft, trace with trace, and the two sleighs came to a sudden rough stop.

"Who are you?" Vainamoinen shouted. "What clan, rude one?"

"I am Joukahaimen. Now name your own lowly clan!"

"I am Vainamoinen. Move aside, youngster. I have no quarrel with a boy."

"My youth is a small matter!" Joukahaimen retorted. "It's our knowledge that's the point, our magic skill. It's he who is the master there who should have the right of way."

"What do I know?" Vainamoinen said with great sarcasm. "I have always lived my life as a farmer, sowing crops. And what, young man, do you know?"

Joukahaimen never heard the sarcasm, never saw how he was being baited. He boasted of the wondrous things he'd seen and heard, expecting this old graybeard to cringe in fright. He told of knowing the trees in every forest, the fish in every stream. He told of knowing how the North plowed with a reindeer, the South with a mare.

But all Vainamoinen said was, "Childish knowledge. Easy things. What else do you know?"

Stung, Joukahaimen boasted of more and wondrous things he'd learned. He told of knowing the origin of birds, the language of snakes, the heart of water from a mountain, the heart of fire from the lightning, the heart of rust in iron.

Vainamoinen heard him out, all these young man's boastings, then asked mildly, "Is this all? Has your ranting come at last to its end?"

Still not seeing how the old man baited him, Joukahaimen boasted wildly, claiming that he had plowed the sea, set the land in place, sowed it with seed—even that he'd guided the Sun and Moon and set the stars in the sky.

"Now I know you lie," Vainamoinen said. "No one saw you plow the sea; nor were you there when the world was made. Small wit, yours, if you claim such things."

"If I have small wit," Joukahaimen snapped, "then I'll let my sword speak for me!"

Vainamoinen only looked at him with scorn. "I'm not afraid of you, youngster, nor of your sword or wit. Enough of this game. Be off with you."

Joukahaimen nearly roared with rage. "Whoever fears to fight a duel, him will I sing into the shape of a pig! A dead pig in a dunghill!"

Vainamoinen hissed in sudden fury. That this mere child should dare insult him thus! He began to sing—began to sing the magic songs. No children's rhymes were these, no boyish things. Pure magic were they, so mighty that the land around him shook and mountains trembled.

And he sang magic over young Joukahaimen, sang green sprouts onto his bow, willows onto his sleigh's shafts, sang the sleigh itself into a pond and the horse into a rock, sang Joukahaimen's sword into lightning, his

arrows into hawks, sang Joukahaimen's cap into a cloud, his gloves into lilies in the pond, his coat into a patch of sky.

And still Vainamoinen sang, his fury yet unabated, sang against Joukahaimen himself, sang the young man into the ground to his ankles, his knees, his armpits. All the while, Joukahaimen tried his best to fight back, to sing a spell song in self-defense, but not a word would come. He could not pull so much as a foot free from the earth, and, all the while, Vainamoinen was singing him deeper, ever deeper!

"Wait! Good, kind, wise Vainamoinen, wait. Reverse your spells; release me. I will give you any payment you desire, any ransom you may name."

That pierced the cloud of Vainamoinen's wrath, though it did not dissolve it utterly. "What payment would you make?"

"I have two fine bows—"

"I have no need of your bows." And he sang Joukahaimen deeper into the earth.

"I have two swift boats—"

"I have no need of your boats." And he sang Joukahaimen deeper into the earth.

"Horses, then! I have fine stallions, mighty steeds—"

"I have no need of horses." And he sang Joukahaimen deeper yet into the earth.

On and on Joukahaimen ranted, offering anything that was his to give and many things that were not. But Vainamoinen was not moved.

At last, despairing, buried to his chin and spitting out mud, the young man pleaded, "Reverse your spells. Sing them backward and release me, oh, wondrous wizard. In my mother's house there lives my sister, fairest Aino. Sing me free, Vainamoinen, and she shall be your wife."

Vainamoinen paused. A wife. He had been lonely, alone of his kind. A wife would warm his days and nights. Vainamoinen sang the young man free, restoring clothes and weapons, sleigh and horse.

Joukahaimen stammered out nervous thanks, no longer the arrogant young wizard.

He hurried home in such haste that he crashed the sleigh against the side of his parents' house.

And so ended the duel. But alas, when she heard she was to wed the ancient, mighty wizard, Aino heard nothing of "mighty" or "wizard." She listened to no word about how kind Vainamoinen would be to her, how easy and happy her life would be. No, Aino heard only "ancient." Crying that she would not be married off to an old, old man, and one who was not even truly human, Aino cast herself into the sea.

Vainamoinen wept for her, grieved for her, and, in the grieving, maybe wept a bit for himself, so old, so wise, yet so lonely. Aino stayed in the ocean, transformed into a fish. And there Vainamoinen was forced to leave her.

Aino's tale ends in the sea. Vainamoinen, though, the mighty wizard, Vainamoinen went on to more adventures.

But never did he, greatest of spell singers, wisest of heroes, win a wife for himself.

Guigemar

A Medieval French Hero Tale

"Guigemar," one of Marie de France's twelfth-century heroic romances, shows some of the roots of the modern romance as well as many of the traditions of medieval folktales and chansons de geste. The tale contains familiar folk themes, such as the hero who does not know love and the knot that cannot be untied by any but the lover.

In the case of the hero who does not know love, examples can be found in mythology and folklore, such as in the Teutonic story of Siegfried, in which the hero does not know love until he sees Brynhild and is smitten, and in European folktales such as "The Boy Who Never Shuddered." The knot that cannot be untied is an echo of the bow that can be drawn only by Odysseus or Rama, or the sword that can be drawn only by the rightful king. There is also the twelfth-century image of courtly love, in which a young man and woman are ideally to love each other truly, without the burden of marriage. As an educated woman, Marie de France would have been well aware of these themes.

Guigemar was a handsome, brave young man with only one flaw: He had never known love and had no real interest in the subject. Then, in a hunting accident, he was wounded by an arrow and told by the hind that he had wounded that nothing could cure him but the woman he loved.

Since Guigemar wanted to be healed, he went questing for a woman to love. But when he took shelter for the night in an abandoned ship, he awoke to find himself helplessly adrift. Since he had no idea how to sail a ship, he prayed to God for help.

The ship sailed straight into a castle's harbor. The ruler of that castle was an old man who kept his young wife a prisoner locked in her chambers. But her attendants were sympathetic to her plight, and when they found the handsome young Guigemar, they spirited him to her. She healed his wound, and the two young people fell utterly in love. They spent a deliriously happy time together, but of course the old man found out.

The young woman tied a knot in Guigemar's shirt, telling him that only the woman he loved would be able to untie it. He fastened his belt (symbolizing a chastity belt) about her waist, saying that only the one who loved her would be able to remove it.

Then, Guigemar was captured by the old man's guards and thrown into his ship, which was cast adrift. Everyone was sure that the young man would die.

But the old man made a mistake; one day, he neglected to lock the door. His wife stole away, found a small boat, and cast off, hoping to join Guigemar in death. Instead, the boat took her to another castle.

This castle was ruled over by Meriaduc, a strong lord who instantly fell in love with the beautiful young woman. He wanted to take her to bed but could not unfasten Guigemar's belt. Frustrated, he told her that there was an-other like her, a young man with a knotted shirt that no woman could remove. Learning that Guigemar was still alive, the young woman nearly fainted with joy.

Now that Meriaduc knew that she loved Guigemar, he planned a tournament, knowing that it would lure Guigemar to the castle. Sure enough, the young man arrived, and there was a joyous but brief reunion between him and his love.

As soon as the knot was untied and the belt removed, Meriaduc stated that he would not give the young woman up.

Guigemar left and later returned with an army. He captured the castle and killed Meriaduc. Guigemar and his love went off to-gether with much rejoicing.

A Story of Gwydion

A Medieval Welsh Mythic Tale

Gwydion is a powerful but good-hearted magician-prince who is a major character in the Welsh medieval collection of tales called the *Mabinogion*. Gwydion originally may have been a deity, like his uncle Math, but this point is still being debated by scholars.

This is only part of the long and complex tale of Gwydion, whose adventures are included in the *Mabinogion*. The first four stories of this work, which predate the written *Mabinogion*, are referred to as the "four branches." There is much debate about just how old the "four branches" are, but elements in the four tales make a good case for roots in the pre-Christian era. This assessment could place the stories as far back as the first millennium B.C.E.

Gwydion came from a magical family. His uncle Math was the son of Mathonwy, ruler of the land of Gwynedd in present-day northern Wales. Math was a powerful magician, the strongest in all the realm. And Gwydion was no weak conjurer.

Ah no, Gwydion could transform sticks to boars, weeds to shoes, whatever he wished into whatever he wished, himself included, without any difficulty at all. Since he was a good man at heart, this great talent was generally no problem to Gwydion or to others. Generally, that is.

Gwydion had gotten himself into trouble by sympathizing with his lovesick brother. Gwydion had used his magic to win a young woman for his brother. She had been the ritual foot-holder for Math, whose power was such that his feet must never touch the bare earth. The young magician had spent time in animal shape after helping his brother, thanks to his angry uncle's greater magic.

So now another foot-holder had to be found. No easy matter that, since the young woman chosen must be pure of heart and body. Aranhrod came forward, she who was Gwydion's sister (though, truth to tell, they had little enough to do with each other, she like chill winter, he like bright summer), to claim the title. Gwydion wondered at that, since he knew his sister was hardly pure in either sense. But come forward she did—to her shame.

Any candidate for foot-holder must first step over a magic wand, and the moment Aranhrod did so, she cried out and gave birth on the spot to two children. One, a finely formed boy, was named Dylan, son of the wave (for, as it turned out later, he was a child of the fair folk of the sea). The second was barely formed at all, a baby too soon torn from the womb.

Aranhrod fled without a backward glance, but Gwydion, his heart aching with pity for his too-new nephew, swept the poor thing up in his cloak and rushed off for his quarters. There, he magicked a chest into a warming container, as close to a womb as his magic could make it, and placed the baby safely within.

"Live, little one," he whispered. "Grow strong and healthy."

And so the baby did. Taken at last from the chest, he was as healthy and lusty lunged as any baby normally born. Gwydion found a nurse for him, a cheerful woman with milk for more than her own baby. The only thing Gwydion could not do for his nephew was name him. That task, by law and magic, must be done by the boy's mother.

"In time," Gwydion said. "In time."

And time passed. The baby grew to a fine, handsome boy, as fair as Gwydion and warm of heart.

"Now, what woman would not be joyous to see so fine a son?" Gwydion thought, watching the boy laughing and running at play. "Even Aranhrod surely will feel some softening of her cold heart at the sight of him."

But Aranhrod had no desire to be reminded of her humiliation back at Math's court. "That is not my son. In fact, I place this curse on him: He shall have no name save from my lips, and my lips shall never utter a name for him."

The magic in this curse was strong, for Aranhrod had inherited some of the family powers as well. Gwydion drew back in horror, for how could a man without a name ever win honor for himself? "You are a wicked woman to harm one who never harmed you! But I vow that name him you shall."

Back Gwydion went to Caer Dathl, his fortress, and he thought long and long again on what he must do. He walked along the beach below the fortress, now and again staring across the water at Aranhrod's fortress, Caer Aranhrod, on its island, and the gathered dulse and seaweed. From this, he conjured a ship and a great mass of the finest cordovan leather. No one had ever seen more supple, beautiful leather!

"Of course not," Gwydion said with a laugh. "For it comes not from some poor cow but from my own will."

He cast magic over himself and his nephew as well, making them look like nothing more than a common shoemaker and his apprentice, then set sail for Caer Aranhrod. A messenger came scurrying down from the fortress to see who had come, then went scurrying back up to his mistress.

"A shoemaker has come here, lady, and he has the finest leather that ever I've seen."

Aranhrod had her feet outlined on a bit of cowhide. "Give this to the shoemaker. Have him make me a pair of shoes."

But Gwydion cleverly made them far too big. The next pair he made too small. Then he grumbled, as a real shoemaker might, "I cannot work from charts alone! I must work from the lady's living foot."

Aranhrod was not about to let a stranger into her fortress. She went down to him. And while Gwydion was pretending to measure her foot, the boy, her son, played at hunting. A wren landed on the boat's mast, and the boy shot it down with a stone from his sling so neatly that Aranhrod cried out, "What a sure hand that fair-haired child has shown!"

"And what a fine name you have given him!" Gwydion cried, dropping his magical disguise. "Lleu Llaw Gyffes, Fair-haired Sure of Hand, shall he be!"

Raging, Aranhrod shouted, "I put this curse on him, then: He shall never take arms till I arm him—and that, I shall never do!"

For a man in that warrior world not to be able to use weapons was a harsh curse, indeed. "A wicked woman you were; a wicked woman you are," Gwydion told her. "But I swear this: He shall take arms!"

Gwydion sailed back to his fortress with his newly named nephew, soothing the boy's fear. "You have a name. I will win you arms; never fear. Have I not given my word?"

But first some time had to pass, time in which Lleu Llaw Gyffes grew into a fine youngster just on the edge of manhood. But Gwydion saw the pain in his eyes when the other boys Lleu's age practiced with sword or spear.

"Come," he said to his nephew. "Time for you to be armed."

He cast a spell over them both, making them look like a world-weary bard and his apprentice, then traveled back to Caer Aranhrod. Bards were always welcome in those days, so it was with no difficulty at all that Gwydion and Lleu won entry. Gwydion happened to be a fine teller of tales, so Aranhrod listened to him without the slightest doubt that he was, indeed, a bard. And, as a bard, he and his "apprentice" were given a fine sleeping chamber that night.

Long before dawn, Gwydion arose and called his magic powers to him. As the sun rose, the air filled with the sounds of war: trumpets blared; men shouted; weapons clashed. It was not long before Aranhrod herself came to the chamber and said, "Bards, I will not deny that we're in a sorry fix. There is no way out for you—for any of us—but to fight. And we need every able-bodied man. Will you fight?"

"Gladly," Gwydion said, and began donning the armor Aranhrod's men had brought. "Och, but my lad there is still new to weaponry. Won't you help him with his armor, lady?"

Now Aranhrod was in such a frantic state, she thought nothing of it. But as she finished helping the "apprentice" don armor, the clamor of battle stopped as suddenly as though cut off by a wall. The disguise fell from Gwydion and Lleu. "Thank you, Sister!" the magician cried ironically. "For now Lleu is armed, and by your own hands."

"May you suffer for what you've done!"

"I? I've done nothing but help your son."

"Many a boy could have come to grief during your magical tricks!"

"Nary a one. And it's you who should suffer, Sister, for the harm you wished on Lleu. But now—"

"But now my curse on him! May he never find a wife of any race known in this world!"

"He has a name, no thanks to you, he bears arms, no thanks to you, and he shall yet find a wife, no thanks to you!"

But Gwydion left that fortress saddened. This time no simple trick of illusion would help. Where would Lleu find a wife if not among the races of the world?

"If I cannot help Lleu," Gwydion thought, "then perhaps Math can. He is, after all, the most powerful magician in the realm."

So off Gwydion went to his uncle, to tell him all that had befallen. "All is not lost, not yet," Math said after a while. "Come, nephew. We must gather flowers."

"Flowers?"

"If we cannot find a bride for Lleu, then we shall make one."

Math and Gwydion worked long hours over the flowers they had gathered. What spells they said, what charms they wove, none can guess. But at the end of it all, there were two very weary magicians—and one woman, as new as the springtime, as lovely as the flowers. Blodeuedd, they named her, and gave her to Lleu as his bride. Math gave them both Cantref Dinoding to rule over, and, for a time, all went well with Lleu and his strange lady.

But Blodeuedd was, after all, made of flowers. She lacked the deep soul of a true human woman. One day, Gronw Pebyr, Lord of Penllyn, stopped by Lleu's fortress when he was not at home. Blodeuedd gave Gronw hospitality. And after the two of them had spent some time in staring hotly at each other, she gave him a great deal more.

"But I have a husband," she murmured to Gronw.

"Such can be removed."

"Not he. He is the nephew and great-nephew of magicians, and not vulnerable as are ordinary men."

"He still breathes like ordinary men. There must be a way to slay him. Find it, Blodeuedd."

That night, Lleu returned home, and Blodeuedd pretended to be joyous. But later, she pretended just as easily to be sorrowful.

"Why, now, wife, what's wrong?"

"If you must know, husband, I am worrying about your death. If someone should kill you—"

"Och, foolish! It is not easy to kill me."

"Why not? Are you not a man? Love, please, please, don't jest with me!"

Lleu saw the worry in her eyes and thought—how not?—that it was all for him. "Love, hear me: It would not be easy to kill me even with a cast of a spear. For that spear could only be made by someone working on it a year, and only on each holy day at that."

"But then you could be slain!"

"Not easily. For I cannot be killed in a house nor outside, neither on horse nor on foot."

"Then—then, how *could* you be slain?"

He still thought the worry in her eyes was for him, all for him, and Lleu smiled at his wife and told her, "One must make a bath for me on the river bank, and construct a roof over the tub, as though to make it a good shelter. Then, that one must find a goat and bring it beside the tub. I must stand with one foot on the goat's back, the other on the edge of the tub. Only then can I be slain."

Of course, Blodeuedd pretended to be greatly relieved—and, of course, she sent word to Gronw, who set about making the spear. A year passed, and then, when Blodeuedd heard that the spear was done, she said to Lleu, "This is foolish of me, my lord, I know it. But . . . och, I cannot picture how one could possibly stand with one foot on a goat's back and the other on the edge of a tub! Surely that's impossible!"

In that year, she had given Lleu nothing but assurances of her love. And he, young man that he was, never thought once of how foolish he was being. "Come, love, I'll show you how it can be done."

So he stood with one foot on the edge of the tub placed at the riverbank and all roofed over, and the other foot on the goat.

And Gronw cast the fatal spear. Lleu screamed as it pierced him. But Lleu had just enough magic in his blood to change to an eagle's form and fly away.

Gwydion, far from there at the court of Math, felt his nephew's cry in every nerve and sinew. "Uncle—"

"I felt it, too."

"I will find him," Gwydion swore. "I will know no rest till I find him."

He wandered here and there and here again, and rested one night in the hut of a swineherd. Gwydion, waking early, saw one sow set off from the pen at a good clip and followed, wondering. She came to a tree, where she fed on that which fell from it. And that was a terrible thing: rotten flesh. Gwydion looked sharply up, and there in that tree, on the uppermost branch, was a sickly eagle, weak and all but dead, and it was from this bird that the rotten flesh fell.

"Lleu," Gwydion breathed. "You don't even remember being human, poor wounded lad, do you?"

He began, very softly and carefully, to sing the eagle out of the tree, his magic tender. At the first verse, the eagle slid down from the upper branch to a lower. At the second verse, the eagle slipped down to the lowest branch. And at the third verse, he landed weakly on Gwydion's knee. Gwydion touched him with magic, and the eagle was Lleu again, but Lleu was so gravely thin and sick that Gwydion feared he would die. Hastily, the magician brought him home, and all the doctors in Gwynedd tended him.

And at the end of the year, Lleu was healthy again.

"Now," Gwydion murmured to Math, "is the time for justice."

"Indeed," Math agreed, and mustered his men.

Off they rode for Cantref Dinoding, which had all this while been in the hands of Gronw Pebyr and the treacherous Blodeuedd. When Blodeuedd saw the army, she cried out in terror, "Gwydion has come for me!"

She fled out across the wilderness, but no matter how she ran, Gwydion was right behind her. At last, she could go no farther. "Don't kill me!"

"I won't," Gwydion agreed grimly. "But for the shame and harm you brought upon Lleu, you shall never see the light of day again. You shall fly only by night, and all the other birds shall hate you. Yes, birds, Blodeuedd. No longer flowers, but owl, no longer Blodeuedd but Blodeuwedd." And Blodeuwedd, "flower face," she became, for that is the look of an owl's face, and she flew despairingly away.

As for Gronw Pebyr, it was Lleu who cornered that villain. "What fine will you accept?" Gronw cried. "Copper? Silver? Gold? Name your blood price, and I will pay it!"

"No blood price save this," Lleu replied coldly. "A cast of a spear as you gave to me."

Gronw snatched up a great stone to shield himself, but so powerful was the fury of Lleu Llaw Gyffes that his spear stabbed right through the stone—and through Gronw, too.

Lleu Llaw Gyffes took possession of his land once more, and ruled it well. And as for Gwydion and his adventures after—that tale is not known.

Raven Steals the Sun

An American Myth from the Pacific Northwest

Raven is a major trickster figure and religious personage in the mythic traditions of most of the indigenous peoples of the Pacific Northwest. This particular tale is told with only minor variations by all the cultural groups of the region.

In the days before the rules of things were set down, the world and sky alike were forever dark, so dark that nothing could be seen—so dark, in fact, that Raven could not see to hunt. He quickly grew weary of flying into rocks and tripping over roots.

"This will never do," he said.

So Raven listened. He heard, from where no one knows, that there was one source of light, one bright golden ball kept by a greedy old man who would not share it with anyone.

"This will never do," Raven repeated, and went in search of the old man.

At last, he came to the old man's lodge, and waited in hiding to see what he would learn.

So, now! The old man had a young daughter. Quick-witted Raven swiftly designed a plan.

"May I be a pine needle floating upon the water," he said.

And instantly, he became a pine needle floating upon the water.

"May the old man's daughter have a great thirst," Raven whispered, "and may she drink me right down."

Instantly, the old man's daughter was seized by a great thirst. Grabbing up a cedar-wood drinking cup, she gulped down water—and drank down Raven with the water.

Soon after that, the belly of the old man's daughter began to swell with child.

"Who is the father?" the old man shouted. "Name him!"

But his daughter wept and swore that she had never met another man nor given anyone her love.

So time passed with no solving of the mystery. At last, she gave birth to a plump, handsome baby boy. The old man was so delighted with his new grandson that he forgot to be angry with his daughter. He was so delighted that he wanted to fulfill his grandson's every wish.

He was so delighted that he never noticed that the baby had clever black eyes—the eyes of Raven reborn.

One day, Raven began to wail. He began to whine. He began to shout and beat his arms and legs on the ground. "Gimmee!" he shrieked. "Gimmee!"

The sound was horrible. Hands over his ears, the old man asked, "Give you *what*? What do you want, Grandson?"

"Gimmee! Gimmee!"

The old man gave Raven toy after toy, but Raven batted them all away.

"Gimmee! Gimmee!"

The old man was at his wits' end. "What do you want?" he shouted.

"Ball! Want golden ball!"

"No!"

"Want! Want! Want!"

With each shriek, Raven's voice grew shriller. At last, the old man could stand no more of it. Warily, he opened the cedar chest in which he kept the golden ball. Instantly, a beautiful golden glow spread throughout the darkness.

"Here," the old man said. "But be careful with it!"

"Oh, I will!" Raven cried.

Suddenly, he was bird-Raven again. The golden ball firmly clutched in his talons, he flapped up and away.

"Come back!" the old man cried.

"Sorry, but no!" Raven called back.

Now, Raven had a rival, Eagle. In the days before light, Eagle couldn't find Raven easily. But all at once he could see Raven clearly! He flew after his rival, his mighty wings gaining with every stroke. And Raven, oh, Raven was burdened by the weight of the golden ball. Eagle would catch him!

"No!" Raven shouted.

Angrily, he broke off a piece of the golden ball and hurled it into the sky.

And that was the birth of the Sun.

But Eagle still pursued Raven, and his mighty wings were gaining with every stroke. Raven was still burdened by the weight of the golden ball.

"No!" he shouted.

Angrily, he broke off another piece of the golden ball and hurled it into the sky.

And that was the birth of the Moon.

But Eagle still pursued Raven, and his mighty wings were gaining with every stroke. Raven was still burdened by the weight of what was left of the golden ball.

"So be it!" he shouted.

Crumbling up what was left of the golden ball, he threw the gleaming, glittering pieces into the sky. Lighter now, he quickly outflew Eagle.

And in the sky . . . well, now, that was the birth of the stars

Orpheus and Eurydice

An Ancient Greek Myth

Orpheus was an Argonaut, one of Jason's crew aboard the ship *Argo* in the heroic quest for the Golden Fleece, but he is best known for this tragic tale of his love for Eurydice. It is a tale type found throughout the world: the quest to the underworld to save a loved one from death. The tale type can be found in the Sumerian myth of Inanna's descent to the underworld. It also can be found in folktales from around the world, including one from the American Southwest in which a man tries to rescue his wife from the afterlife, only to learn that she does not want to leave.

Orpheus was the son of Apollo, god of music, and the muse Calliope. With so noble a heritage, he was born with amazing talent. Orpheus's father presented him with a lyre and taught the boy to play it. Soon Orpheus was such a wondrous musician that men and women wept to hear him, and even the wildest beasts grew tame hearing him play.

Lovely young Eurydice and he met, and loved, and became joyous husband and wife. But not long after their marriage, a shepherd made advances to Eurydice. She ran from him—and, in her haste, she stepped on a snake lying hidden in the grass. It bit her, and poor Eurydice died.

Orpheus released his grief in song, expressing bitter sorrow in music to gods and men alike. But no one could aid him. At last, his grief unchecked, Orpheus vowed to snatch Eurydice back from the realm of the dead.

So Orpheus traveled down to the underworld. His song moved all who heard it, and even Cerberus, the terrible three-headed dog-guardian, whined and crouched down to let Orpheus pass. At last, Orpheus sang before Hades, the king of the underworld, and Persephone, Hades's wife. Persephone wept to hear his sorrow, and even Hades bowed his proud head.

"You may take Eurydice away with you. But there is one condition. You must lead her, but you must not so much as glance back at her until you both have reached the upper air and the land of the living."

"I shall do it," Orpheus swore.

He led Eurydice up the dark, rocky, steep passages. Utter silence surrounded them, wearing on Orpheus's nerves. What if Eurydice wasn't following him? What if Hades had tricked him?

No! He would not look back.

They climbed farther up in the darkness and heavy silence. What if it wasn't Eurydice following him? What if it was some demon of the underworld?

No! He would not look back!

They were almost at the entrance to the upper world, the world of the living. Was Eurydice still following? Was it Eurydice? Was she—

Orpheus glanced behind him. Instantly, Eurydice was swept away from him, back to the underworld. Orpheus was left alone once more.

Perseus

A Greek Myth of a Culture Hero

Perseus is a culture hero of ancient Greece. His story includes several folk motifs. First is the princess locked away in a tower where no one but a hero (or, in this case, a god) can reach her. Then there is the prophecy that a king will be killed by his son or grandson, which the king tries in vain to overturn. In another familiar motif, Perseus performs a classic hero quest, slaying Medusa and then rescuing a princess from a dragon. All these elements make him of particular interest to folklorists and storytellers alike.

There once lived a king named Acrisius whose daughter was named Danae. But an oracle warned Acrisius that a son of Danae would be the one to kill him. Loving life more than his daughter, Acrisius locked Danae in a bronze tower with no door and only one small window. Now, the king thought, his daughter would never marry or have children. He would be safe from the prophecy.

Acrisius had reckoned without considering the gods. A bright shower of gold blazed in through the window in Danae's tower and turned into the splendid Zeus, chief of the gods. God and mortal woman loved each other, and, in time, Danae bore a son, whom she named Perseus.

When Acrisius found Danae with her son, he was terrified and furious. He would not let the prophecy come true! So he had Danae and Perseus shut in a large chest and cast out to sea.

But the chest did not sink. It floated safely over the waves to the island of Seriphos, where mother and son were rescued by King Polydectes.

Perseus grew up to become a fine, clever young man. But King Polydectes grew obsessed with Danae's beauty. He asked for her hand, but she refused him. Polydectes would have wed her by force, but Perseus stood between them.

What could the furious Polydectes do? He couldn't simply have Perseus slain. That would not be a kingly act. Instead, he secretly plotted to be rid of the inconvenient young man.

The king announced that he would be marrying another royal woman, and that everyone who was loyal to him must bring a suitably noble present. Perseus alone could bring nothing because, as Polydectes knew very well, Perseus owned nothing. But this was the king's chance. He pretended to be offended, claiming that the young man to whom he'd given hospitality was useless and disloyal—knowing perfectly well what would happen.

Sure enough, the insulted Perseus cried that he could bring Polydectes anything the king might wish.

"Then bring me the head of the Gorgon Medusa!" King Polydectes stated.

"Done!" Perseus retorted.

Only as he set out on his quest for the Gorgon did Perseus discover what he was hunting. There were three Gorgons, Eryale, Stheno, and Medusa. They had once been human sisters, but they had offended the gods, and now they laired together, three monsters. Medusa was the most terrible of the three, but also the only one who was still mortal. She had writhing serpents for hair, and her stare could turn a man instantly to stone. Perseus secretly despaired, wondering how he could ever take her head.

Fortunately for Perseus, the goddess Athene hated Medusa. She appeared before the startled Perseus, a tall, handsome, cool-eyed woman. Beside her stood a golden-haired young man wearing winged sandals. This was Hermes, the messenger of the gods.

"We have decided to help you slay Medusa," Perseus was told.

Hermes gave Perseus the winged sandals and the deadly metal sickle that Cronos had once used to overpower his father, Uranus. Athene gave him a highly polished shield, as shiny as a mirror. Perseus would be able to slay Medusa by looking only at her reflection, and would not be turned to stone.

"Now you must find the Graeae," Hermes said. "You must win from them the way to the Stygian Nymphs."

With that, the two gods vanished.

Perseus set out to find the Graeae. When he reached their cave, he hid, watching them. What strange beings they were! They seemed almost like ancient women, but they had only one eye among the three of them, and took turns using it—when they weren't busy fighting over whose turn it was.

As soon as one took out the eye to give to another, Perseus sprang from his hiding place and snatched the eye from them. "Tell me how to find the Stygian Nymphs, or I won't give you back your eye," he said.

Grumbling, the Graeae gave him directions. Giving them back their eye, Perseus flew off on the winged sandals.

The Stygian Nymphs were friendlier than the Graeae. They gave Perseus the Cap of Darkness to make him invisible and a magic wallet in which he could safely place Medusa's head, then told him how to reach the Gorgons' lair.

Perseus flew on, following their directions, until he came to a mountainous island. To his horror, what he had taken to be rocks were stone figures that used to be men. He'd reached the Gorgons' lair.

Perseus raised his shield, using it as a mirror, and saw Medusa and her sisters asleep. Hastily, he put on the Cap of Darkness and flew down. Still watching only in the shield-mirror, he swung the sickle and felt it cut through Medusa's neck. Not daring to look away from the image in the shield, he forced Medusa's head into the magic wallet. As Medusa's sisters woke to attack, Perseus quickly flew away.

Perseus performed one act of kindness on the flight back to Seriphos. He met Atlas, the huge Titan who had been sentenced by Zeus to hold up the sky. At the Titan's weary request, he showed Atlas Medusa's head, turning him to stone so that he could no longer feel the weight of his burden.

Perseus flew on, skimming the seacoast. Suddenly, he saw what looked like a lovely statue chained to a rock. But as Perseus flew lower, he realized that it wasn't a statue, but a beautiful young woman.

"Who are you?" he cried. "Why are you chained here?"

She turned a tearful face up to him. "I am Andromeda, and I am here because my mother boasted about me. She claimed that I was more beautiful than the Nereids, the nymphs of the sea. That angered Poseidon, who proclaimed that I must be sacrificed to a sea monster."

Even as she finished, a hideous creature rose from the sea, tentacles waving and beak clashing. Andromeda screamed, but Perseus simply pulled Medusa's head out of the wallet, and the sea monster turned to stone. The monster crumbled to pieces and fell back into the sea.

"It, not you, was the sacrifice," Perseus said.

Cutting Andromeda's chains, Perseus flew with her to her father, King Cepheus of Phoenicia. By this time, the young people were clinging to each other happily. And when Perseus asked for Andromeda's hand in marriage, Cepheus gladly agreed.

So Perseus took Andromeda in his arms once more and set off for Seriphos. But he wasn't Hermes, who could fly around the world without getting weary. On the way, Perseus and Andromeda stopped to rest at Larisa. There, Perseus tried his hand in some athletic games. But when he threw the discus, the wind caught it. The discus hit an old man in the head and slew him.

It was none other than King Acrisius, he who had tried to prevent Danae from having a child. The prophecy had come true, despite what the king had done to prevent it. Perseus mourned for the proper length of time, though it might have been difficult to mourn for a grandfather who had cast his daughter and grandson into the sea to die.

When Perseus and Andromeda arrived at Seriphos, Perseus learned that King Poly-dectes had never married but had forced Danae to serve as his handmaiden.

Furious, Perseus strode into the palace and shouted, "Let all who are my friends shield their eyes!"

With that, he raised Medusa's head. In an instant, Polydectes and his courtiers were changed to statues. Danae happily rushed into her son's arms.

Perseus and Andromeda lived happily for many years, and their descendants became great kings. Perhaps the greatest of these was the famous Heracles, the strongest man in the world.

Spider Woman

Creation Myth of the Hopi People

Spider Woman is a supernatural being, a creator figure for the Hopi people. She is also an important figure to the Diné (Navajo) people. Many of the stories about Spider Woman portray her as very powerful and generally as a very commonsensical being.

Spider Woman was not born of mortal parents. Indeed, no one knows the details of her birth; she was simply there at the beginning of things, a grown woman or (if the fancy took her) a spider, full of magic. She liked to wander among the people, helping this person, teaching that one. Spider Woman was, in fact, helping the Pinon Maidens, along with Mole, when Kwataka, the Man-Eagle, first appeared.

Kwataka was a terrible monster, a merging, as his name implies, of bird and a human, with all the worst aspects of both. He killed for the joy of it. Kwataka stole women away, and then, when he grew bored with them, slew and ate them. Whenever Kwataka left his mountain lair he wore a magical shirt, a flint-arrowhead shirt that no weapon could pierce, so he had no fear of humans.

Now, Kwataka soared over the Hopi, just high enough over one particular village so that no one saw him, just low enough so he could watch one young woman who took his fancy. She was Lakone Mana, new wife of the young hero Puukonhoya, and husband and wife were very much in love.

Kwataka knew nothing of love. What he wanted, he took. He swooped down, snatched up Lakone Mana, and soared back up into the sky before anyone on the ground realized what had happened. Puukonhoya cried out his wife's name in anguish. Sighting Kwataka's path in the sky, the warrior ran after him as best he could. But what earthbound man could chase Kwataka?

But here sat Spider Woman with the Pinon Maidens. "Where are you going in such a rush, Puukonhoya?"

"Kwataka has stolen away my wife!"

"That is bad," Spider Woman agreed gently. "But it can be made better. I will help you. You, Pinon Maidens, gather pine resin. Make me an exact copy of Kwataka's flint-arrowhead shirt. Be quick about it!"

Sure enough, the Pinon Maidens quickly gathered the resin and quickly made an exact copy of the flint-arrowhead shirt. "Excellent!" Spider Woman said. "Mole, make ready. We will need your help as well."

Mole agreed.

Spider Woman sprinkled sacred corn pollen over the shirt, chanting an invocation; then she changed into her other true shape, becoming a tiny spider sitting on Puukonhoya's ear. "I'm here," she said in her now piping little voice. "Now, let us be off. Kwataka's lair is at the top of that mountain."

They reached the mountain, but Puukonhoya frowned with worry. "How can I get up there? I don't see any way to climb."

"No need," Spider Woman said in his ear. "Mole, dig us a tunnel, please."

Mole dug a tunnel into the mountain, sloping up and up. Puukonhoya, with Spider Woman on his ear, climbed up after Mole and found himself coming out of the mountain onto a ledge far above the ground. "But Kwataka's lair is higher still," Spider Woman said. "Now I shall call some good birds to help."

Several came. An eagle carried Spider Woman, Puukonhoya, and Mole part of the way up. When the eagle wearied, a gray hawk took them higher still. When the gray hawk wearied, a red hawk took them higher still, right to the white house on the mountain peak that was Kwataka's lair. Spider Woman thanked the red hawk, as she had thanked the gray hawk and the eagle.

"Wait," she said to Puukonhoya, who was about to climb the ladder into the white house. "You can't climb that yet! The rungs are lined with sharp obsidian, like row after row of terrible knives."

"Then, what am I to do?"

"Wait for Horned Toad. Ah, here he is. Puukonhoya, pick some berries, please, and feed them to Horned Toad."

The young man did as Spider Woman instructed him. Horned Toad chewed the berries into a sticky paste. "Good," Spider Woman said. "Now, Puukonhoya, smear that paste on the ladder rungs. Be careful!"

He smeared the berry paste over the rungs, and the sharp edges were blunted. Puukonhoya rushed up the ladder, with Spider Woman on his ear and Mole hiding in his hair, and entered Kwataka's lair. "There's his flint-arrowhead shirt!"

"Softly!" Spider Woman warned. "Kwataka is home, asleep in another room. I will cast a spell to keep him from hearing you, but you must still be careful!"

Puukonhoya quickly switched the real flint-arrowhead shirt with the counterfeit, slipping on the real shirt. He stole into the next room, and there was Lakone Mana, her hands and feet bound. Her eyes flashed with joy and alarm, and she whispered, "You mustn't stay! He kills anyone who enters!"

"I'm not leaving without you," Puukonhoya said, and he cut her bonds.

But even though they were trying to be quiet, even though Spider Woman had cast that spell to keep Kwataka from hearing them, the Man-Eagle woke—and found himself facing Puukonhoya. "Who are you?" Kwataka asked sharply. "What are you doing here?"

"I am Puukonhoya, and I've come to rescue my wife!"

"Maybe you have and maybe you haven't," Kwataka snapped. "First, you must win her from me. You must win a smoking contest with me. Do you see this tobacco pouch? We will both smoke, and the first to faint loses. If I lose, you may take back your wife. If I win, you die!"

"That tobacco is poisonous to humans," Spider Woman whispered in Puukonhoya's ear, "and Kwataka knows it. Mole, dig us a hole, if you would."

Mole dug a hole right where Puukonhoya stood, an airhole to the outside world so that when the young man took his turn at the smoking pipe, fresh air kept his head clear. Kwataka had no such airhole, and so it was he who nearly fainted. Hastily, the Man-Eagle hurried outside to clear his head. How had the human managed that? How had the human won?

"So, you won the first contest," Kwataka snarled. "But that was only the first. There must be three."

Puukonhoya sighed. "If there must, there must. What is the second contest?"

"A simple thing," Kwataka said. "We shall each take up one of these great elk antlers. He who can break his antler with one snap wins."

"This is a trick," Spider Woman said to herself, and scuttled down to study the antlers.

Sure enough, the one intended for Kwataka was half rotten, ready to fall apart at a touch, while the one meant for Puukonhoya was as hard as stone. Spider Woman switched the two, so quickly and magically that Kwataka never suspected it. He snatched up what he thought was his antler and nearly tore his arms from their sockets trying to break it. Puukonhoya snapped the half-rotten antler with one slight twist of his hands.

Kwataka stared. How had the human done that? "Very well," the Man-Eagle muttered, "you have won the second contest. But the third remains!"

"What is the third contest?" Puukonhoya asked.

"Do you see those two trees? Well, we both shall try to uproot them, leaves, branches, trunks, and all. The one who can lift his tree free wins. The tree on the left is mine," he added, picking the one that had the shallowest roots.

Spider Woman whispered to Mole, "Loosen the roots of the tree on the right. Hurry!"

Mole hurried. He did such a fine job that when Puukonhoya pulled, the tree came up almost easily. Kwataka, meanwhile, could hardly budge his tree at all.

"I win," Puukonhoya panted. "Now, let my wife go."

"Not so fast; not so fast!" Kwataka cried. "I am hungry after all this work, and so, I guess, are you. That shall be the final contest. Yes, the fourth contest will be it! We shall both eat, and whoever eats the most, wins!"

"Hurry," Spider Woman whispered to Mole; "dig a hole next to Puukonhoya!"

Puukonhoya did eat some of the food, since he really *was* hungry, but the rest of it he let fall into the hole, bit by bit, till his plate was clean. Kwataka never guessed a thing. At last, too full to eat another bite, Kwataka said, "Enough!"

"Can't eat any more?" Puukonhoya asked. "Now I'll take my wife and—"

"Not so fast!" Kwataka cried. "One last test; one last test! Which of us is invulnerable,

eh? Which of us can stand in a fire unscathed?"

He gathered two great piles of wood. Kwataka sat on one, Puukonhoya on the other. "Now your wife can light them," the Man-Eagle said, "and we shall see who survives this!"

Nervously, Lakone Mana lit the fires. But, of course, Puukonhoya was wearing the magical flint-arrowhead shirt, while Kwataka had only the counterfeit. The magical shirt produced ice to keep Puukonhoya nicely cool, but the resin shirt burned up in a flash, and Kwataka burned with it.

"Quickly," Spider Woman said to Puukonhoya, "take this magical cornmeal in your mouth and blow it all over Kwataka's ashes."

Puukonhoya obeyed. And a handsome man rose from the ashes. Spider Woman turned back into her woman form and scolded him. "Have you learned your lesson? Have you?"

"I have," he who had been Kwataka murmured, like a little boy being scolded by his grandmother.

"Will you swear to stop killing people? Will you swear to stop carrying them off and eating them? Well? Will you swear that?"

"I swear it. I will never do evil deeds again."

"Then, that's that," Spider Woman said with satisfaction. "Now we can all go home."

A Creation

An Iroquois Myth

Every culture has its creation myth, its myth of how things came to be. This myth, "A Creation," is from the Iroquois Confederacy (also known as the Five Nations), a group of five indigenous North American groups: the Mohawk, Onondaga, Oneida, Cayuga, and Seneca. After the original confederacy was created, a sixth group, the Tuscarora, was added.

An unlimited expanse of water once filled the space inhabited by the world today. There was total darkness, and the human family dwelt in a country in the upper regions of the air, abounding in every comfort and convenience. The forests were full of game, the rivers full of fish, and fowl and vegetables grew abundantly. The Sun shone without fail, and storms were unknown. The people were happy, and death, pain, and disease were unknown to them. The people were without a care, until one day when anxiety was introduced to them.

A youth had become withdrawn. He became solitary and avoided his social circle as his body wasted away. By his face and countenance, it was certain something troubled him, but he would reveal nothing though his friends questioned him. At last, he agreed to tell. He would speak, however, only if they dug up the roots of a certain white pine tree and lay him on a blanket by the hole with his wife seated by his side.

Everyone eagerly complied with the strange request, and soon the great tree was uprooted, and the man and his wife placed by the hole, which opened into the great abyss below. Suddenly, to everyone's amazement and horror, he seized his pregnant wife, threw her through the hole, and told the people that he had long suspected his wife's chastity, but now that she was gone, he would soon recover.

Down the woman fell toward the watery world below. The loon first observed her falling and cried out that the council should meet to prepare for her coming. They knew that she was a human being and must have Earth to stand upon. First, they decided to find someone who could support her weight. The sea bear tried first and the other animals climbed on his back, but he sank beneath their weight. Several other animals tried and failed. At last, the turtle volunteered, and the animals were unable to sink him.

Next, the animals decided they must obtain Earth, which might be found at the bottom of the sea. The mink volunteered to seek Earth, and dove down below the water. After a long absence, he floated to the surface, dead. The animals, after inspecting him closely, found that clutched in his tiny paw was a small amount of dirt. They placed it on the turtle's back, and it began to grow as the woman from the sky continued to fall. By the time she landed, there was enough dirt for her to stand with one foot over the other, but soon there was room enough to stand on both feet, and soon after that, there was enough dirt for her to be seated. Earth continued to grow and grow, and soon there were plants, and plains, and rivers headed toward the sea.

The woman traveled toward the water and built a small dwelling. In a short while, she gave birth to a baby girl, and the two of them lived on the products of the earth until the girl became a woman. Then, animals changed themselves into the form of men and came as suitors to ask for the young woman's hand in marriage. First came the loon, in the form of a tall, well-dressed, attractive man, but after the woman consulted with her mother, this suitor was rejected. Others came, and they, too, were rejected. At last, the turtle came with his short neck, humped back, and bandy legs to offer himself as a suitor, and he was accepted.

After the young woman had gone to sleep, the turtle came and placed two arrows on her abdomen in the shape of a cross. One arrow was tipped with flint, and the other with the rough bark of a tree. Then the turtle left. Time passed, and the young woman became pregnant with twins. The twins spoke to each other about the best way to be born. The younger twin decided to exit the usual way, but the older wished instead to be born through his mother's side, thus taking her life.

The grandmother was enraged at her daughter's death and determined that she would destroy the twins in revenge. She grabbed the two of them and tossed them into the sea, but when she returned to her home, they had arrived before her at her own door. She threw them into the sea several more times, and finally decided that the two would live. Then, the grandmother divided her daughter's corpse into two sections and threw them into the sky. One part of her body became the Sun, and the other half became the Moon, and so day and night began.

The boys soon became men and excelled at archery. The older twin was called Than-wisk-a law (Flint) and had a malignant nature and the turtle's arrow pointed with flint. This son was a favorite with his grandmother. The younger twin was called Tan-lon-ghy-au-wan-goon and had a benevolent nature and the turtle's arrow headed with bark. The older son, with his flint-tipped arrow, lived in abundance with his grandmother but would share nothing with his younger brother, who could kill little with his bark-point arrow.

One day, Tan-lon-ghy-au-wan-goon was hunting, and his bark-tipped arrow flew wide of the mark and sank into the ocean. He followed it, hoping to recover the arrow, and found himself by a cottage at the bottom of the sea. An old man greeted him in front of the cottage and said, "Welcome, my son, to the home of your father." The old man offered Tan-lon-ghy-au-wan-goon an ear of corn, and told him he had witnessed his brother's behavior. While the older brother lived, he said, the world could never be peopled. Tan-lon-ghy-au-wan-goon must kill him.

His father instructed him to collect all the flint he could find into heaps, and hang up all the buck horns, as they were the only things that could affect his brother's body, which was made of flint. Tan-lon-ghy-au-wan-goon did so, and on a hunting excursion, he falsely told his brother that nothing affected him more than bulrushes and beech boughs, and asked him what he was most afraid of. Flint answered that only flint stones and buck horns could affect him.

The brothers had a meal, and Flint retired to his hut to rest. While he slept, his brother built a fire at the entrance. Soon, Flint found himself expanding with the heat. In his discomfort, he ran from the hut. Seeking revenge, he grabbed a beech bough to beat his brother, but to no effect. Tan-lon-ghy-au-wan-goon pelted Flint with flint stones and beat him with buck horns. Flint rushed at him armed with bulrushes, but these were unable to injure his younger brother. At last, Flint fled.

The land was at that time a vast green plain, but as Flint fled across it, deep valleys and high mountains were formed. Peaceful streams formed violent cataracts and foamed through rocky channels. Tan-lon-ghy-au-wan-goon followed Flint, beating him with buck horns until his brother breathed his last breath and fell to Earth, forming what are now the Rocky Mountains.

With the enemy of the turtles destroyed, the turtles came out of the earth in human form and multiplied over the years, living in peace and prosperity.

The grandmother was furious that her favorite had been destroyed and caused torrents of rain to descend upon Earth until even the highest mountains were below water. The inhabitants fled in their canoes to avoid destruction. At last, the grandmother caused the rain to cease and the waters to subside, and the inhabitants returned to their former homes. Then the angry grandmother covered Earth with snow. The inhabitants took to their snowshoes and avoided her vengeance.

At last, the grandmother gave up hope of destroying the entire race at one time and instead inflicted upon humankind all the evils that are suffered in the present world.

Tan-lon-ghy-au-wan-goon displays infinite benevolence by bestowing upon humankind an abundance of blessings.

Balder

A Norse Myth

Balder was the most glorious of the Norse gods. He was fair of skin and hair, and so handsome and pure in spirit that none could equal him. The Norse god Balder may, in fact, be a later incarnation of a minor deity. The main myth about him, as retold here, reveals a Christian influence in its portrayal of Balder as more of a figure from a Christian story than a pagan Norse character. The myth also portrays Loki, the Norse trickster deity, as closer to a demonic figure than is usual for him.

Balder was the much-loved son of Odin and Frigga. Indeed, it seemed as though every creature that lived loved him. Yet Odin knew a sad prophesy. His son was fated to die an early death. To protect him and try to ward off the prophesy, Frigga traveled far and wide, speaking with all, whether they be living or mere objects, exacting promises from each and all not to harm Balder. Only the mistletoe was missed, and only the mistletoe never swore the vow.

But there was one who did not love Balder. Loki grew more and more jealous of the handsome young man who was so very pure and good. At last, Loki came to hate Balder, and he swore to destroy him. Loki searched, and at last found that one thing that could harm Balder, that one plant—that mistletoe.

Meanwhile, the Norse gods rejoiced to know that Balder was safe from all harm. He challenged them to throw whatever they would at him, knowing he would not be hurt.

While all the gods hurled things at Balder, Balder's blind brother, Hoder, sat by himself, unable to join in what he could not see. Loki slipped a sprig of mistletoe into Hoder's hand and offered to guide him. Blind Hoder threw the sprig—and it pierced Balder to the heart, slaying him on the spot.

Odin and Frigga mourned the death of their glorious son. They sent an envoy to Hel, goddess of the underworld and the dead, to ask whether Balder could be ransomed from her. Hel at last agreed, but only if all creation wept for the slain god. The gods sent out messengers throughout all creation, and all things wept for Balder—all but one old woman. It was Loki in disguise who refused to weep, so Balder was lost to death.

The gods took their revenge upon Loki. They bound him to a rock in a deep cave and set a poisonous serpent to drop venom on his face. Loki's faithful wife sat at his side, catching as much of the venom as she could in a cup. But whenever she had to empty the cup, the venom struck Loki, and his anguish caused earthquakes.

From then on, Loki allied himself against the gods, and he would fight against them when Ragnarok, the final battle, came.

Thor Catches the Midgard Serpent

A Norse Myth

Thor was the Norse god of thunder, usually portrayed as a tall, muscular man, somewhat of a brawler compared to the more dignified deities. As a result, he was the chosen god of the common man. Thor was married, happily, to the golden-haired goddess Sif.

One day, Thor, god of thunder, took it into his head to go fishing. He disguised himself as a young man, left the gods' palace of Asgard, and wandered until night, when he met up with a giant named Hymir. Thor spent that night in Hymir's home.

When the day came, Hymir made ready to go fishing in the sea. Thor said, "Let me go rowing with you."

Hymir laughed. "What, such a scrap of a youngster go out on the open ocean? The cold and wet will make you catch cold if we row out as far as I usually do."

Thor promptly forgot all about his disguise, and let Hymir know his true identity. "I am well able to row a long way out, and it won't be me who first demands to be rowed back! Now, what are we going to use for bait?"

"Get your own," Hymir muttered.

So Thor went to a herd of oxen owned by Hymir, selected the largest ox, and struck off its head with his powerful hammer, Mjollnir. Taking the ox head with him, Thor climbed into Hymir's boat and rowed them both out with amazing speed.

"This is far enough," Hymir said.

"Not yet," Thor replied, and began rowing again.

"This is far enough!" Hymir repeated when Thor stopped. "We're so far out that we are in danger. The Midgard Serpent might surface under us! We're too far out!"

The Midgard Serpent was the enormous snake that encircled the globe underwater, and little did Hymir suspect that catching the serpent was Thor's goal.

"No, we're not," Thor replied, and once again began rowing.

Hymir wasn't at all pleased with this. He went right on complaining, until, at last, Thor said, "This is far enough."

Thor shipped his oars and prepared a strong fishing line and a stronger hook. Baiting the hook with the ox head, he cast the line and waited.

Sure enough, it wasn't long at all before the Midgard Serpent snapped at the ox-head bait—and got caught by the hook. It gave so powerful a jerk, trying to get free, that it nearly dragged Thor overboard. Thor dug in his heels so hard that his legs went right through the boat and his feet were braced on the bottom of the ocean. Hand over hand, he drew up the serpent till he was staring right at it. The Midgard Serpent stared right back, spitting poison.

"Have you gone mad?" Hymir cried in terror.

Thor merely raised his hammer, readying to strike the serpent over the head and finish it off. But Hymir was too frightened to think. Before Thor could strike, Hymir grabbed his bait knife and sliced the fishing line.

The Midgard Serpent dove back into the sea. Thor flung his hammer after it but missed.

The Midgard Serpent is still down there, encircling the earth.

"I had to do it!" Hymir began.

He got no further. The furious Thor struck him a blow that hurled him overboard. By the time Hymir had floundered back aboard, Thor, god of thunder and frustrated fisherman, had waded ashore.

Maui Snares the Sun

A Polynesian Myth

The Polynesian culture hero Maui is both hero and trickster. Half human, half god, he wanders much of the Pacific Ocean, particularly the islands of Hawaii—including Maui, the island that bears his name—setting matters right and enjoying himself hugely in the process.

Maui was special right from birth. He was not even created in the usual way. Maui's mother, Hina, began to fall asleep on the nice, warm sands of the island that would someday bear her son's name. Half asleep as she was, Hina didn't realize that the loincloth she'd pulled over herself wasn't hers, but belonged to a god.

And from the magic in that simple cloth, from that simple coming together of the human and the divine, Maui was begun.

Maui was more clever and daring than any child ever seen, and he began almost right away to make sure that the world ran the way it should. In those long-ago days, the Sun sped across the sky so quickly that Hina, Maui's mother, grew angry. She was a skillful maker of tapa, the cloth that is pounded out of mulberry bark—but the tapa needed to fully dry if it was to be of any use as cloth.

"I beat out my tapa," she told Maui, "but before it has even the slightest chance to dry, the Sun is gone from the sky, and the Sun's warmth with it."

Maui was still a child in those days, but he said as bravely as any man, "I will go and cut off the Sun's legs."

Hina glanced warily at him. She already knew that her son could do amazing deeds. "But are you strong enough?" Hina asked.

"Oh, I am," Maui answered boldly. "And I am clever enough, as well."

Hina believed him. Carefully, she told him what he must do; then she gave him fif-teen strong ropes of coconut fiber and sent him on his way.

Maui had listened well to everything his mother had said. At last, as she had told him, he came to a huge wiliwili tree. In this tree, Maui knew, one of his ancestors lived, the old blind woman Wiliwilipuha, which means "hollow wiliwili." He sat at the foot of the tree and waited. The night came, and the night went, and a rooster began to crow. Once it crowed; twice it crowed; three times it crowed.

On the third crow, Maui tensed, watching to see what would happen next. An old woman came out of the wiliwili tree to cook bananas for the Sun's meal. This woman was Wili-wilipuha. As she lit her cooking fire, Maui snatched away the bananas.

"Humph!" Wiliwilipuha snorted in annoy-ance. "Where did the bananas go?"

She went to fetch more. But Maui stole these, too. A third time, Wiliwilipuha brought bananas to be cooked; a third time, Maui stole them.

"This must be the work of a trouble-maker," Wiliwilipuha said, and sniffed the air until she found Maui. "Whose mischievous one are you?" the old woman asked.

"Yours," Maui answered.

"Mine? By whom?"

"By Hina," Maui answered. "I am your grandson, Grandmother."

Wiliwilipuha's old, strong face showed no emotion. "What brings you here?"

"I've come to keep the Sun from racing across the sky. It runs so quickly that my mother's tapa cloth cannot dry."

"That would be a feat, indeed."

Wiliwilipuha gave Maui a sharp stone and one more rope. She told Maui that the Sun came there every morning for a breakfast of fried bananas.

Maui dug a pit in which to hide. He hadn't hidden there for long before the Sun came blazing to the wiliwili tree. Maui cast the first of his ropes—and he snared the Sun. Oh, it fought him! Oh, it burned at him! But Maui was small and quick, quicker almost than thought.

And quicker than thought, Maui used his sixteen ropes to bind the Sun and all its squirming legs. He bound it fast to the wiliwili tree, then picked up the stone.

"I will cut off your legs!" he threatened.

"No!" the Sun cried in terror. "Spare me!"

"Why? Why should I spare someone who is so selfish? You race across the sky to please yourself and think nothing of the folk below who need your light and warmth." Maui picked up the sharp stone again. "No, I shall cut off your legs."

"No!" the Sun screamed. "Maybe we can strike a bargain."

"Maybe we can." Maui pretended to be thinking things over. But his clever mind had already worked out what he wanted to say. "What if you go slowly across the sky—but only for half the year?"

"And for the other half?"

"For the other half of the year," Maui said, "you may go as swiftly as you please."

"I don't know. . . ."

Maui raised the stone once more.

"I agree!" the Sun shrieked. "We have a bargain."

Maui used the stone to cut the Sun free. The Sun shot back up into the sky.

And so it is that the days are short for half the year. Those are the days when the Sun races across the sky. But for the other half of the year, the Sun moves slowly, and that, or so this story says, is the work of Maui the clever.

Inanna's Descent to the Underworld

An Ancient Sumerian Myth

Inanna was the Sumerian goddess of love and war, a very important goddess who was later known as Ishtar and Astarte. The story of Inanna and Dumuzi is the oldest form of the tale type known by the Greeks as "Venus and Adonis." But Inanna's descent and return also has a link to rituals of a shaman's voluntary (symbolic) death and rebirth.

There was the strongest love between the goddess Inanna, who is love and lust together, and the mortal Dumuzi. But mortals die, and gods may sometimes mourn. And, sometimes, some of them determine to do more than mourn. They will not let their lovers go.

Kurnugi is the land from which no one returns. It is the dark house wherein dwells Erkalla's god, the house wherein those who enter never leave, where dust is their only food and darkness their only way.

To Kurnugi, that land from which no one returns, that place of the dead, was great Inanna determined to go. No other god could stop her or persuade her otherwise.

When she arrived at the gate of Kurnugi, Inanna commanded, "Gatekeeper, open your gate for me! Let me come in! If you do not open the gate for me to come in, I shall smash the door and shatter the bolt; I shall raise up the dead, and they shall eat the living! The dead shall outnumber the living!"

The gatekeeper cried out, "Stop, lady; do not break it down! Let me go and report your words to Queen Ereshkigal."

The gatekeeper hurried to Queen Ereshkigal. "Inanna is here!"

When Ereshkigal heard this, her face turned as pale with anger as a cut-down tamarisk, while her lips turned as dark as a bruised kuninu-reed. "What drove her here to me? What impelled her spirit hither? I am as I should be! Should I drink water with the spirits of the dead? Should I eat clay for bread, drink muddy water for beer? Should I bemoan the men who left their wives behind? Should I bemoan the maidens wrenched from their lovers' laps? Or should I bemoan the tender babe sent off before his time?

"Go, Gatekeeper; open the gate for her," the queen concluded in a voice as cold as clay. "Let her enter. Treat her in accordance with the ancient rules."

The gatekeeper went and opened the gate to Inanna.

"Enter, my lady. May the palace of Kurnugi be glad to see you."

He let her in through the first door, but stripped off and took away the great crown from her head.

"Gatekeeper, why have you taken away the great crown from my head?"

"Go in, my lady. Such are the rites of the mistress of the underworld."

He let her in through the second door, but stripped off and took away her earrings.

"Gatekeeper, why have you taken away my earrings?"

"Go in, my lady. Such are the rites of the mistress of the underworld."

He let her in through the third door, but stripped off and took away the beads from around her neck.

"Gatekeeper, why have you taken away the beads from around my neck?"

"Go in, my lady. Such are the rites of the mistress of the underworld."

He let her in through the fourth door, but stripped off and took away the ornaments from her breast.

"Gatekeeper, why have you taken away the ornaments from my breast?"

"Go in, my lady. Such are the rites of the mistress of the underworld."

He let her in through the fifth door, but stripped off and took away the girdle of birthstones from around her waist.

"Gatekeeper, why have you taken the girdle of birthstones from around my waist?"

"Go in, my lady. Such are the rites of the mistress of the underworld."

He let her in through the sixth door, but stripped off and took away the bangles from her wrists and ankles.

"Gatekeeper, why have you taken away the bangles from my wrists and ankles?"

"Go in, my lady. Such are the rites of the mistress of the underworld."

He let her in through the seventh door, but stripped off and took away the robes from her body.

"Gatekeeper, why have you taken away the robes from my body?"

"Go in, my lady. Such are the rites of the mistress of the underworld."

Naked and unafraid, Inanna went down to Kurnugi. As soon as Inanna had descended to the Land of No Return, Ereshkigal saw her. Inanna, heedless of all but rage, flew at her, and the queen cried to her vizier:

Go, Namtar, lock her up in my palace!
Release against her the sixty miseries:
Misery of the eyes against her eyes,
Misery of the sides against her sides,
Misery of the heart against her heart,
Misery of the feet against her feet,
Misery of the head against her head—
Against every part of her, against her
*   whole body!*

Now, back in the mortal realm sadness reigned, for there could be no love or lust with Inanna gone to the underworld. The bull ignored the cow; the boy and girl ignored each other; the man slept in one room and the woman in another.

Papsukkal, vizier of the great gods, hung his head. Dressed in mourning clothes, his hair unkempt, he went before the gods and wept.

"Inanna has gone down to the underworld and has not come up again."

The wise god Ea created a person, an image, Asushunamir, which means "good looks."

"Go, Asushunamir, set thy face to the gate of the Land of No Return. The seven gates of the Land of No Return shall be opened for thee. Ereshkigal shall see thee and rejoice. When her heart has calmed, and her mood is happy, let her utter the oath of the great gods.

"Then ask her this: 'Pray, lady, let them give me the life-water bag so that I may drink from it.'"

So he went, and so it happened. As soon as Ereshkigal heard his request, she struck her thigh and bit her finger, restless with worry. "You have asked of me something that should not be asked. Asushunamir, I will curse thee with a mighty curse!"

The food of the city's gutters shall be
*   thy food;*
The sewers of the city shall be thy drink.
The threshold shall be thy habitation;
The besotted and the thirsty shall smite
*   thy cheek!*

She knew that as soon as Asushunamir was hers, she must keep a balance by returning Inanna. She did not know that Asushunamir was a mere image, not reality.

So Ereshkigal told her vizier, Namtar, "Sprinkle Inanna with the water of life and take her from my sight!"

And Namtar sprinkled Inanna with the water of life and took her from the queen's presence.

When through the first gate he had made her go out, he returned to her the robes for her body.

When through the second gate he had made her go out, he returned to her the bangles for her wrists and ankles.

When through the third gate he had made her go out, he returned to her the girdle of birthstones for her waist.

When through the fourth gate he had made her go out, he returned to her the ornaments for her breast.

When through the fifth gate he had made her go out, he returned to her the beads for her neck.

When through the sixth gate he had made her go out, he returned to her the earrings for her ears.

When through the seventh gate he had made her go out, he returned to her the great crown for her head.

But Inanna knew her rebirth was not in vain. As she was reborn, so would Dumuzi return to her every spring.

"You shall not rob me forever of my only love!" And so indeed, they did not.

Prince Wicked and the Grateful Animals

A Parable from the *Jataka*

"Prince Wicked and the Grateful Animals" is a prime example of the "grateful animals" folk motif, in which animals that are helped by a human repay the kindness in turn. The *Jataka*, or *Jatakas*, is a collection of moral tales of the previous lives of the Buddha. They are said to have been compiled sometime between the third century B.C.E. and the fifth century C.E.

Once upon a time, a king had a son named Prince Wicked. He was fierce and cruel, and he spoke to nobody without abuse or blows. Like grit in the eye was Prince Wicked to everyone, both in the palace and out of it.

His people said to one another, "If he acts this way while he is a prince, how will he act when he is king?"

One day when the prince was swimming in the river, suddenly, a great storm came on, and it grew very dark. In the darkness, the servants who were with the prince swam from him, saying to themselves, "Let us leave him alone in the river, and he may drown."

When they reached the shore, some of the servants who had not gone into the river said, "Where is Prince Wicked?"

"Isn't he here?" the prince's attendants asked. "Perhaps he came out of the river in the darkness and went home." Then, the servants all went back to the palace.

The king asked where his son was, and again the servants said, "Isn't he here, O King? A great storm came on soon after we went into the water. It grew very dark. When we came out of the water, the prince was not with us."

At once, the king had the gates thrown open. He and all his men searched up and down the banks of the river for the missing prince. But no trace of him could be found.

In the darkness, the prince had been swept down the river. He was crying for fear he would drown when he came across a log. He climbed up on the log and floated farther down the river.

When the great storm arose, the water rushed into the homes of a rat and a snake who lived on the riverbank. The rat and the snake swam out into the river and found the same log the prince had found. The snake climbed up on one end of the log, and the rat climbed up on the other.

On the river's bank, a cottonwood tree grew, and a young parrot lived in its branches. The storm pulled up this tree, and it fell into the river. The heavy rain beat down the parrot when it tried to fly, and it could not go far. Looking down, it saw the log and flew down to rest. Now, there were four on the log floating downstream together.

Just around the bend in the river, a certain poor man had built himself a hut. As he walked to and fro late at night listening to the storm, he heard the loud cries of the prince. The poor man said to himself, "I must get that man out of the water. I must save his life." So he shouted, "I will save you! I will save you!" as he swam out in the river.

Soon, he reached the log, and pushing it by one end, he soon pushed it into the bank. The prince jumped up and down, he was so glad to be safe and sound on dry land.

Then the poor man saw the snake, the rat, and the parrot, and he carried them to his hut. He built a fire and put the animals near it so they could get dry. He took care of them first, because they were the weaker, and afterward he looked after the comfort of the prince.

Then, the poor man brought food and set it before them, looking after the animals first and the prince afterward. This made the young prince angry, and he said to himself, "This poor man does not treat me like a prince. He takes care of the animals before taking care of me." Then, the prince began to hate the poor man.

A few days later, when the prince, the snake, the rat, and the parrot were rested and the storm was all over, the snake said good-bye to the poor man with these words: "Father, you have been very kind to me. I know where there is some buried gold. If ever you want gold, you have only to come to my home and call, 'Snake!' and I will show you the buried gold. It shall all be yours."

Next, the rat said good-bye to the poor man. "If ever you want money," said the rat, "come to my home and call out, 'Rat!' and I will show you where a great deal of money is buried near my home. It shall all be yours."

Then the parrot went to the poor man, saying: "Father, silver and gold have I none, but if you ever want choice rice, come to where I live and call, 'Parrot!' and I will call all my family and friends together, and we will gather the choicest rice in the fields for you."

Last came the prince. In his heart, he hated the poor man who had saved his life. But he pretended to be as thankful as the animals had been, saying, "Come to me when I am king, and I will give you great riches." So saying, he went away.

Not long after this, the prince's father died, and Prince Wicked was made king. He was then very rich.

By and by, the poor man said to himself, "Each of the four whose lives I saved made a promise to me. I will see if they will keep their promises."

First of all, he went to the snake, and standing near his hole, the poor man called out, "Snake!"

At once, the snake darted forth, and with every mark of respect he said, "Father, in this place there is much gold. Dig it up and take it all."

"Very well," said the poor man. "When I need it, I will not forget."

After visiting for a while, the poor man said good-bye to the snake and went to where the rat lived, calling out, "Rat!"

The rat came at once and did as the snake had done, showing the poor man where the money was buried.

"When I need it, I will come for it," said the poor man.

Going next to the parrot, the poor man called out, "Parrot!" and the bird flew down from the treetop as soon as he heard the call.

"Oh, Father," said the parrot, "shall I call together all my family and friends to gather choice rice for you?"

The poor man, seeing that the parrot was willing and ready to keep his promise, said, "I do not need rice now. If ever I do, I will not forget your offer."

Last of all, the poor man went into the city where the king lived. The king, seated on his great white elephant, was riding through the city. The king saw the poor man and said to himself, "That poor man has come to ask me for the great riches I promised to give him. I must have his head cut off before he can tell the people how he saved my life when I was the prince."

So the king called his servants to him and said, "You see that poor man over there? Seize him and bind him, beat him at every corner of the street as you march him out of the city, and then chop off his head."

The servants had to obey their king. So they seized and bound the poor man. They beat him at every corner of the street. The poor man did not cry out, but he said, over and over again, "It is better to save poor, weak animals than to save a prince."

At last, some wise men among the crowds along the street asked the poor man what prince he had saved. Then, the poor man told the whole story, ending with the words, "By saving your king, I brought all this pain upon myself."

The wise men and all the rest of the crowd cried out, "This poor man saved the life of our king, and now the king has ordered him to be killed. How can we be sure that he will not have any, or all, of us killed? Let us kill him." And in their anger, they rushed from every side upon the king as he rode on his elephant, and, with arrows and stones, they killed him then and there.

Then, they made the poor man king, and set him to rule over them.

The poor man ruled his people well. One day, he decided once more to try the snake, the rat, and the parrot. So, followed by many servants, the king went to where the snake lived.

At the call of "Snake!" out came the snake from his hole, saying, "Here, O King, is your treasure; take it."

"I will," said the king. "And I want you to come with me."

Then, the king had his servants dig up the gold.

Going to where the rat lived, the king called, "Rat!" Out came the rat, and bowing low to the king, the rat said, "Take all the money buried here and have your servants carry it away."

"I will," said the king, and he asked the rat to go with him and the snake.

Then, the king went to where the parrot lived, and called, "Parrot!" The parrot flew down to the king's feet and said, "O King, shall I and my family and my friends gather choice rice for you?"

"Not now, not until rice is needed," said the king. "Will you come with us?" The parrot was glad to join them.

So with the gold and the money, and with the snake, the rat, and the parrot as well, the king went back to the city.

The king had the gold and the money hidden away in the palace. He had a tube of gold made for the snake to live in. He had a glass box made for the rat's home, and a cage of gold for the parrot. Each had the food he liked best of all to eat every day, and so these four lived happily all their lives.

The Lady, or the Tiger?

An American Riddle Tale

> The story "The Lady, or the Tiger?" is perhaps the most classic example of a riddle tale, a story with an ending left to the audience to debate. It was written in 1884 by American author and humorist Frank R. Stockton (1834–1902).

In the very olden time there lived a semi-barbaric king, whose ideas, though somewhat polished and sharpened by the progressiveness of distant Latin neighbors, were still large, florid, and untrammeled, as became the half of him which was barbaric. He was a man of exuberant fancy, and, withal, of an authority so irresistible that, at his will, he turned his varied fancies into facts. He was greatly given to self-communing, and, when he and himself agreed upon anything, the thing was done. When every member of his domestic and political systems moved smoothly in its appointed course, his nature was bland and genial; but, whenever there was a little hitch, and some of his orbs got out of their orbits, he was blander and more genial still, for nothing pleased him so much as to make the crooked straight and crush down uneven places.

Among the borrowed notions by which his barbarism had become semified was that of the public arena, in which, by exhibitions of manly and beastly valor, the minds of his subjects were refined and cultured.

But even here the exuberant and barbaric fancy asserted itself. The arena of the king was built, not to give the people an opportunity of hearing the rhapsodies of dying gladiators, nor to enable them to view the inevitable conclusion of a conflict between religious opinions and hungry jaws, but for purposes far better adapted to widen and develop the mental energies of the people. This vast amphitheater, with its encircling galleries, its mysterious vaults, and its unseen passages, was an agent of poetic justice, in which crime was punished, or virtue rewarded, by the decrees of an impartial and incorruptible chance.

When a subject was accused of a crime of sufficient importance to interest the king, public notice was given that on an appointed day the fate of the accused person would be decided in the king's arena, a structure which well deserved its name, for, although its form and plan were borrowed from afar, its purpose emanated solely from the brain of this man, who, every barleycorn a king, knew no tradition to which he owed more allegiance than pleased his fancy, and who ingrafted on every adopted form of human thought and action the rich growth of his barbaric idealism.

When all the people had assembled in the galleries, and the king, surrounded by his court, sat high up on his throne of royal state on one side of the arena, he gave a signal, a door beneath him opened, and the accused subject stepped out into the amphitheater. Directly opposite him, on the other side of the inclosed space, were two doors, exactly alike and side by side. It was the duty and the privilege of the person on trial to walk directly to these doors and open one of them. He could open either door he pleased; he was subject to no guidance or influence but that of the aforementioned impartial and incorruptible chance. If he opened the one, there came out of it a hungry tiger, the fiercest and most cruel that could be procured, which immediately sprang upon him and tore him to pieces as a punishment for his guilt. The moment that the case of the criminal was thus decided, doleful iron bells were clanged, great wails went up from the hired mourners posted on the outer rim of the arena, and the vast audience, with bowed heads and downcast hearts, wended slowly their homeward way, mourning greatly that one so young and fair, or so old and respected, should have merited so dire a fate.

But, if the accused person opened the other door, there came forth from it a lady, the most suitable to his years and station that his majesty could select among his fair subjects, and to this lady he was immediately married, as a reward of his innocence. It mattered not that he might already possess a wife and family, or that his affections might be engaged upon an object of his own selection; the king allowed no such subordinate arrangements to interfere with his great scheme of retribution and reward. The exercises, as in the other instance, took place immediately, and in the arena. Another door opened beneath the king, and a priest, followed by a band of choristers, and dancing maidens blowing joyous airs on golden horns and treading an epithalamic measure, advanced to where the pair stood, side by side, and the wedding was promptly and cheerily solemnized. Then the gay brass bells rang forth their merry peals, the people shouted glad hurrahs, and the innocent man, preceded by children strewing flowers on his path, led his bride to his home.

This was the king's semi-barbaric method of administering justice. Its perfect fairness is obvious. The criminal could not know out of which door would come the lady; he opened either he pleased, without having the slightest idea whether, in the next instant, he was to be devoured or married. On some occasions the tiger came out of one door, and on some out of the other. The decisions of this tribunal were not only fair, they were positively determinate: The accused person was instantly punished if he found himself guilty, and, if innocent, he was rewarded on the spot, whether he liked it or not. There was no escape from the judgments of the king's arena.

The institution was a very popular one. When the people gathered together on one of the great trial days, they never knew whether they were to witness a bloody slaughter or a hilarious wedding. This element of uncertainty lent an interest to the occasion which it could not otherwise have attained. Thus, the masses were entertained and pleased, and the thinking part of the community could bring no charge of unfairness against this plan, for did not the accused person have the whole matter in his own hands?

This semi-barbaric king had a daughter as blooming as his most florid fancies, and with a soul as fervent and imperious as his own. As is usual in such cases, she was the apple of his eye, and was loved by him above all humanity. Among his courtiers was a young man of that fineness of blood and lowness of station common to the conventional heroes of romance who love royal maidens. This royal maiden was well satisfied with her lover, for he was handsome and brave to a degree unsurpassed in all this kingdom, and she loved him with an ardor that had enough of barbarism in it to make it exceedingly warm and strong. This love affair moved on happily for many months, until one day the king happened to discover its existence. He did not hesitate nor waver in regard to his duty in the premises. The youth was immediately cast into prison, and a day was appointed for his trial in the king's arena. This, of course, was an especially important occasion, and his majesty, as well as all the people, was greatly interested in the workings and development of this trial. Never before had such a case occurred; never before had a subject dared to love the daughter of the king. In after years such things became commonplace enough, but then they were in no slight degree novel and startling.

The tiger cages of the kingdom were searched for the most savage and relentless beasts, from which the fiercest monster might be selected for the arena; and the ranks of maiden youth and beauty throughout the land were carefully surveyed by competent judges in order that the young man might have a fitting bride in case fate did not determine for him a different destiny. Of course, everybody knew that the deed with which the accused was charged had been done. He had loved the princess, and neither he, she, nor any one else, thought of denying the fact; but the king would not think of allowing any fact of this kind to interfere with the workings of the tribunal, in which he took such great delight and satisfaction. No matter how the affair turned out, the youth would be disposed of, and the king would take an aesthetic pleasure in watching the course of events, which would determine whether or not the young man had done wrong in allowing himself to love the princess.

The appointed day arrived. From far and near the people gathered, and thronged the great galleries of the arena, and crowds, unable to gain admittance, massed themselves against its outside walls. The king and his court were in their places, opposite the twin doors, those fateful portals, so terrible in their similarity.

All was ready. The signal was given. A door beneath the royal party opened, and the lover of the princess walked into the arena. Tall, beautiful, fair, his appearance was greeted with a low hum of admiration and anxiety. Half the audience had not known so grand a youth had lived among them. No wonder the princess loved him! What a terrible thing for him to be there!

As the youth advanced into the arena he turned, as the custom was, to bow to the king, but he did not think at all of that royal personage. His eyes were fixed upon the princess, who sat to the right of her father. Had it not been for the moiety of barbarism in her nature it is probable that lady would not have been there, but her intense and fervid soul would not allow her to be absent on an occasion in which she was so terribly interested. From the moment that the decree had gone forth that her lover should decide his fate in the king's arena, she had thought of nothing, night or day, but this great event and the various subjects connected with it. Possessed of more power, influence, and force of character than

any one who had ever before been interested in such a case, she had done what no other person had done,—she had possessed herself of the secret of the doors. She knew in which of the two rooms, that lay behind those doors, stood the cage of the tiger, with its open front, and in which waited the lady. Through these thick doors, heavily curtained with skins on the inside, it was impossible that any noise or suggestion should come from within to the person who should approach to raise the latch of one of them. But gold, and the power of a woman's will, had brought the secret to the princess.

And not only did she know in which room stood the lady ready to emerge, all blushing and radiant, should her door be opened, but she knew who the lady was. It was one of the fairest and loveliest of the damsels of the court who had been selected as the reward of the accused youth, should he be proved innocent of the crime of aspiring to one so far above him; and the princess hated her. Often had she seen, or imagined that she had seen, this fair creature throwing glances of admiration upon the person of her lover, and sometimes she thought these glances were perceived, and even returned. Now and then she had seen them talking together; it was but for a moment or two, but much can be said in a brief space; it may have been on most unimportant topics, but how could she know that? The girl was lovely, but she had dared to raise her eyes to the loved one of the princess; and, with all the intensity of the savage blood transmitted to her through long lines of wholly barbaric ancestors, she hated the woman who blushed and trembled behind that silent door.

When her lover turned and looked at her, and his eye met hers as she sat there, paler and whiter than any one in the vast ocean of anxious faces about her, he saw, by that power of quick perception which is given to those whose souls are one, that she knew behind which door crouched the tiger, and behind which stood the lady. He had expected her to know it. He understood her nature, and his soul was assured that she would never rest until she had made plain to herself this thing, hidden to all other lookers-on, even to the king. The only hope for the youth in which there was any element of certainty was based upon the success of the princess in discovering this mystery; and the moment he looked upon her, he saw she had succeeded, as in his soul he knew she would succeed.

Then it was that his quick and anxious glance asked the question: "Which?" It was as plain to her as if he shouted it from where he stood. There was not an instant to be lost. The question was asked in a flash; it must be answered in another.

Her right arm lay on the cushioned parapet before her. She raised her hand, and made a slight, quick movement toward the right. No one but her lover saw her. Every eye but his was fixed on the man in the arena.

He turned, and with a firm and rapid step he walked across the empty space. Every heart stopped beating, every breath was held, every eye was fixed immovably upon that man. Without the slightest hesitation, he went to the door on the right, and opened it.

Now, the point of the story is this: Did the tiger come out of that door, or did the lady?

The more we reflect upon this question, the harder it is to answer. It involves a study of the human heart which leads us through devious mazes of passion, out of which it is difficult to find our way. Think of it, fair reader, not as if the decision of the question depended upon yourself, but upon that hot-blooded, semi-barbaric princess, her soul at a white heat beneath the combined fires of despair and jealousy. She had lost him, but who should have him?

How often, in her waking hours and in her dreams, had she started in wild horror, and covered her face with her hands as she thought of her lover opening the door on the other side of which waited the cruel fangs of the tiger!

But how much oftener had she seen him at the other door! How in her grievous reveries had she gnashed her teeth, and torn her hair, when she saw his start of rapturous delight as he opened the door of the lady! How her soul had burned in agony when she had seen him rush to meet that woman, with her flushing cheek and sparkling eye of triumph; when she had seen him lead her forth, his whole frame kindled with the joy of recovered life; when she had heard the glad shouts from the multitude, and the wild ringing of the happy bells; when she had seen the priest, with his joyous followers, advance to the couple, and make them man and wife before her very eyes; and when she had seen them walk away together upon their path of flowers, followed by the tremendous shouts of the hilarious multitude, in which her one despairing shriek was lost and drowned!

Would it not be better for him to die at once, and go to wait for her in the blessed regions of semi-barbaric futurity?

And yet, that awful tiger, those shrieks, that blood!

Her decision had been indicated in an instant, but it had been made after days and nights of anguished deliberation. She had known she would be asked, she had decided what she would answer, and, without the slightest hesitation, she had moved her hand to the right. The question of her decision is one not to be lightly considered, and it is not for me to presume to set myself up as the one person able to answer it. And so I leave it with all of you: Which came out of the opened door,— the lady, or the tiger?

Storytelling Resources

Worldwide List of Courses In and/or About Storytelling at Colleges and Universities

This list began in 1998 when Eric Miller, then a doctoral student in folklore at the University of Pennsylvania, felt there was a need for such a list and began compiling it. In 2002, Miller embarked on two years of field-work in south India and passed on compiling duties to Millie Jackson. Jackson, who had earned a Ph.D. from Michigan State University, began studies in storytelling at East Tennessee State University during her sabbatical in 2004; updating the list became part of her research on storytelling. Although Miller is now settled in Chennai, on India's southeast coast, Jackson continues to update the list, which is accessible at http://shesig.pbwiki.com.

Both of these scholars believe that storytelling studies is an interdisciplinary field of study, or a discipline unto itself. For introductions to storytelling studies, please see Miller's comments at http://ccat.sas.upenn.edu/storytelling/definition.html and the *Storytelling, Self, and Society*'s editorial policy statement at http://www.courses.unt.edu/efiga/SSS/SSS _Journal.htm.

The full text of what is considered to be a founding article of storytelling studies, "Once Upon a Time: An Introduction to the Inaugural Issue," by Joseph Sobol, John S. Gentile, and Sunwolf, can be found at http://www. courses.unt.edu/efiga/SSS/IntroInaugural IssueSSSJournal.htm.

The following list includes courses in a number of disciplines; international offerings are listed first, followed by courses offered by universities within the United States. The address, specific contact information, website, and a brief description are given for each program as applicable. Note that many courses are taught by adjuncts and are not taught every semester; check with the university to determine the status of current courses and future offerings.

Australia

Parsifal College (a Rudolf Steiner training college), Sydney
P.O. Box 231, West Pennant Hills
Sydney 2125
Australia
Phone: +61 (0) 2 9680 9533
Courses: Storytelling for Early Childhood Teachers, and Storytelling and Puppetry.

Southern Cross University
P.O. Box 157
Lismore, NSW 2480
Australia
http://www.scu.edu.au/index.php
Course: ENG 355: Storytelling: Emphasizes the importance of storytelling as a method of transmitting culture, and enables students to enjoy, prepare, and tell stories to children.

Canada

Cape Breton University
Folklore (Community Studies)
P.O. Box 5300, 1250 Grand Lake Road
Sydney, Nova Scotia, B1P 6L2
Canada
Contact: Afra Kavanagh,
    afra_kavanagh@uccb.ca
http://faculty.cbu.ca/afrak/storytelling/
default.htm
*Offers courses and sponsors annual Universal Child
Care Benefit (UCCB) Storytelling Symposium.*

Memorial University of Newfoundland,
    St. John's
Department of Folklore
St. John's, Newfoundland A1C 5S7
Canada
Phone: 709-737-8402
Contact: folklore@morgan.ucs.mun.ca
http://www.mun.ca/folklore/
*Offers courses in folk literature, folk tales,
and mythology.*

University of Alberta, Edmonton
School of Library and Information Studies
3-20 Rutherford South
Edmonton, Alberta T6G 2J4
Canada
Contact: Gail de Vos,
    storyteller.devos@telusplanet.net
http://www.slis.ualberta.ca/

Germany

Richard Martin
Bornstrasse 83 Darmstadt
Phone: +49 (0) 6151 377 175
Contact: info@tellatale.eu
www.tellatale.eu
*Offers teacher training workshops in "Using
Storytelling in the Classroom" at various
universities in Germany and other countries.*

United Kingdom

Artemis School of Speech and Drama
Perdue Centre for the Arts

West Hoathly Road
East Grinstead, West Sussex RH19 4NF
England, UK
Phone: +44 (0) 1342 321330
Contact: Christopher Garvey, Director
http://www.artemisspeechanddrama.org.uk/

Emerson College (Rudolf Steiner College)
School for Storytelling
Forest Row
East Sussex RH18 5JX
England, UK
Contact: Ashley Ramsden, Director
http://www.emerson.org.uk/index.php?id=21
*Courses are offered full time, part time, and
on weekends.*

University of Kent
School of Drama, Film and Visual Art
Canterbury CT2 7NB
England, UK
Contact: Vayu Naidu
http://www.kent.ac.uk/sdfva/
*Applicable courses are related to performance
and cinema.*

University of Glamorgan
Drama
Pontypridd, CF37 1DL
Wales, UK
Phone: +44 (0) 1443 482693
Contact: Mike Wilson, mwilson@glam.ac.uk
*Courses are offered through the Drama
department and as part of the continuing
education program. Opportunities for indepen-
dent study also are available at the graduate
level.*

University of Glasgow
Dumfries Campus
Rutherford McCowan Buildings
Dumfries DG1 4ZL
Scotland, UK
Contact: Tom Pow, t.pow@crichton.gla.ac.uk
http://www.cc.gla.ac.uk/layer2/
    creativeculture.htm
*Courses in storytelling offered through the Creative
and Cultural Studies Program.*

United States

Note: Additional lists of U.S. higher education Folklore and Folklife programs are kept by the American Folklife Center, Library of Congress Research Center (http://www.loc.gov/folklife/source/grad.html) and the American Folklore Society (http://www.afsnet.org/aboutfolklore/wherestudyFL.cfm).

Alaska

University of Alaska, Fairbanks
Alaska Native Studies Program
319 Brooks Building
Fairbanks, AK 99775-6300
Phone: 907-474-7181
http://www.uaf.edu/ans/index.html
Selected courses included storytelling by indigenous cultures.

Arizona

Glendale Community College
Building 02, Room 121
6000 West Olive Avenue
Glendale, AZ 85302
Phone: 623-845-3686
Contact: Joyce Story,
   Joyce.story@gcmail.maricopa.edu
Course: The Art of Storytelling.

South Mountain Community College
Storytelling Institute in the Communications
   and Fine Arts Division
7050 South 24th Street
Phoenix, AZ 85040
Phone: 602-243-8000
Contacts: Lorraine Calbow; LynnAnn
   Wojciechowicz; Liz Warren,
   liz.warren@smcmail.maricopa.edu.
http://eport.maricopa.edu/published/l/yn/lynnannw/home/1/
The Storytelling Program of Study involves six required courses and various electives. Students need not be matriculated in a B.A. program. Courses include: The Art of Storytelling, Life Stories, Multicultural Folktales, Mythology,

Using Story in Business Settings, Using Story in Educational Settings, and Using Story in Healing Settings.

California

Antelope Valley College
Communication Arts
3041 West Avenue K
Lancaster, CA 93536
Phone: 661-722-6300, ext. 6477
Contact: Debra Olson Tolar, dtolar@avc.edu

California State University, Los Angeles
Charter College of Education
Division of Curriculum and Instruction
King Hall D2069
Los Angeles, CA 90032
Contact: Ambika Gopalakrishnan,
   agopala@calstatela.edu
http://www.calstatela.edu/academic/ccoe/
This university offers courses in storytelling, digital storytelling, and folklore. Certificate in Storytelling: This program is designed for persons with an interest in the techniques, theories, and literature associated with the ancient and modern art of storytelling. The certificate is valuable for teacher use in language arts instruction and for improving communications skills; it also can be used effectively by librarians and recreation leaders. This program is open to matriculated, upper division undergraduate and postbaccalaureate students. Completion of this credit certificate program requires thirty-two units in core and elective courses.

Chapman University College
Professional Development Center
3001 Lava Ridge Court
Roseville, CA 95661
Phone: 916-984-6248
Contact: Susan M. Osborn,
sosborn@ix.netcom.com

San Jose State University
Television, Radio, Film, Theatre
One Washington Square
San Jose, CA 95192-0098

Phone: 408-924-4568
Contact: Beverly Swanson,
    Beverly1007@aol.com
*Theater Arts 131: Storytelling & Creative
Dramatics.*

University of California, Los Angeles
    (UCLA)
Information Studies
220GSE&IS
Los Angeles, CA 90095
Phone: 310-206-9363
Contact: Virginia Walter, vwalter@ucla.edu
www.ucla.edu

Connecticut

The Graduate Institute
701 North Street
Milford, CT 06460
Phone: 203-874-4252; 860-701-7708
Contacts: Wendy Cook, Robin Moore,
    graduateinstitute@learn.edu
www.learn.edu/ot/
Offers a Master of Arts degree in Oral Traditions.

Southern Connecticut State University
School of Communication, Information and
    Library Science
501 Crescent Street
New Haven, CT 06575
Phone: 203-392-5711
Contact: Gwendolin Nowlan, Director,
    nowlan@scsu.ctstate.edu
http://www.southernct.edu/programs/
    storytelling
*Offers a master's program in Oral Tradition.
Courses include: Fostering the Multiple
Intelligences through the Oral Tradition,
Historical and Cultural Integration of Music and
Oral Tradition, History and Development of the
Folktale in the Oral Tradition, History and
Development of the Oral Tradition, Integrating
Enhanced Learning Techniques and Movement
into the Oral Tradition, Integrating the Oral
Tradition into the Elementary Curriculum,
Integrating the Oral Tradition into the Middle
and High School Curriculum, Methods of*

*Storytelling for the Elementary School, The Oral
Tradition in Ancient and Modern Mythology,
Storytelling in Art and Legend, and Storytelling
in Art and Technique. The school also offers
special programs, field projects, and independent
studies in storytelling.*

University of Bridgeport
School of Education and Human Resources
Carlson Hall
303 University Avenue
Bridgeport, CT 06604
Contact: Connie Rockman,
    connie.rock@snet.net
Course: Storytelling for Teachers.

Florida

Florida Atlantic University
South Florida Storytelling Project
Communications
777 Glades Road
Boca Raton, FL 33431
Phone: 561-297-0042
Contact: Caren S. Neile, cneile@fau.edu,
    carenina@bellsouth.net
http://www.fau.edu/storytelling/index.htm

Georgia

Kennesaw State University
Department of Theatre and Performance
    Studies
1000 Chastain Road, Box #3103
Kennesaw State University
Kennesaw, GA 30144
Phone: 770-423-6338
Contacts: John S. Gentile (Chair),
    jgentile@kennesaw.edu; Hannah B.
    Harvey, hharvey3@kennesaw.edu
http://www.kennesaw.edu/theatre/
    monkeyking/
*Courses: 1) Storytelling I: Folktale and Legend:
The study of folk narrative forms of folktale and
legend through storytelling performance. Introduces
student to folkloristics as a field of study; to the
nature, structure, and function of narrative; and to
the aesthetics, methods, and practice of storytelling.
2) Storytelling II: Myth and Epic: The study of*

folk narrative forms of myth and epic through storytelling performance. Introduces students to the various approaches to the study and interpretation of world mythologies and to the aesthetics, methods, and practice of storytelling.

Hawaii

University of Hawaii, Manoa
Academy for Creative Media
2550 Campus Road
Honolulu, HI 96822
Contact: Chris Lee, Chair, Academy for
    Creative Media, cpl@hawaii.edu
http://acm.hawaii.edu/
Courses in Storytelling and Story Theater.

Illinois

Dominican University
Graduate School of Library and Information
    Science
Crown 323, 7900 West Division Street
River Forest, IL 60305
Phone: 708-524-6871
Contact: Janice M. Del Negro,
    jdclnegro@dom.edu
Course: Storytelling for Adults & Children.

Northern Illinois University
School of Theatre and Dance
Dekalb, IL 60115
Phone: 815-753-8074
Contact. Patricia Ridge, pridge@niu.edu
http://www.vpa.niu.edu/theatre.html

Northwestern University
Department of Theatre, in the School of
    Speech
Chicago and Evanston, IL
Phone: 847-491-3163
Contact: Rives Collins, r-collins@nwu.edu
*Courses include Adapting Folk Tales and
Other Sources, and Intensive Coaching for
Storytellers.*

University of Illinois
Graduate School of Library and Information
    Studies

501 East Daniel
Champaign, IL 61820
Phone: 217-244-7451
Contact: Betsy Hearne, ehearne@uiuc.edu
http://www.lis.uiuc.edu/~hearne/
*Courses offered in person and online through
LEEP (an online scheduling option).*

Indiana

Indiana University
School of Library and Information Science
755 West Michigan Street, UL 3100N
Indianapolis, IN 46202-5195
Contact: Hope Baugh, bryteller@yahoo.com
http://www.slis.iupui.edu/
*Course: S603: Workshop in Youth Services
Librarianship—Storytelling (1.5 credits).
The course is a special topics course taught by
several instructors in various locations around
Indiana.*

Indiana University
Department of Folklore, M.A. and Ph.D.
504 North Fess
Bloomington, IN 47405
Phone: 812-855-0395
Contact: Richard Bauman,
    bauman@indiana.edu

Iowa

University of Iowa
College of Education
Department of Curriculum and Instruction
Program in Literature, Science & the Arts
13-E North Hall
Iowa City, IA 52242
Phone: 319-335-3011
Contact: Steve McGuire,
    s-mcguire@uiowa.edu

Kentucky

Western Kentucky University
Folk Narrative
Department of Folk Studies and
    Anthropology
Bowling Green, KY 42101

Phone: 270-745-5896
Contact: Chris Antonsen,
    Chris.antonsen@wku.edu

Louisiana

Lousiana State University
School of Library and Information Science
276 Coates Hall
Baton Rouge, LA 70803
Phone: 225-578-1467
Contact: Dr. Margie J. Thomas, Faculty
    Coordinator, Mthom39@lsu.edu

Maine

University of Southern Maine
Center for the Study of Lives
400 Bailey Hall
Gorham, ME 04038
Phone: 207-780-5078
Contact: Robert Atkinson
Teaching the telling of sacred stories.

Maryland

Garrett Community College
166 Lodge Circle
Swanton, MD 21561
Phone: 301-387-9199
Contact: Gail N. Herman
*Offers courses on using storytelling in education
and business.*

Western Maryland College
School Library Media Program
Hill Hall
Westminster, MD 21157
Contact: Joanne Hay, jhay@cvn.net
http://www2.yk.psu.edu/~mer7/storytel.html
Course: Art of Storytelling.

Massachusetts

Fitchburg State College
160 Pearl Street
Fitchburg, MA 01420
Contact: Laurie DeRosa, Chair of Education,
    Lderosa@fsc.edu
www.fsc.edu

*Courses are offered through the Department of
Education (Early Childhood), the Department of
English, and the Center for Professional Studies.*

Harvard University
Folklore and Mythology Program
11 Prescott Street
Cambridge, MA 02138
Phone: 617-495-4788
Contact: folkmyth@fas.harvard.edu
http://www.fas.harvard.edu/~folkmyth/

Lesley University
29 Everett Street
Cambridge, MA 02138
Phone: 617-349-8740; 800-999-1959 ext. 8426
Contact: Lisa Donovan
http://www.lesley.edu/offcampus/term/
    nmagss_cal.html
*The Creative Arts in Learning program offers
storytelling specialization as part of master's of arts
and master's of education degrees.*

Simmons College
Graduate School of Library and Information
    Science
Room P-204D
300 The Fenway
Boston, MA 02115
Phone: 617-521-2793
Contact: Maggie Bush,
    Margaret.bush@simmons.edu
Course: LIS 423: Storytelling.

Michigan

Grand Valley State University
Lake Superior Hall 121
Allendale, MI 49401
Phone: 616-331-3510
Contact: Karen Libman, libmank@gvsu.edu
Course: CTH 300: Storytelling.

Wayne State University
Teacher Education Division
241 Education Building
Detroit, MI 48202
Phone: 313-577-0928

Contact: R. Craig Roney, rroney@wayne.edu
Graduate course in storytelling are cross-listed with the School of Information and Library Science; this university also offers related special topics courses.

Minnesota

Metropolitan State University
Communication, Writing, and the Arts
	Department
Suite 205, Energy Park Place
1380 Energy Lane
St. Paul, MN 55108
Contacts: Loren Niemi, niemistory@aol.com,
	Loren.Niemi@metrostate.edu, 651-793-
	1439; Nancy Donoval, 651-999-5940
http://www.metrostate.edu/cas/cwa/index.
html
Courses: Storytelling as a Modern Communications Art, and Storytelling as Presentation & Performance (both analytic and performance skills).

University of Minnesota, Twin Cities
205 Folwell Hall
Minneapolis, MN
Phone: 612-624-1041
Contact: Jack Zipes, Zipes001@umn.edu
Course offered in the summer: Storytelling, Critical Literacy, and Creative Drama.

Missouri

University of Missouri—Columbia.
Center for Studies in Oral Tradition
66 McReynolds Hall
Columbia, MO 65211-2370
Phone: 573-882-9720
Contact: John Miles Foley, Director,
	csot@missouri.edu
http://oraltradition.org/

Nebraska

University of Nebraska, Omaha
Teacher Education
Kayser Hall 314
6001 Dodge Street
Omaha, NE 68182

Phone: 402-558-0864
Contact: Rita Paskowitz, storywitz@juno.com
Course: Storytelling and Education.

New Jersey

Rutgers, the State University of New Jersey
School of Communication, Information, and
	Library Studies
4 Huntington Street
New Brunswick, NJ 08901-1071
Phone: 732-932-7500
Contact: lis@scils.rutgers.edu
http://www.scils.rutgers.edu
Course: Traditions in Oral Narration.

New Mexico

New Mexico State University
Department of Management
Las Cruces, NM 88003-8003
Contact: David Boje, dboje@nmsu.edu
http://business.nmsu.edu/~dboje/
Courses on business and storytelling.

New York

Bank Street Graduate School of Education
Main Campus Location
610 West 112th Street
New York, NY 10025-1898
Phone: 212-875-4492
Contact: Nina Jaffe, njaffe@bankstreet.edu
http://www.bankstreet.edu/gs/
Graduate courses: Storytelling for Children, Folklore in the Classroom, and Human Development I: Programming for Young Audiences.

Ithaca College
Department of Speech Communication
422 Muller Center
Ithaca, NY 14850
Phone: 607-274-3931
Contact: Bruce Henderson,
	henderso@ithaca.edu

Palmer School of Library and Information
	Science
720 Northern Boulevard

Brookville, NY 11548-1300
Phone: 516-299-2866
Contact: Amy Spaulding,
    amy.spaulding@liu.edu
Courses include Storytelling and Folk Literature, and Myth and the Age of Information (the roles of story and storytelling in the modern world).

New York University
Department of Performance Studies
721 Broadway, 6th Floor
New York, NY 10003
Phone: 212-998-1620
Contact: Barbara Kirshenblatt-Gimblett,
    bkg@nyu.edu
http://performance.tisch.nyu.edu/page/home.
html

Yeshiva University, Stern College for
    Women
525 West End Avenue
New York, NY 10024
Phone: 917-326-4810
Contact: Peninnah Schram,
    Peninnah1@aol.com

North Carolina

The University of North Carolina—Chapel
    Hill
School of Library and Information Science
CB#3360 Manning Hall
Chapel Hill, NC 27599
Phone: 919-962-7622
Contact: Brian Sturm, sturm@ils.unc.edu
http://ils.unc.edu/~sturm/
Course: INLS 121: Principles and Techniques of Storytelling.

The University of North Carolina,
    Greensboro
University Speaking Center
3211 MHRA Building
Greensboro, NC 27403
Contact: Kim Cuny, kmcuny@uncg.edu
Course: Storytelling Across Cultures (Freshman Seminars).

Ohio

Ashland University
Communication Arts
Ashland, OH 44805
Phone: 419-289-5143
Contact: Deleasa Randall-Griffiths,
    DRANDALL@ashland.edu
Course in International Storytelling is offered in Communications and Education.

The Ohio State University
Enarson Hall
154 West 12th Avenue
Columbus, OH 43210
www.osu.edu
Storytelling courses are offered through Freshman Seminars and through Folklore and Area Studies (i.e., Near Eastern Language & Culture).

Pennsylvania

Allegheny College
Psychology
520 N. Main Street
Meadville, PA 16335
Contact: Joshua Searle-White,
    jsearle@allegheny.edu
Course: FS 101: Adventures, Mysteries, and Just Plain Lies: The Art of Telling Stories.

Kutztown University
Performance Studies/Speech and Theatre
Speech Communication
15200 Kutztown Road
Kutztown, PA 19530
Phone: 610-683-4251
Contact: Deryl Johnson,
    Johnson@kutztown.edu

University of Pittsburgh
School of Information Sciences
135 North Bellefield
Pittsburgh, PA 15260
Phone: 412-624-3988
http://www.ischool.pitt.edu/
Course: LIS 2326: Storytelling.

Tennessee

East Tennessee State University
Department of Curriculum and Instruction
P.O. Box 70784
Johnson City, TN 37614-1709
Phone: 423-439-7863
Contact: Joseph Sobol, Director of
    Storytelling Program, sobol@etsu.edu
http://www.etsu.edu/stories
*Offers a master's of arts in Reading with a
Concentration in Storytelling. Courses include:
Advanced Storytelling, Basic Storytelling,
Historical and Psychological Foundations of
Storytelling, Linguistics of Reading (section
focusing on storytelling), and Practicum. Electives
include Storytelling Institutes, Story Performance,
and special topics courses. Capstone Project and
thesis options are available.*

University of Tennessee, Knoxville
School of Information Science
451 Comm UEB
Knoxville, TN 37996
Contact: Tena Litherland, clither1@utk.edu
*Course: IS 576: Storytelling in the Library and
Classroom.*

Texas

University of North Texas
School of Library and Information Sciences
Information Sciences Building, Room 216
P.O. Box 311068
Denton, TX 76203-1068
Phone: 940-565-2187
Contact: Elizabeth Figa,
    efiga@lis.admin.unt.edu, slis@unt.edu
http://www.unt.edu/slis; http://www.courses.
    unt.edu/efiga/Figa/
Graduate Academic Certificate in
    Storytelling: http://www.unt.edu/slis/
    programs/storytellingcert.htm
*Courses: SLIS 5440, Storytelling, and SLIS 5611,
Advanced Storytelling. The first course is offered
each semester, 100 percent online; the second course
also is taught online, but has an optional on-site
component and is offered just once a year.*

Vermont

Goddard College
123 Pitkin Road
Plainfield, VT 05667
Phone: 785-843-0253
Contact: Caryn Mirriam-Goldberg,
    Coordinator, carynken@mindspring.com
http://www.goddard.edu/masterarts_
    transformative
*Offers master's of arts in Individualized Studies,
concentration in Transformative Language Arts.*

Virginia

George Mason University
Department of English
Robinson A439
4400 University Drive, MSN 3E4
Fairfax, VA 22030
Phone: 703-993-1172
Contact: Margaret R. Yocom,
    myocom@gmu.edu

Washington

Shoreline Community College
Humanities Division, Speech
    Communication
16101 Greenwood Avenue North
Shoreline, WA 98133-5696
Phone: 206-546-4795
Contact: Brooke Zimmers,
    bzimmers@shoreline.edu
*Course: Speech Communications: The Art of
Storytelling.*

Western Washington University
Woodring College of Education
Miller Hall 265
Bellingham, WA 98225
Phone: 360-650-6446
Contact: Rosemary Scott Vohs,
    Rosemary.Vohs@wwu.edu
www.wwu.edu/~rvohs
*Courses offered include Advanced Storytelling,
The Power of Storytelling in Action, Reader's
Theatre in the Classroom, and Storytelling:*

Practical Field Applications, as well as summer workshops and independent studies.

Wisconsin

University of Wisconsin, Milwaukee
Theatre 278
P.O. Box 413
Milwaukee, WI 53201
Phone: 414-229-6066
Contact: Robin Mello, rmello@uwm.edu

Offers storytelling courses in the Theatre department (460) and School of Information Studies.

University of Wisconsin, Madison
American Indian Studies Program
315 Ingraham Hall
1155 Observatory Drive
Madison, WI 53706
Phone: 608-263-5501
Contact: aisp@mailplus.wisc.edu
Courses in American Indian Oral Literature.

Storytelling Festivals

Following is a list of storytelling festivals. The international festivals are listed first, followed by those held in the United States. The location, contact information, website, and month or season are listed for each festival as applicable. All events are annual unless otherwise noted.

Those wishing to attend any of the festivals listed here should be aware that storytelling festivals may be cancelled, rescheduled, or have their organizers or sites changed. While the events included represent many major events, this is not to be considered a comprehensive list, since storytelling events may be held in other areas, and new storytelling festivals may be started up after this list is published.

Australia

Australian National Storytelling Conference/Festival. Perth. 61-0-35333-4347. astewart@netconnect.com.au.

Canada

Alberta

T.A.L.E.S. Fort Edmonton Storytelling Festival. Edmonton. holly.gilmour@interbaun.com; mamclean@shaw.ca. www.ecn.ab.ca/~tales/. September.

British Columbia

Kootenay Storytelling Festival. Proctor. 888-422-1123. www.kootenaystory.org. July.
Vancouver Storytelling Festival. Vancouver. 604-876-2272. info@vancouverstorytelling. org. www.vancouverstorytelling.org. Time varies.

Manitoba

Sundog Storytelling Festival. Winnipeg. 204-956-2830. February.

Newfoundland

St. John's Storytelling Festival. St. John's. 866-576-8508. office@sjfac.nf.net. www. nlfolk.com/storytelling/storytelling.html. November.

Ontario

Brantford Storytelling Festival. Brantford. 519-756-0727. taletellers@bizbrant.com. www.tales.bizbrant.com. October.
Ottawa Storytelling Festival. Ottawa. 613-722-2606. ruth@rasputins.ca. Autumn.
The Toronto Festival of Storytelling. Toronto. 416-656-2445. admin@storytellingtoronto. org. March/April.

Quebec

Note: The Quebec festivals, though bilingual, are mostly for French speakers.
De Bouche à Oreille (From the Mouth to the Ear). Montreal. info@andrelemelin.com. Time varies.
Festival du Conte (Storytelling Festival). West Brome. Time varies.
Le Festival Intercultural du Conte du Quebec (The International Storytelling Festival of Quebec), Montreal. 514-272-4494. rosebudc@sympatico.ca. http://festival-contc.qc.ca/. Bi-annually in October.

Yukon Territory

Yukon International Storytelling Festival. Whitehorse. yukonstory@yknet.yk.ca. Time varies.

Ireland

Féile Scéalaíochta Chléire/The Cape Clear Island International Storytelling Festival. Cape Clear Island, Skibbereen, County Cork. http://indigo.ie/~stories/. September.

New Zealand

Glistening Waters Storytelling Festival. Masterton. gw@waireap.org.nz. Time varies.

United Kingdom

Festival at the Edge. Much Wenlock, Shropshire. www.festivalattheedge.com. July.
North Pennines Storytelling Festival. Teesdale, Tynedale, Wear Valley, Eden. www.npenninestorytelling.org.uk/. October.

United States

Arizona

Mesa Storytelling Festival. Mesa. 480-644-6500. www.mesaartscenter.com. October.

California

Ananda Storytelling Festival. Nevada City. www.livingwisdom.org. Autumn.
Bay Area Storytelling Festival. San Francisco. www.bayareastorytelling.org/. May.
Mariposa Storytelling Festival. Mariposa. www.arts-mariposa.org/storytelling.html. March.

Colorado

Rocky Mountain Storytelling Festival. Palmer Lake. www.colo-performingartists.com/Festival/homepage.html. Mid-summer.

Connecticut

Connecticut Storytelling Festival. New London. www.connstorycenter.org/festival.html. Late April or early May.

Florida

Cracker Storytelling Festival. Homeland Heritage Park. 863-834-4274. October.
Tampa Hillsborough County Storytelling Festival. www.tampastory.org/. April.

Georgia

Azalea Storytelling Festival. La Grange College, La Grange. www.lagrange.edu/azalea/index.html. March.
Winter Storytelling Festival. Southern Order of Storytellers. Atlanta. www.southernorderofstorytellers.org/. January.

Illinois

Annual Sterling Storytelling Festival. Sterling. 815-625-1370. akpeach54@hotmail.com. August/September.
Fox Valley Folk Music & Storytelling Festival. Geneva. 630-897-3655. September.
Illinois Storytelling Festival. Spring Grove. 630-877-0931. info@storytelling.org. August.

Indiana

Hoosier Storytelling Festival. Indianapolis.
  317-576-9848. Ellen@storytellingarts.org.
  October.

Iowa

Iowa Storytelling Festival. Clear Lake.
  641-357-6134. clplib@netins.net. July.

Kansas

Kansas Storytelling Festival. Downs. http://
  www.downsks.net/. April.

Kentucky

Cave Run Storytelling Festival. Morehead.
  606-780-4342; 800-654-1944.
  caverunstoryfest.org/. September.
Corn Island Storytelling Festival.
  Louisville. 502-245-0643.
  www.cornislandstorytellingfestival.org/.
  September.

Massachusetts

Three Apples Storytelling Festival. Bedford.
  617-499-9529. www.threeapples.org.
  September or October.

Michigan

Detroit Storytelling Festival. Livonia. http://
  www.detroitstorytelling.org/. September.
Michigan Storytellers Festival. Flint. 810-232-
  7111. www.flint.lib.mi.us/msf. July.

Mississippi

Mississippi Blueberry Jubilee Storytelling
  Festival. Poplarville Storytelling Guild.
  Poplarville. www.blueberryjubilee.org.
  June.

Missouri

St. Louis Storytelling Festival. St. Louis. 314-
  516-5961. www.umsl.edu/divisions/conted/
  storyfes/. April/May.

Montana

Montana Story Telling Roundup. Cut Bank.
  406-336-3253; 406-873-2295. www.
  northerntel.net/~cbchambe/storytel/. April.

Nebraska

Buffalo Commons Storytelling Festival.
  McCook. http://www.buffalocommons.
  org/. May.

New Mexico

Taos Storytelling Festival. Taos. 877-758-7343;
  575-758-0081. www.somostaos.org.
  October.

New York

Riverway Storytelling Festival. Albany. 518-
  383-4620. www.riverwaystorytellingfestival.
  org. April/May.

Oregon

Stories by the Sea. Newport. 541-265-ARTS.
  September.
Tapestry of Tales Storytelling Festival.
  Portland. 503-988-5402. November.

Pennsylvania

Three Rivers Storytelling Festival. Pittsburgh.
  smith6@einetwork.net. August.

South Carolina

Patchwork Tales Storytelling Festival. York
  County Public Library, Rock Hill. www.
  patchworktales.org. March.

Tennessee

Haunting in the Hills, a Storytelling Event. Big
  South Fork National River and Recreation
  Area, Big South Fork. 423-569-9778.
  September.
National Storytelling Festival. International
  Storytelling Foundation, Jonesborough.
  www.storytellingfoundation.net/festival/
  festival.htm. October.

Texas

George West Storyfest. George West. http://georgeweststoryfest.org/. November.

Squatty Pines Storytelling Retreat. Whitehouse. 903-510-6400. http://www.easttexastellers.homestead.com/Squatty.html. March.

Utah

Timpanogos Storytelling Festival. Orem. 801-229-7050. www.timpfest.org. August/September.

Washington

Bellingham Storytelling Festival. Bellingham. 360-714-9631. November.

Forest Storytelling Festival. Port Angeles. 360-417-5031; 206-935-5308. forestfest@yahoo.com. October.

Wisconsin

Northlands Annual Conference and Storytelling Workshop. Location varies. www.northlands.net. April.

Riverbend Storytelling Festival. West Bend. info@riverbendstorytelling.org. October.

Bibliography

Storytelling Books

Baker, Augusta, and Ellin Greene. *Storytelling: Art and Technique.* New York: R.R. Bowker, 1977.

Barton, Bob. *Tell Me Another: Storytelling and Reading Aloud at Home, at School, and in the Community.* Portsmouth, NH: Heineman. 1986.

Barton, Bob, and David Booth. *Stories in the Classroom: Storytelling, Reading Aloud and Roleplaying with Children.* Portsmouth, NH: Heineman. 1990.

Bauer, Caroline Feller. *Caroline Feller Bauer's New Handbook for Storytellers.* Chicago: American Library Association, 1993.

———. *Handbook for Storytellers.* Chicago: American Library Association, 1977.

Breneman, Lucille N., and Bren Breneman. *Once Upon a Time: A Storytelling Handbook.* Chicago: Nelson-Hall, 1983.

Bruchac, Joseph. *Tell Me a Tale: A Book About Storytelling.* New York: Harcourt Brace, 1997.

Cassady, Marsh. *The Art of Storytelling: Creative Ideas for Preparation and Performance.* San Francisco: Meriwether, 1994.

———. *Storytelling Step by Step.* San Jose, CA: Resource, 1990.

Collins, Chase. *Tell Me a Story: Creating Bedtime Tales Your Children Will Dream On.* Boston: Houghton Mifflin, 1992.

Cullum, Carolyn N. *The Storytime Sourcebook: A Compendium of Ideas and Resources for Storytellers.* New York: Neal-Schuman, 1990.

Dart, Archa O. *Tips for Storytellers.* Nashville, TN: Southern Publishers Association, 1966.

Davis, Donald. *Telling Your Own Stories.* Little Rock, AR: August House, 1994.

Geisler, Harlynne. *Storytelling Professionally: The Nuts and Bolts of a Working Performer.* Littleton, CO: Libraries Unlimited, 1997.

Gillard, Marni. *Storyteller, Storyteacher: Discovering the Power of Storytelling for Teaching and Living.* York, ME: Stenhouse, 1996.

Greene, Ellin. *Storytelling: Art and Technique.* Westport, CT: Greenwood, 1996.

Haven, Kendall. *Super Simple Storytelling: A Can-Do Guide for Every Classroom, Every Day.* Englewood, CO: Teacher Ideas, 2000.

Kinghorn, Harriet R., and Mary Helen Pelton. *Every Child a Storyteller: A Handbook of Ideas.* Englewood, CO: Teacher Ideas, 1991.

Lipman, Doug. *Improving Your Storytelling: Beyond the Basics for All Who Tell Stories in Work or Play.* Little Rock, AR: August House, 1999.

———. *The Storytelling Coach: How to Listen, Praise, and Bring Out People's Best.* Little Rock, AR: August House, 1995.

———. *Storytelling Games: Creative Activities for Language, Communication, and Composition Across the Curriculum.* Westport, CT: Oryx, 1994.

Livo, Norma, and Sandra Reitz. *Storytelling: Process and Practice.* Littleton, CO: Libraries Unlimited, 1986.

MacDonald, Margaret Read. *The Storyteller's Start-Up Book: Finding, Learning, Performing, and Using Folktales: Including Twelve Tellable Tales.* Little Rock, AR: August House, 1993.

Mellon, Nancy. *Storytelling and the Art of Imagination.* Rockport, MA: Element, 1992.

Mooney, Bill, and David Holt. *The Storyteller's Guide: Storytellers Share Advice for the Classroom, Boardroom, Showroom, Podium, Pulpit and Central Stage.* Little Rock, AR: August House, 1996.

Moore, Robin. *Creating a Family Storytelling Tradition: Awakening the Hidden Storyteller.* Little Rock, AR: August House, 1999.

National Storytelling Association. *Tales as Tools: The Power of Story in the Classroom.* Jonesborough, TN: National Storytelling, 1994.

Pellowski, Anne. *The Family Storytelling Handbook: How to Use Stories, Anecdotes, Rhymes, Handkerchiefs, Paper, and Other Objects to Enrich Your Family Traditions.* New York and London: Collier Macmillan, 1987.

———. *The World of Storytelling.* New York: R.R. Bowker, 1977.

Ross, Ramon Royal. *Storyteller.* Columbus, OH: Charles E. Merrill. 1980.

Sawyer, Ruth. *The Way of the Storyteller.* New York: Penguin, 1977.

Schimmel, Nancy. *Just Enough to Make a Story: A Sourcebook for Storytelling.* Berkeley, CA: Sisters' Choice, 1982.

Shedlock, Marie. *The Art of the Storyteller.* New York: Dover. 1951.

Simmons, Annette. *The Story Factor: Inspiration, Influence, and Persuasion Through the Art of Storytelling.* Boulder, CO: Perseus, 2002.

Winch, Gordon, and Barbara Poston-Anderson. *Now for a Story: Sharing Stories with Young Children.* Alberta Park, Australia: Phoenix Education, 1993.

Zipes, Jack. *Creative Storytelling: Building Community, Changing Lives.* New York: Routledge. 1995.

Folktale Books

Afanas'ev, Aleksandr. *Russian Fairy Tales.* New York: Pantheon, 1976.

Ausubel, Nathan. *A Treasury of Jewish Folklore.* New York: Crown, 1975.

Barchers, Suzanne I. *Wise Women.* Englewood, CO: Libraries Unlimited, 1990.

Bierhorst, John. *Latin American Folktales.* New York: Pantheon, 2001.

Briggs, Katharine M. *A Dictionary of British Folk-Tales in the English Language.* 2 vols. London: Routledge and Kegan Paul, 1970.

———. *An Encyclopedia of Fairies.* New York: Pantheon, 1978.

Briggs, Katharine M., and Ruth Tongue. *Folktales of England.* Chicago: University of Chicago Press, 1968.

Calvino, Italo. *Italian Folktales.* New York: Pantheon, 1980.

Christiansen, Reidar T. *Folktales of Norway.* Chicago: University of Chicago Press, 1968.

Clarkson, Atelia, and Gilbert B. Cross. *World Folktales.* New York: Charles Scribner's Sons, 1980.

Cole, Joanna. *Best-Loved Folktales of the World.* New York: Doubleday, 1983.

De Caro, Frank. *The Folktale Cat.* Little Rock, AR: August House, 1993.

Degh, Linda. *Folktales of Hungary.* Chicago: University of Chicago Press, 1965.

DeSpain, Pleasant. *Thirty-three Multicultural Tales to Tell.* Little Rock, AR: August House, 1993.

———. *Twenty-two Splendid Tales to Tell from Around the World.* Little Rock, AR: August House, 1994.

Dorson, Richard. *Folktales Told Around the World.* Chicago: University of Chicago, 1975.

El-Shamy, Hasan M. *Folktales of Egypt.* Chicago: University of Chicago Press, 1982.

Erdoes, Richard. *Legends and Tales of the American West.* New York: Pantheon, 1998.

Fenner, Phyllis. *There Was a Horse.* New York: Alfred A. Knopf, 1941.

Grimm, Brothers. *The Complete Fairytales of the Brothers Grimm.* Trans. Jack Zipes. New York: Bantam, 1992.

Hall, Edwin S. *The Eskimo Storyteller: Folktales from Noatak, Alaska.* Fairbanks: University of Alaska Press, 1998.

Massignon, Genevieve. *Folktales of France.* Chicago: University of Chicago Press, 1969.

Milord, Susan. *Tales Alive! Bird Tales from Near and Far.* Charlotte, VA: Williamson, 1998.

Noy, Dov. *Folktales of Israel.* Chicago: University of Chicago Press, 1969.

O'Sullivan, Sean. *Folktales of Ireland.* Chicago: University of Chicago Press, 1968.

Paredes, Americo. *Folktales of Mexico.* Chicago: University of Chicago Press, 1970.

Pino-Saavedra, Yolando. *Folktales of Chile.* Chicago: University of Chicago Press, 1968.

Ragan, Kathleen. *Fearless Girls, Wise Women, and Beloved Sisters: Heroines in Folktales from Around the World.* New York: W.W. Norton, 2000.

Ramanujan, A.K. *Folktales from India.* New York: Pantheon, 1994.

Ranke, Kurt. *Folktales of Germany.* Chicago: University of Chicago Press, 1966.

Roberts, Moss. *Chinese Fairy Tales and Fantasies.* New York: Pantheon, 1980.

Shah, Idris. *World Tales.* San Diego, CA: Harcourt Brace Jovanovich, 1979.

Thompson, Stith. *One Hundred Favorite Folktales.* Bloomington: Indiana University Press, 1976.

Wolkstein, Diane. *The Magic Orange Tree and Other Haitian Folktales.* New York: Random House, 1997.

Yolen, Jane. *Favorite Folktales from Around the World.* New York: Pantheon, 1987.

———. *Gray Heroes: Elder Tales from Around the World.* New York: Penguin, 1999.

Tale Type and Motif Indexes

Aarne, Antti. *Verzeichnis der Märchentypen (The Types of the Folktale).* FFC 3. Helsinki, Finland: Folklore Fellows Communications, 1910.

Aarne, Antti, and Stith Thompson. *The Types of the Folktale: A Classification and Bibliography.* FFC 74. Helsinki, Finland: Folklore Fellows Communications, 1961.

Ashliman, D.L. *A Guide to Folktales in the English Language: Based on the Aarne-Thompson Classification System.* New York: Greenwood, 1987.

Azzolina, David S. *Tale Type and Motif Indexes: An Annotated Bibliography.* New York: Garland, 1987.

Baughman, Ernest W. *Types and Motif-Index of the Folktales of England and North America.* Indiana University Folklore Series, No. 20. The Hague: Mouton, 1966.

Boberg, Inger. *Motif-Index of Early Icelandic Literature.* Bibliotheca Arnamagnaeana, 27. Copenhagen, Denmark: Munksgaard, 1966.

Bødker, Lauritus. *Indian Animal Tales, A Preliminary Study.* Helsinki, Finland: Suomalainen Tiedeakatemia, 1957.

Boggs, Ralph Steele. *Index of Spanish Folktales.* FFC 190. Helsinki, Finland: Folklore Fellows Communications, 1963.

Bordman, Gerald. *Motif-Index of the English Metrical Romances.* FFC 190. Helsinki, Finland: Folklore Fellows Communications, 1963.

Childers, James Wesley. *Motif-Index of the Cuentos of Juan Timoneda.* Indiana University Folklore Series, No. 5. Bloomington: Indiana University Press, 1948.

———. *Tales from Spanish Picaresque Novels: A Motif Index.* Albany: State University of New York Press, 1977.

Chòe In-hak. *A Type Index of Korean Folktales.* Seoul, South Korea: Myong Ji University Publications, 1979.

Cross, Tom Peete. *Motif-Index of Early Irish Literature.* Indiana University Folklore Series, No. 7. Bloomington: Indiana University Press, 1952.

El Shamy, Hassan. *Folk Traditions of the Arab World: A Guide to Motif Classification.* 2 vols. Bloomington: Indiana University Press, 1995.

Flowers, Helen L. *A Classification of the Folktales of the West Indies by Types and Motifs.* New York: Arno, 1980.

Goldberg, Harriet. *Motif-Index of Medieval Spanish Folk Narratives.* Tempe, AZ: Medieval and Renaissance Texts and Studies, 1998.

Hansen, Terrence Leslie. *The Types of the Folktale in Cuba, Puerto Rico, the Dominican Republic, and Spanish South America.* Folklore Studies, 8. Berkeley: University of California Press, 1957.

Haring, Lee. *Malagasy Tale Index: A Type and Motif Index of Japanese Folk-Literature.* FFC 231. Helsinki, Finland: Folklore Fellows Communications, 1982.

Hødne, Ornulf. *The Types of the Norwegian Folktale.* Oslo, Norway: Universitesforlaget, 1984.

Ikeda, Hireko. *A Type and Motif Index of Japanese Folk-Literature.* FFC 209. Helsinki, Finland: Folklore Fellows Communications, 1971.

Jason, Heda. *Types of Oral Tales in Israel.* Jerusalem: Israel Ethnographic Society, 1975.

Keller, John Esten. *Motif-Index of Mediaeval Spanish Exempla.* Knoxville: University of Tennessee Press, 1949.

Kirtley, Basil Flemming. *A Motif Index of Polynesian, Melanesian, and Micronesian Narratives.* New York: Arno, 1980.

———. *A Motif Index of Traditional Polynesian Narratives.* Honolulu: University of Hawaii Press, 1971.

Lambrecht, Winifred. *A Tale Type Index for Central Africa.* Ph.D. dissertation. Berkeley: University of California Press, 1967.

MacDonald, Margaret Read. *Storyteller's Sourcebook: A Subject, Title and Motif Index to Folklore Collections for Children.* Detroit, MI: Gale Research, 1982.

MacDonald, Margaret Read, and Brian Sturm. *Storyteller's Sourcebook: A Subject, Title and Motif Index to Folklore Collections for Children, 1983–1999.* Farmington Hills, MI: Gale Group, 2001.

Neugard, Edward J. *A Motif-Index of Medieval Catalan Folktales.* Binghamton, NY: Medieval & Renaissance Texts & Studies, 1993.

Neuland, Lena. *Motif-Index of Latvian Folktales and Legends.* FFC 229. Helsinki, Finland: Folklore Fellows Communications, 1981.

O'Súilleabháin, Sean, and Reider Th. Christiansen. *The Types of the Irish Folktale.* FFC 118. Helsinki, Finland: Folklore Fellows Communications, 1963.

Robe, Stanley. *Index of Mexican Folktales.* Folklore Studies, 26. Berkeley: University of California Press, 1973.

Rotunda, D.P. *Motif-Index of the Italian Novella in Prose.* Indiana University Folklore Series, No. 2. Bloomington: Indiana University Press, 1942.

Seki, Keigo. *Types of Japanese Folktales.* Asian Folklore Studies, vol. 25. Tokyo, Japan: Shorai, 1966.

Thompson, Stith. *Motif-Index of Folk Literature.* Revised edition. 6 vols. Bloomington: Indiana University Press, 1955–1958.

———. *The Types of the Folktale.* FFC 184. Helsinki, Finland: Folklore Fellows Communications, 1961.

Thompson, Stith, and Jonas Balys. *The Oral Tales of India: A Motif-Index of the Oral Tales of India.* Bloomington: Indiana University Press, 1958.

Thompson, Stith, and Warren E. Roberts. *Types of Indic Tales: India, Pakistan and Ceylon.* FFC 180. Helsinki, Finland: Folklore Fellows Communications, 1960.

Ting, Nai-Tung. *A Type Index of Chinese Folktales.* FFC 223. Helsinki, Finland: Folklore Fellows Communications, 1978.

Waterman, Patricia P. *A Tale-Type Index of Australian Aboriginal Oral Narratives.* Helsinki, Finland: Suomalainen Tiedeakatemia, 1987.

Wilbert, Johannes, and Karen Simoneau, eds. *Folk Literature of the Ayoreo Indians.* Los Angeles: University of California, 1989.

———. *Folk Literature of the Bororo Indians.* Los Angeles: University of California, 1983.

———. *Folk Literature of the Caduveo Indians.* Los Angeles: University of California, 1989.

———. *Folk Literature of the Chamacoco Indians.* Los Angeles: University of California, 1987.

———. *Folk Literature of the Chorote Indians.* Los Angeles: University of California, 1985.

———. *Folk Literature of the Cuiva Indians.* Los Angeles: University of California, 1991.

———. *Folk Literature of the Gê Indians.* Vols. 1 and 2. Los Angeles: University of California, 1978; 1984.

———. *Folk Literature of the Guajiro Indians.* Vols. 1 and 2. Los Angeles: University of California, 1986.

———. *Folk Literature of the Makka Indians.* Los Angeles: University of California, 1991.

———. *Folk Literature of the Mataco Indians.* Los Angeles: University of California, 1982.

———. *Folk Literature of the Mocovi Indians.* Los Angeles: University of California, 1988.

———. *Folk Literature of the Nivaklé Indians.* Los Angeles: University of California, 1987.

———. *Folk Literature of the Selknam Indians.* Los Angeles: University of California, 1975.

————. *Folk Literature of the Sikuani Indians.* Los Angeles: University of California, 1992.

————. *Folk Literature of the South American Indians.* Los Angeles: University of California, 1992.

————. *Folk Literature of the Tehuelche Indians.* Los Angeles: University of California, 1984.

————. *Folk Literature of the Toba Indians.* Vols. 1 and 2. Los Angeles: University of California, 1982; 1989.

————. *Folk Literature of the Warao Indians.* Los Angeles: University of California, 1970.

————. *Folk Literature of the Yamana Indians.* Los Angeles: University of California, 1977.

————. *Folk Literature of the Yanomami Indians.* Los Angeles: University of California, 1990.

————. *Folk Literature of the Yaruro Indians.* Los Angeles: University of California, 1990.

Wurzbach, Natasha. *Motif-Index of the Child Corpus: The English and Scottish Popular Ballad.* Translated by Gayna Walls. Berlin, Germany, and New York: W. de Gruyter, 1995.

Index